1993

WHITE MEN DON'T
HAVE JUJU

WHITE MEN DON'T HAVE JUJU

An American Couple's Adventure Through Africa

Pam Ascanio

The Noble Press, Inc.
Chicago

Printed in the United States of America.

Library of Congress Cataloging-in-Publication Data:

Ascanio, Pam, 1950-
    White men don't have juju : an American couple's adventure through Africa / Pam Ascanio
        p. cm.
    ISBN 1-879360-12-8 (pbk.) : $12.95
    1. Africa—Description and travel. 2. Ascanio, Pam, 1950-
    —Journeys—Africa. I. Title.
    DT12.25.A8 1992
    916.04'327—dc20
                                                              91-5220
                                                                  CIP

Noble Press books are available in bulk at discount prices
Single copies are available prepaid direct from the publisher:

The Noble Press, Inc.
213 W. Institute Place, Suite 508
Chicago, Illinois 60610
(800) 486-7737

To The Supervisor
Thanks, I love you.

CONTENTS

PART IV

PART V

Acknowledgments

This is the special thanks section. So here they go. Special thanks to my manuscript readers Mary Eschbach, Linda Smith, Sally Sange, and my husband Robb Annable for their helpful comments, "You make the same stupid mistakes over and over."

To our many friends who provided us with physical and moral support from the very beginning of our craziness.

To Linda and Charles Smith who nurtured us in their cottage.

Thanks to Noble Press and my editors, Suzanne Roe and Doug Seibold, for teaching me the ways of the publishing world.

Grateful homage to the Mother Goddess of the Universe who produced more miracles than I produced grammatical errors.

To our families who are a constant source of strength and inspiration. Thanks for not revoking our passports.

Profound thanks to my "sweet, wonderful husband Robb" (his words). For taking me with him (his words again) and supporting me while I wrote my "memoirs." He kept me honest in my retelling. So any mistakes are his. (Guess who said that?)

And very special thanks to our African teachers.

Preface

The great temptation is to hype the tales into daring escapades replete with cauldrons of juju headshrinkers and tussles with the deadly green mamba snake. In truth, we had scrapes with these and more, but I cannot bring myself to exaggerate the experience. This is a disappointment for adventure readers but a happy nonevent for us. Beryl Markham wrote in *West with the Wind*, "The only disadvantage in surviving a dangerous experience lies in the fact that your story tends to be anticlimactic...."

This book is for everyone who dreams of dropping out, who values experience over possessions, who hears the whispers of Africa. When preparing for this trip, we had no idea what to expect on a daily basis, how we would manage it, if we could, or where we would go. We had nothing to return to if we failed. From 1989 to 1990, we crossed twenty-two countries and 28,000 continental miles, with the help of hundreds of new friends along the way.

As a career advisor in a community college, I encouraged students to pursue their dreams. "Do in life what you most enjoy," I would tell them. Robb, my husband, had been a social services supervisor in a Florida hospital, which meant his days were spent putting people of all ages into nursing homes. He was often touched by those whose dreams of "doing" were never realized because of an unexpected illness or accident. Together, this was a compelling combination of forces. We enjoyed travel—admittedly, we were experienced wanderers—and our dream was to take an open-ended journey together. We were attracted to "third world nations" because of the frailty of traditional cultures and volatility of change. Africa lured us. The immensity of the continent as well as the expense in getting there required a long-term commitment. We knew the journey would be physically challenging. We needed to do it while we were still young and strong enough to adapt to discomfort.

There are as many different realities of Africa as there are people on the continent. Likewise, for every statistic you'll find ten others that refute it. I have attempted to give an accurate portrayal of our reality. The endurance of travel literature is not in its fiction but in its faithfulness.

I have included perhaps too many stories of border crossings and rides. Border crossings and police patrols were always a point of tension because something always went wrong. They are ubiquitous obstacles to the movement of goods and people. I think they are partially to blame for Africa's failure to develop its resource potential. The rides illustrate peoples' responses to authority. Also, it was in the trucks that we felt the greatest kinship with people and met some of our best friends on the trip.

Many of our African teachers send messages to the Western world. They are printed here as promised. Because political recriminations are a real threat, I have used only first names. Further, more quotes are directly attributed to Europeans than to Africans. Anonymity is crucial to the Africans' survival.

Names in Africa are not used the same way they are in Western countries. Because of the high infant mortality rate, babies are often not named until they have survived into their fifth year of life. Names are intimate. Yet, with intimacy, the necessity for a name diminishes. Arguably, in the cities, name pronunciation is accepted. More respectful and more endearing were the names we heard most often: chief, mother, father, grandmother, sister, or brother.

That place names vary in spelling from map to map can be very confusing. I have tried to stick with the spellings most common to the English-speaking world.

An appendix was created for miscellaneous comments and specific travel information that you will not find in travel guides. In some cases, the endnotes supplement the narrative, but often they address the most fundamental problems encountered by Western travelers to Africa. I like to think that this information, this story, will put you safely on the road without the bulk of a planned itinerary.

When in Africa expect the unexpected. Behave with honor and patience, and the most magical things will come your way. Do white men have juju? Magical powers and beliefs? Do black men have juju? It is all in your reality.

Walk well. As you walk, we would love to hear your tales.

PART I

Africa with author's route

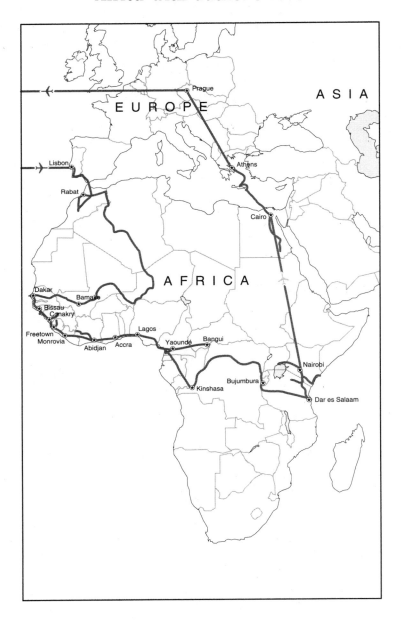

- 1 -
Africa at Last!

If we'd gone off to fight a war in a foreign country or to convert Pygmies to Christianity, no one would have questioned our plans to travel through Africa for a year. We wish we could have invented a reason, a simple and pragmatic response to, "Why are you doing this? And why Africa?" But we could no more satisfy incredulous friends and colleagues than a ghost can explain life on the other side to a skeptic.

October 16 was not a good day for travel. But had an oracle warned us against it, I would have spit in its eye. To hesitate, to wait one more day and chance another delay, was beyond our endurance. We had already struggled against scrawny finances, a lackluster real estate market, vehement objections, and several thwarted starts.

Just three days earlier the sun had illuminated the hills of Africa across the Straits of Gibraltar from Spain. The distant coastline had winked coyly and beckoned with romantic promises. But then winter had dropped an opaque shroud, and the gray sea began clawing the southern coast of Spain. Since then cold bullets of rain had pelted our eyes and ripped paint from the garish marquees of Tarifa, "Wind Surfing Capital of the World."

On October 16, a sturdy ferry battled the Straits of Gibraltar between Spain and Ceuta, Morocco.[1] Thirty-foot swells gnashed at the bow of the boat. Plates shattered in the galley with each violent pitch and roll. Two hundred fifty seasick passengers crawled down aisles to get to the bathrooms. A few Westerners clung to the posh bar trying to catch a slosh of alcohol before reaching the abstemious shores of Morocco.

The majority of passengers, however, were djellaba-draped Arabs who could care less about beer. Their prayers intertwined with their nauseous moans. They were certain this was the day they would be called to the side of Allah.

We had envisioned a sedate, quixotic crossing between the pillars of Hercules that antagonistically guarded opposite shores: The rock of British Gibraltar to our backs and Mt. Acho in Spanish-owned Ceuta, Morocco, facing us. Robb and I would curl in each others arms under the Mediterranean sun, like models in a slick travel magazine. We'd shiver with growing excitement at the approaching shoreline and our first view of Africa.

Instead, our fingernails splintered as we clung not to each other, but to chairs, tables, portholes, anything immovable. All that could be seen through the windows were frothy waterfalls and mountainous waves.

We overheard the crew discussing lowering the lifeboats. The crossing was supposed to take one-and-a-half hours, but I was certain we had been under way for five. The crew seemed startled when I interrupted them to order lunch. "Well, we're hungry," I responded. If the ferry was going down, I wanted fuel for the long swim. I thought about telling the crew we were sailors from Florida, that we were accustomed to the sea. Then I remembered that was in a past life. Now we were nomads with no forwarding address.

I became determined that our craft would dock safely. We *would* touch the shores of Africa. Naysayers would not have the satisfaction of boasting, "I told them to stay at home" or "I knew they'd die. This proves the only safe place is here in America. If they had only taken a gun...." I expected there to be a clear beginning to our trip: a banner, or credits rolled across a screen to a fanfare of trumpets, "This is Your Trip." But nothing like that ever happened. When did our journey begin? Was it with the germination of the idea, with a parquet of maps spread over the floor? Was it when we sold our house and quit our jobs? Or was it when the wheels of the plane retracted from the airstrip at La Guardia and I said, "Now it really begins." I said it again in Portugal. And again, in the ferry, "When we touch Africa the trip really begins." I suppose I was hoping for a fresh start.

Before our trip, Robb was a social work director for a hospital. His days were spent putting people of all ages into nursing homes. He often came home distraught by a person whose dreams of "doing" had been severed by an accident or a sudden illness. "Life is short, and it is fickle," he would say. "We need to live our dreams now and not save them for the future because the future probably won't get any better."

I worked with college students who were confused about their career decisions. At the start of each day I would repeat to myself, "Recognize each person as an individual. Never give advice that you wouldn't take yourself." So each time I asked a client, "What do you enjoy doing? What do you value in life?" I heard myself encouraging them to dream big, to make a plan, and to go for it.

Robb and I were burned out. Our strategies for professional and personal enrichment no longer worked. Six-week vacations no longer renewed our energies. We had everything we wanted: sports cars, sailboat, a house with a pool, good jobs, retirement, good health. But, contrary to our own advice, we were not living our own dreams.

Like most people, we'd talked about taking a year or two in our lives to do as we wanted. We were travelers when we'd met fifteen years earlier. This shared passion put our feet on the road for several months each year. Like malaria, travel was in our blood, a recurring burning fever that required treatment. We listened to our own advice and made a plan.

The timing seemed right: Our families were healthy, and, by living in cloistered frugality, we had managed to save some money. The bulk of the money for our trip, however, would come by selling much of what we owned. We wanted nothing to hold us back, so we sold everything except what we needed for our trip.

Unexpectedly, the house sold the first month it was on the market. We scrambled to pack ten years of junk, and we were in the process of moving when, within hours of closing, the buyers were disqualified. Too disheartened to unpack, we lived the next year among boxes and bare walls. It was bleak. And when thieves smashed our back door, it was all too easy for them to read the neat labels on the boxes and cart away our best treasures. In one afternoon, we lost $15,000 in assets! Since what was left had little resale value, books and clothes were donated, and sentimental memorabilia wrapped and distributed as gifts to family members.

When the house ultimately sold, every appliance from the pool pump to the refrigerator broke down, lightning struck a tree that had to be removed, and the roof started leaking. Financially, mentally, and physically drained, we limped to my mother's house to act out the final two months of work.

When we thought the house had sold the first time, we confided in our supervisors our plans to leave. As happens in organizations, the gossip mills buzzed and within hours ambitious upcomers were maneuvering for our positions. After the house deal fell through, it took months to resolidify work effectiveness and credibility. Bitter at our carelessness, we swore never to mention our plan again—not to anyone.

I am not sure what sustained us during that year. Our spirits were depleted. We tried to make jokes of the setbacks, but artificial laughter often ended in tears. Yet, somehow, the dream thrived and became a more powerful force than all the other challenges. Each penny that clanked into the savings jar represented an icon of determination. National Geographic maps and library books on countries of the world filled the emptiness of our house. We would go to China! We would sail! We would go to Africa! We changed our minds each day. But by the end of that long Florida winter, all the maps were down but one: Africa.

We were baffled by the apparent inconsistencies in what we read about Africa and by its diverse geography. It is called a rich continent, a potential powerhouse. Yet with an annual average per capita income of $365, it is the poorest of all seven continents. Also, if there is so much death by starvation and illness, how could a population of 646 million double by the year 2001? How could people so often described as kind and gentle beget such atrocious bloodshed as when the Tutsis murdered 200,000 Hutus in Burundi?

Our tongues tangled over place names like Ouagadougou and Mbandaka, while we searched the maps for lost places like Upper Volta, Rhodesia, Stanleyville, and the Congo River. When was rainy season? Was it migratory? How did two thousand languages communicate? Why did so many expatriates curse the land and yet stay there to become alcoholics?

Africa and her inconsistencies challenged our understanding of the world like no other continent. Her art, music, and history captivated us. It would be expensive to get to Africa. It was too big to incorporate as a layover en route to somewhere else. We would need good health to travel its rural backroads and to adapt to discomfort. Yes, we would go to Africa!

For months we tried to trace a route on the map, to make a plan. Despite, and because of, inconsistent information in books, our route never progressed beyond a vague fluttering wave of the hand. "We'll fly to wherever is cheapest—probably Western Europe.[2] From there we'll cross the Sahara, probably through Algeria because the other North African routes are closed to travelers— Libya to the east is closed to Americans, and the borders between Morocco and Mauritania are out because of the Polisario guerilla war. Somehow we'll get to West Africa and spend most of our time there, where art and culture are supposedly more intact than in other regions. Now this section here in the center, the Congo, would be interesting, too. It's the only green area of the map. It's also the land of legend—the deep, dark heart of Africa. The east or south? Well, we'll see how it goes when we get there...if we get there." That's as close as we got to a travel plan. We had more questions than we had answers.

We shrugged and said, "Why decide our experience in advance? We'll let Africa be our teacher and shape the outcome for us."

Our main debate was over transportation: should we ship our VW camper, buy a vehicle there, or take public transportation? A private vehicle would allow the luxury of freedom of movement; it would also require maintenance. We had traveled self-contained in our own vehicle and knew the greatest risk was insularity. It's too easy to lock the doors and strut down the road in a race against the earth's rotation. "Just a few miles more. . . ." It's like watching a documentary through the car windows. Public transportation would force us into experiences. We decided to go with the public transportation and the uncertainty of never knowing where we would end up, how, or when.

Food was another unknown. I'm fastidious about my diet. I eat mostly veggies. Okay, truth: gourmet food is my weakness. I'll walk miles to find it. I'll roam a town and sniff kitchens until they all close, and we get stuck hungry. This habit irritates Robb, so he crusaded against it. "I won't go with you if you're going to act up about food. With so much starvation and malnutrition you'll have to eat anything and everything—even if you don't like it." I promised I would change. Neither of us believed me.

The most widely spoken languages in Africa are French, English, and Arabic. Another two thousand languages, not dialects, are also spoken. Our high school French barely made it off the pages of grammar books, and all we knew of Arabic was the equivalent of "What's happening?" I was fluent in Spanish, but with the possible exception of Portuguese-speaking Guinea-Bissau and Guinea, it would not help. French and Arabic language tapes replaced Madonna at home and in the car, but few words stuck from the effort. "No one in Africa can communicate all the time. We'll learn as we go."

French and British Commonwealth citizens don't need visas for their former colonies. America never really colonized Africa. Technical exceptions are Coca-Cola and Liberia, which was "founded" by freed slaves who the United States repatriated in 1822. As a result, Americans must buy visas for nearly every African nation.[3] They are taxation gimmicks, stamps in a passport that give the bearer permission to enter a country if local immigration officials can't find any reason to refuse entry. African visas are usually valid for three months. Since our itinerary was rather nebulous, we decided to pick them up along the way. That meant we would have to visit the capital of each country we visited for an unknown period of time while our visas were processed. Being backwater folk who are uncomfortable in the grime and noise of cities, we looked upon this as a penalty.

Money was our next concern. There's nothing about money that makes sense, especially when it comes to travel. Financiers advocated traveling with a mix of yen, marks, pounds, and dollars; budget travelers touted investing in blue jeans to barter with at the local markets. We put our money in a market fund and linked an American Express account to it. It took a little finagling, and we had to budget our funds between American Express offices but this was no big deal since most of them are located in capital cities anyway. We also distributed six hundred dollars in American cash between our passport cases, along with traveler's checks and local currencies that exceeded our daily needs. Robb carried only "mugger money" in his wallet. Together we budgeted thirty dollars a day.[4]

Almost one-third of any African guidebook is devoted to a litany of what is dangerous to life: yellow fever, typhoid, hepatitis A through Z, cholera, malaria, polio, AIDS, lesser venereal diseases, rabies, tetanus, leprosy, encephalitis, meningitis, trypanosomiasis (sleeping sickness), bilharzia (river blindness), schistosomiasis (blood flukes), blackwater fever, worms, giardia, malnutrition, ulcers, diarrhea, dysentery, tumba bugs, bedbugs, lice, alcoholism and drugs, fatal accidents and wars. Avoid food, soft drinks, water, insects, cuts, the sun, hours between sunset and dawn, breathing chicken or bat guano, swimming in fresh water, swimming in the ocean, and physical contact with other people. Whew!

It was not easy to sort out all the conflicting advice about unpronounceable diseases and medications. The Florida medical establishment was not up on it. "Pepto Bismol is all you need" and "Dearie, you don't need a hepatitis shot unless you're a drug addict" were some of the pieces of advice we got from local physicians. One doctor claimed that polio vaccinations were dangerous to adults, and another blatantly called him misinformed. "Take Paludrine as a malaria prophylaxis. You'll have to buy it in Europe though, the FDA hasn't finished testing it, although the British have been using it for forty years." "You need a shot for malaria, whoever told you to take pills is crazy." We finally got a comprehensive plan and immunizations from the Traveler's Advisory Clinic at Massachusetts General Hospital in Boston.

Medical insurance was a snarl of clauses and exclusions, and the policy premiums were high. Underwriters laughed. The best of the American lot required a five-day qualifying stay in a local hospital before they would remunerate for air evacuation. We considered the state of medical care in Africa and our route through remote bush land. Under those conditions, if either of us were to qualify for air evacuation after five days in a local hospital it would fall under another category: body repatriation. Somewhat dubiously, we decided against medical insurance. Life insurance was more practical.

Packing was another gnarly problem. How do you fit a house, emergency ambulance, kitchen, closet, photography studio, and library into one backpack? You don't. Big items like the pool, the boat, and the microwave were relatively easy to eliminate; the closet and the library were more difficult.

We reduced our clothing to cheap cottons from discount outlets. We packed casual but dressable long- and short-sleeved shirts, baggy pants, shorts, long underwear, socks, windbreaker jackets, an ankle-length skirt, sturdy sandals, and rain parkas. Miscellaneous items included compact sleeping bags, sheets, a tape recorder with earphones and miniature speakers, two cameras, a first aid kit and medicines, a pocket knife, a sewing kit, a wristwatch with alarm, film, flashlights, sunglasses, a canteen, and a small day pack. Our backpacks had internal frames, yet they could be transformed into respectable looking suitcases.[5]

With great despair we stared lovingly at a stack of forty books that would not fit into the leftover space. We knew books would be hard to come by in Africa. Ultimately, we packed ten of an eclectic range. The books comprised almost half the total weight and volume of the backpacks.

We kept our planning and preparations secret. Even close friends ceased to notice the "For Sale" sign in our yard. As our private lives became a separate reality from our public facade, our impatience to get under way grew. We used the delay to teach ourselves patience: we knew we would need plenty of it in Africa. And to work off frustrations, we exercised to the point of fanaticism. We knew it would be to our advantage to start our journey with strong, healthy bodies.

The day the house sold and the keys passed to the new owner, we both submitted requests for leaves of absence from our jobs—

no reason specified. Whereas nothing in our employee policy manuals encouraged it, nothing prohibited it.

The news triggered a minor gossip wave in Spaceport USA, Brevard County, Florida. Everyone was shocked. They assumed that we had abandoned our plan of taking a year off to travel. I guess that's because most people only talk big and never follow through.

"But why Africa?" everyone asked. At first we tried to explain the lure. But it was as if we were talking in Mandinga. No one understood a single word of what we ineptly tried to explain. The concept was either too abstract or too intimidating to people who counted each day as one day closer to retirement. Travel was something you did in a camper when you retired, or after you won the lottery.

"You're making a big mistake! Think about what you're giving up...a nice house, retirement, security. You'll never get it back again!" Our friends' admonishments eventually changed to protests: "I would go with you, but I've got a house mortgage, a wife, kids, bills....I couldn't leave my job." We came to realize that it wasn't just Africa that perplexed them, but that our very act of selling everything for an open-ended journey, a dream, threatened their perception of security and order.

We wished we could have lied and said, "We have Fulbrights." When people asked us where we would go, what we would do, we would respond with a vague fluttering of the hand. This didn't elucidate anything to people who thought Africa was below the meridian, that we could drive there, and that we should take guns.

By the time higher-ups at work interviewed us about our leaves, we didn't know what to tell them. We were as vaguely honest with them as we were with ourselves. Our hands fluttered, our words stuttered. In the end, they went away believing what they wanted to believe: We were going to do missionary work. To teach. To produce a television documentary. One-year leaves of absence were approved.

That's when we became known as the "crazy missionaries going to Africa." Our mothers got closed-lipped—they knew we were going in search of knowledge and that the search would many times take us to the brink of danger. But they also knew none of their protests would stop us.

We boarded our pets with friends, sniffled farewells to our Florida family and colleagues, and headed northeast to visit Robb's family. We thought that in cosmopolitan New England we would meet people who understood why we were going to Africa. However, everyone from the stock brokers who would handle our finances to the doctors in the travel clinic were as incredulous and perplexed as our friends and family in Florida had been. What we hadn't understood at the time is that no one travels through Africa as we were planning to.

No one, that is, until we met Nigel from Britain. He was a prototype Brit, with the kind of austere, physical presence that Americans associate with crumpets, royalty, or Oxford. We were introduced to Nigel on Cape Cod, where Robb's mother lived.

"Where will you travel?" Nigel asked blandly.

"All over," I said as my hand beat the air in a memorized gesture of our imagined route. His eyes glinted, but otherwise Nigel's stoic expression didn't change.

"Interesting," he nodded. "I lived in West Africa for five years. Now tell me how you intend to travel. Will you drive your own car or go by mammy wagon?"

I wasn't sure what a mammy wagon was, but I assumed it was some sort of public transportation. "Mammy wagon," I replied on the bet.

"My God!" he said and stretched his arms overhead as if exhorting heaven as a witness. "Finally, I've met people who are actually doing something with their lives!"

I would have hugged Nigel if it had been proper. At the very least, I wanted to tuck him into my pocket to carry around and whip out each time someone asked, "Why are you going to Africa? Are you crazy? How can you give up so much?"

Unfortunately, Nigel flew back to London before we could shyly plunder his knowledge—before we could even ask him what a mammy wagon was. I looked it up. Many synonyms were listed: taxi brousse, bush taxi, camion, truck, taxi ordinaire, Peugeot, bus, poda-poda, money truck, pirogue or canoe, a lucky ride. Essentially, a mammy wagon is a dilapidated vehicle into which an impossible number of people, babies, chickens, goats, bundles of household goods, and market products are crammed together for a journey lasting anywhere from three hours to a week over equally impossible roads.

When we arrived in Portugal we thought we had finally left our problems behind and were on our way. After several days in Lisbon we went to the Algarve region in the south. From there we would visit all the parts of Spain that we'd missed in previous trips and then find a ferry to Morocco. Africa at last!

But disaster seemed to stalk us. In Tavira, Portugal, we called home from a public pay phone. A neighbor answered my mother's phone. "What kind of daughter are you?" the neighbor berated, "How can you go off and leave her at a time like this?" Mom was in the hospital for an emergency laryngectomy—cancer. We had left the States three days earlier! "Come home right away—she's dying!"

We cried all the way to the airport in Seville, Spain. We cried for my mother, and we cried for ourselves. We had given up everything and had made it only as far as Europe!

Robb wanted to go home with me. It was perhaps the most difficult decision we ever faced. Should we chuck our dream and eighteen agonizing months of planning? We were stunned, stymied, and defeated. With the last breath of reason, I argued for Robb to remain in Spain as a hostage to the trip. I would go home alone and assess the situation.

Mom's shrunken, yellowish frame did not resemble the robust woman I'd known for thirty-eight years. Tubes flowed from every part of her body. A red hole yawned in her neck.

"Surely you didn't get sick overnight, Mom, why didn't you tell me before I left?" I asked.

On a notepad she scribbled, "I knew for a long time, but I was waiting for you to leave. I didn't want to stop your trip." Calm acceptance of what neither of us could change replaced anger, fear, and frustration.

My sister moved home to take care of Mom, and I rejoined Robb in Spain. But not before neighbors and family flayed me with accusations of selfishness. This would be the burden of guilt and fear we would carry throughout Africa.

All my doubts reemerged on the pitching boat from Spain to Morocco. The crew had been deployed to emergency stations. It was not a good day for travel. We should have waited, maybe an-

other year, until Mom was out of danger. Or, at least until the
storms subsided.

It would not be easy to call home again. Nor would they be able
to contact us since we had failed to develop an itinerary. We would
make our way across Africa bit by bit, whenever, however, and
wherever transport or our feet would take us. As our probable
route materialized, we would send addresses for *poste restante*—
general delivery to the main post office of a town. It occurred to
me that no one knew we were on the boat, our names were not on
a passenger manifest. If it sank, no one would know for months
that we were missing.

We wanted to be nomads, to follow the dry season to ever
greener pastures. Were we selfish? We promised our mothers we
would stay out of danger; yet, we had not even reached the shores
of Africa, and we had already broken that promise. I have never
been able to evade my mother's omnipotent sixth sense. She would
say, "You can't fool me for one moment, I know what you're up
to!" She probably knew we were on a boat that was about to cap-
size. I chuckled.

"What's so funny?" Robb said looking up from his book,
Whirlwind, a chilling novel about foreigners caught in Iran during
the Muslim fundamentalist revolution. I didn't think it was a good
choice for Muslim North Africa.

"Nothing, I was just thinking about home."

I'm not the optimist. Robb is. And he expresses it in a dangerous way: "Gee this is great! So far we're still alive!" I believe
boasting invokes problems. So I am always knocking on wood or
thumping my head against bad luck. He hates it when I do that,
which just eggs me on.

"You're reading too fast, you won't have anything left for the
trip," I said. I wanted him to distract me from watching waves
break over the windows and from thinking of home.

"This *is* the trip," he said.

Africa, the place of dreams stretched before us; Europe, America, and other dreams shrunk slowly behind us. Without knowing
it, the trip had begun. Nigel, the Brit and the only person to bless
our endeavor, said we were doing something important with our
lives. We *would* make it.

"Ceuta! All passengers must disembark!" someone shouted.

I peered out the window. Rain obscured the dock.

"Ceuta!" wailed the voice.

I looked at my watch. Only one-and-a-half hours had passed. The ferry was on time. "Robb, put your book away. We're in Africa at last!"

– 2 –

Morocco

Every guidebook and tourist to Morocco warns against the hustlers. To read or listen to them makes you believe hustling is native to Moroccan blood. So, as excited as we were at first, we were leery when we boarded the bus that would take us from Spanish Ceuta to the land border of Morocco. The incessant rain would not let up, and our moods were becoming as dreary as the weather.

The first Moroccan hustler we encountered hawked immigration cards outside the customs office. Rain dripped off his beaked nose. "Buy them here and avoid the wait!" he urged. His spiel might have worked on a more active day, but we were the only foreigners at immigration. Around us, androgynous white forms slithered through the chill, gray morning without lifting their eyes or pausing for formalities.

Inside the customs office we bent open our damp French phrasebook to the "Customs Formalities" section. It was useless. The one rain-sodden official present shrugged his shoulders and turned his back in snobbish refusal to recognize Spanish, English, or our halting attempts to pronounce phonetic French from a book.

As in a Charlie Chan movie, a man materialized from the shadowy interior of the office. His English was as impeccable as his manicured appearance. He was either a high-class hustler or a secret agent. He took over our case with polite efficiency. As we completed the necessary paperwork and exchanged traveler's checks for dirhams ($1 = DH 8.33), he gave us a short lesson on Morocco: a brief-but-formal history of the monarchy, an introduction to Islam and currencies, and a stern warning against hustlers who pose as students. "From here take a shared taxi to Tetoan," he advised, "It's 41 kilometers south, but it's where you get the bus to any place in our country. Don't pay more for the taxi than fourteen dirham." He waved good-bye as we trudged through the rain to the one small, red Toyota squatted among the puddles.

Berlitz failed us again. All I could find in the phrasebook was, "The air conditioner is broken" and "I want a gift for a small child." The driver indicated he spoke only Arabic anyway. I flashed fourteen fingers in the air, signaled Robb and me, and said, "Tetoan." He shook his head and ambled off to suck on a wet cigarette.

A rain-streaked window of the car screeched open, and a man in a leather jacket hollered in English, "Welcome to the Great Kingdom of Morocco. You must learn to speak Arabic here, but I will translate. The driver said you must pay forty dirham." I hadn't heard the driver say anything.

"We'll pay fourteen for the two of us!" I said. The locus of bargaining shifted to "our translator," who spewed a stream of Arabic at the driver.

"No, it is forty!" the driver said, as he whisked our luggage into the trunk and slammed it shut.

"Then we will wait for a bus or take another taxi," we said. Robb and I fumbled at the locked trunk.

"Madame, there is no other way to Tetoan. You can see for yourself. You'll wait all day," the driver replied. Yellow sulphur lights lit the empty car park. "Alright, because you are a visitor I do not want to give you bad impression of my country. I take you for fourteen dirham." The driver made apparent his sacrifice at accepting such an insultingly low fare.

We squashed into the back seat with the translator, and the driver locked the door on the outside. The driver stuck his tea-stained teeth into the open window and said, "You pay extra for your luggage. Twenty dirham for each bag, add that to fourteen for the ride makes fifty-four that you must pay."

"No. No. No. Let us out and give us our luggage!" we protested. Six men—two in worn, gray western clothes, two in sodden djellabas, the driver, and the leather-jacketed translator— argued and gestured wildly over our fare. It sounded violent, and we added to the fracas by climbing over the front seat to get out and pounding the locked trunk.

Suddenly the argument stopped. The translator smiled and said, "We Moroccans are hospitable people and will not let you stand all day in the rain. The driver said he will take you and the luggage for fourteen dirham although it is too little. Get into the car. We go now." The car didn't leave for forty-five minutes.

The ride was as bleak as the weather. Four men in the front seat shared hand-rolled cigarettes. The inside windows fogged with black ashes and perspiration from eight bodies in wet clothing. The windshield wipers didn't work. We squinted out the window. Gray, cascading rain veiled much of what there might have been to see.

"Where are you going?" the translator asked us.

Honestly, we didn't know. It had been enough to get to Africa— to Morocco. With a vague fluttering of our hands we said that we would cross the Sahara into West Africa.

The translator's leather jacket creaked as he lit a cigarette. "You know, you must learn to relax and to trust people," he said. "Throw away your guidebooks and let us help you. Those guide-books lie; they make you believe that everyone in Morocco is a thief and a hustler. As you can see, I am your friend. I am not a hustler. I want to help you understand my country. Relax, trust me, tell me where you are going. It's the only way . . . ."

"We will take a bus somewhere; we just don't know where," we said. I stifled what I was really thinking: "I trust people; I don't trust you." Luckily he didn't require more than an abstract nod. It was barely 9:00 A.M., and we were numbed with premature culture shock. Language was turning out to be a major barrier. Arabic sounded totally hostile, and French bore no resemblance to our cassette lessons or our Berlitz phrasebook.

Outside the window, everything was a rain-smeared blur as the car splashed through the countryside. The ride was disorienting; yet, I felt as vivid as a painted cartoon character in a black-and-white comic strip. Reality came in the form of an occasional pink minaret of a mosque spearing the dark clouds; a donkey cart—the ubiquitous symbol of North Africa; or a fuzzy pyramid that transformed into a camel's hump. White-walled towns effervesced from the gloom. "European resorts," explained the translator. "They're very nice and not so expensive. You should go to them and enjoy our beautiful beaches. Be with other Europeans." My lip curled.

"This is a big day in the Tetoan market because all the Berbers come. It is like Christmas. I will take you to the famous market myself and help you find a place to stay. Founded in 1307, Tetoan is the capital of the Rif province." He was either a hustler or a Chamber of Commerce recruiter.

Tetoan was a gully wash. The narrow roadways of the old city were mined with bottomless pools, and the rain beat people and animals into huddles under eaves and alleyway tents. Even the translator could see it wasn't a good day for a hustle and led us to the bus station. "I leave you now as I promised. See, you must remember to trust people!"

A haze of cigarette smoke, burning coals from tea pots and hashish, and the musty stench of damp bodies assailed our eyes and noses inside the station. Babies squalled amid a cacophony of languages, squealing tape players, and rain reverberating on the tin roof. Everyone seemed to know what they were doing there and where they were going, except us.

Numerous marquees displayed flowing Arabic script. For lack of a better idea, we joined a line in front of the most active ticket counter.

"Where are you going?" asked a man in English.

"Where is this bus going?" we asked.

He read the schedule aloud. Robb looked at me and pronounced, "Fes."

The new translator ordered the tickets then blended into the milling mob of faceless voices. We joined the squatters on the floor of the bus station. A woman boldly peered from her covering into my eyes, found a nerve, then seemed to caress it. She shyly passed us each a cup of tea steeped in mint leaves. Its warmth and the woman's calmness transformed the alien surroundings into a refuge.

The bus conductor wagged his finger. "No smoking hashish on my bus! I do not make joke," he screamed over muffled titters from the back, "you smoke hashish and you walk!" The bus roared into the street laying a black cloud of carbon monoxide over a gang of urchins fist fighting on the loading platform.

The Compagnie Transport de Maroc (CTM) bus, as plush as Spanish buses, careened through a valley and into the sculpted rock of the Rif mountains and then dipped into seas of plowed dirt and green plots of vegetables. Twelve-foot marijuana plants sprouted along the roadside, and barefoot kids with a rock in one hand and a black ball of kif (hashish) in the other threatened drivers to stop for their roving market. The sky had benignly cleared.

At twilight the streets of Fes were crammed with cars loudly braying their passage. A thousand tea salons spilled onto the streets creating an obstacle course of tables and chairs. Blown-out speakers vibrated with Tracy Chapman singing "Revolution" and popular Arabic artists singing praises to Allah. The brisk, rush-hour current swept us along on our search for a cheap hotel.

Two hours later, bedraggled and verging on grumpiness, Robb suggested he might make more progress alone. I waited in a tiny tea parlor with the luggage and a coke. That's when Mohammed strolled in with Joseph Conrad's *Heart of Darkness* tucked under his arm.

"I'm a student of English literature at the university," he said. His dimpled, billboard smile didn't wane when I turned my back to him. "Do you know this book? I'd like to discuss it with you. May I sit down?"

"My husband will be back in a minute." I responded. My words surprised me; I'd never before hidden behind my husband's trousers. I was too tired to invent a direct way to tell this student/ hustler to scram.

"I know, he's gone to look for a hotel." Mohammed had correctly assessed the heap of luggage and my sagging shoulders. "When he returns I will show you a very good, cheap hotel across the street. I just want a few minutes of your time to discuss literature. You see, I'm doing my thesis on the tragic elements of *Tess of the Dubervilles* and *Julius Caesar*." Mohammed's enthusiasm was unstoppable. So was his presumptuousness. I gave in to both.

The Excelsior, the hotel Mohammed recommended, was a palatial sanctuary from translators. Robb unpacked the toiletries and set up the tape recorder. Always his first act in a new place was to transform it into a homey nest. I am as indifferent to nesting as he is to food, so it was a compromise when I pronounced his work "Wonderful," and he took me to an overly lit cafe for liver tajin.

We crawled into bed unreasonably tired and mentally battered. Our bodies had moved, but my mind had been left behind. Absent was any sense of involvement or the ability to process new information. I willed my body to relax and my senses to observe. Through the window wafted smells of sizzling garlic and cumin, excited shouts from what sounded like a bingo game, and cats spatting on the tin roof. A neon sign illuminated the warped mirror and bathed the room in an ephemeral orange.

"Pami," said Robb, patting my hand, "the trip has begun. We're not in Florida anymore." I fell asleep on his chest, solid and familiar, and dreamed of friends from home charging on camelback through our room.

The morning presented us with the first sunny day in two weeks and a message from Mohammed that he would meet us at ten for tea. We went early to a saloon on Boulevard Mohammed V—not the one in Mohammed's note as I wanted to avoid him. We stretched in an almost warm patch of sun. The streets were quiet, easy, and nonthreatening.

"I think I lost it yesterday," I said, filtering coffee grounds between my teeth. "Maybe I need time alone to sort out everything with my mother and the craziness of the past months. We haven't had a moment without crisis in almost a year. Robb, let's leave before Mohammed finds us, I'm sure he's running the student/ hustler scam, and I don't want the hassle. Look, we could catch the bus to Rabat, pick up visas to Algeria, and head out to the Sahara. What do you think?"

"Can't you just relax and enjoy being here? If he shows up, which I doubt, we'll tell him we don't want a guide. Anyway, I don't think he's a hustler. They don't carry books. Relax."

Everyone was telling me to relax. I was relaxed. I tried to look placid to cover a pout. I searched for something to say that would anchor me to the present. "Did you know that Fes is the cultural and spiritual capital of Morocco? And that the world's largest and oldest Koranic university is here?"

"Good morning, Ma-salamma. Did you sleep well at the Excelsior?" inquired a smooth voice. Salem, the translator from the Tetoan bus station, stepped between the tables and glanced at his watch as if late for an appointment. Claustrophobia and suspicion returned. How did Salem know where we stayed?

Soon after, Mohammed showed up clutching Henrik Ibsen's *A Doll's House.*

"Hello! We were released early from drama class, so I hurried here to get your opinion of Nora." Mohammed acted as though he'd expected to find us at this tea saloon even though it was not the one he had indicated in his note. Coincidences were piling up. Both he and Salem seemed to know our every movement.

We introduced Mohammed to Salem and told each of them how we had met the other. I don't think I imagined a suppressed spark of recognition when their eyes met. Maybe it was mutual distrust. If so, we were all on equal footing. None of us trusted the other.

"Last night I offered to teach you about Islam and the Arabic culture in exchange for literary discussions. I know you think that I am a hustler, but you will see that I am not interested in your money, but in your knowledge," Mohammed said, ignoring Salem as he astutely negotiated for our attention.

"You must first learn that in this small country of twenty-six million we are Berbers, Arabs, and other tribes. We all move around like nomads, the desert people, so wherever you go you will meet someone you know. This is not coincidence, we say it is Allah's way of caring for us and watching that we live according to his teachings. One of our duties is to be a host. A guest is given the best room in the house to sleep in and the best food to eat. But on the third day, it is the responsibility of the guest to make an excuse to leave. If he has nowhere to go he must lie and say that he does so not to offend his host. Because we are all both hosts and guests we give freely and do not accept payment or gifts. In this way we serve Allah, and we are happy." He smugly crossed his arms and laughed. "There, that is your first lesson in our culture."

Mohammed's authoritative voice belied his curly-headed cuteness. He knew that he had outwitted any protests we might have uttered against his presence. Soon we were discussing Nora and the feminist movement, religion, and politics. A dangerous mixture by any normal standards. Verbal agility kept us hopping over the Palestinian question, U.S. foreign policy and Israel, and East-West relations. Only when we directed the conversation to Moroccan politics, the Polisario war in western Sahara, skirmishes with Algeria to the east, and King Hassan II did Mohammed and Salem become nervously quiet.

I delighted in this vengeful exercise of control when Mohammed whispered, "The world is full of ears, we must be very cautious of what we say and not trust anyone. Even friends are spies." Salem nodded agreement, and I looked around for eavesdroppers. Across the boulevard a shopkeeper sloshed a bucket of water on the sidewalk. "We can smoke hashish, sleep with our girlfriends, and drink beer, but since the coup attempts against King Hassan II in the seventies, we are not free to talk.

"Enough of this, I want you to be guests in my apartment. We'll move your things from the hotel, then I'll take you to lunch at my family house in the *medina*—the oldest quarter of the city. It was built in the ninth century. There you will see life lived as it has been for a thousand years."

"Mohammed, we don't want a guide, and we won't pay for a guide. We also prefer to remain at our hotel."

"Please, it is not often I meet people who can discuss literature . . . in return I have only my hospitality and what I can teach you," he replied. I felt chastised. "So I insist you first come to lunch in my family home. Then you decide if I am honorable." Salem paid for the tea, and we departed with Mohammed as if led by nose rings.

Abruptly Mohammed stopped in front of the tourist information office. "Please wait for me here. My friend who is a policeman said that I should register you as my guests. It means that I accept full responsibility for you while you're in Morocco. If you do something wrong, I will go to jail for you. Don't let that worry you, I will teach you well." It worried me.

On the way to the *medina*, he pointed out the *mellah*, the Jewish section on the hill, and the *kasbahs*, the old Arabic quarters.

"Where you stay is the *Ville Nouvelle*. It was constructed by the French. Every city is composed of these quarters. The *medinas* were built first and were walled against sand and early invaders. This is a *bab*," he said, paying the taxi fare, "it means gate. The entrances to a *medina* are through *babs*."

His voice droned like a field professor lecturing undergraduates. "You will see many small unpretentious wood doors that open into palaces. The wealthy people tried to hide their riches from the tax collectors by looking poor on the outside.

"See that woman in the window? She just signaled someone to take her bread to the bakery; her husband or son will bring it home to her. Many traditional women never leave their house. She has no need to leave. In our culture, as I told you, we serve Allah by gladly helping or giving to other people.

"When you enter a shop or a home say '*Salaam al lai koum*,' 'may Allah bring peace.' The reply to thank you, *shokaran*, is '*la shokaran Allah wajib*,' 'the thanks all go to God.'"

Since entering the labyrinth of the *medina*, my orientation had disintegrated. Imagine forty miles of tangled spaghetti. Tall brown walls jutted upward at either shoulder, leaving a space only wide enough for a single donkey or black djellaba-draped person to pass. Overhead the sky was a zigzag blue ribbon. Each alleyway appeared to dead end, then it would abruptly twist a corner to a fountain plastered with indigo blue tiles—"the official color of Fes because it is the color of water, life."

A mixture of odors and sounds hung heavy in the air: parsley, coriander, ceder, mint, incense, lamb, donkey dung, fats and tanned leather; the tap-tapping of hammers against chisels as intricate designs were carved into leather, wood, and metal; the clacking and thumping of wooden looms hidden in dark rooms dusty with dyes and tufts of wool; an indistinguishable babble of languages—Arabic, French, and Berber—entwined in a low roar. Then, like a knife rending human passion, "Allah Akbar...God is Great"—the call to noon prayer—bellowed from hundreds of minarets.

Mohammed's father was so brittle and shrunken from age that his white pants, shirt, turban, and chin whiskers billowed around him. His mother retained the beauty and grace found only in the unselfconscious. Her blue chin and tattooed forehead designated her birth into a Rif mountain Berber family. On the floor of their house sprawled their children and their children's spouses: doctors, lawyers, and teachers. We were greeted with hands laid over the heart. It was a courtly scene that could have been played out in a tent as well as in the seven-hundred-year-old room.

The meal was served in a room dominated by a low table, an even lower pillowed couch that ran along three walls, and, for a while, an Egyptian soap opera. We were served gazelle horn pastries stuffed with dates, vegetable couscous, mint tea, and *bastilla*—honey, almonds, and pigeon.

"I feel like a scruffy intruder," I said to Mohammed.

"When my family stays at our farm in the Rif, there isn't much to do except watch the stars and listen to my father's stories. He knows many. He was an *Imam*. I think in your language it means deacon. One story was about a wealthy man who had a big party to show off his riches, his great palace, and his powerful French friends. He invited all the important people, including one man famous in all the land for his wisdom. The fine guests arrived glittering in gold and diamonds, but the wise man was sent away at the gate because his clothes were too humble. He was insulted, but he went home and changed into rich robes. This time he was welcomed and seated prominently at the table. The first course was soup. The wise man pulled his sleeve over his hand and began dipping the cloth into the soup while saying loudly, 'Eat! Eat!' The host was horrified, 'Why are you behaving this way?' he asked. The wise man replied, 'You made it clear that it was not me that you invited here tonight but my clothes. So they might as well enjoy your food.'"

For many days we were never far from Mohammed's sight. His attentiveness was both a blessing and a curse, but we were never sure which it was in any given situation. The few times we explored the city without him, we found our path blocked by a real hustler: "Hey mister, friend. Welcome to Morocco. What's your name? Are you French? English? German? Do you need something? I can help you no problem. I am a student. Do you want me to walk with you? You know my city? Where is your car? Your other friends? Where are you staying?" There is only one way to shake a hustler and that is to enter a hotel or an expensive restaurant. They're not allowed in those places.

We spent our evenings with Mohammed in the one-room apartment that he shared with a cat, books, and a charcoal burner. His many friends contributed to our various lessons: literature, French, Arabic, religion, and cooking. Dinner was a feast of food and stories. After the fifth recitation of "The History of Our Great Kings" I asked, "What is the criteria of a great king?" Hamid, a carpet salesman, rose to his feet and repeated in schoolboy fashion, "The responsibility of a great king is to build public monuments and to name the streets." I couldn't tell if he was serious or not.

One night, we finally announced, "We have overstayed the three days allowed to guests. Tomorrow we go to Rabat on the 7:30 train." In Rabat, the capital, we would get visas to enter Algeria, which flanked Morocco on the east.[1] It was a perfect excuse to get on our own again.

"What luck!" exclaimed Mohammed. "I told you this is a small country of coincidences. My brother and I will be on the same train. We can travel together!"

Rabat was a city without an identity. It was completely lackluster after the unshakable confidence of Fes. It had been the French administrative capital and is the present-day seat of the monarchy. The large *Ville Nouvelle* gave the impression that the inhabitants had suddenly fled, leaving it to aspiring impostors.

Mohammed accompanied us in our search for a cheap hotel near the *medina*. Then he rejoined his brother. Robb and I were finally released on our own.

The *medina* was shut tightly in the afternoon, but by nightfall it literally hopped with vendors packed shoulder-to-shoulder. Many merchants were legitimately licensed, but many more were squatters who displayed their wares on large pieces of cloth or inside boxes that snapped shut at the first sight of police batons thrashing the air. As soon as the police swaggered past, the itinerant shops reopened. It was a true open market: a place where cama-

raderie and conspiracy united the sellers and buyers against the
authorities.

Mohammed had taught us scraps of classical and street Arabic.
I tried them both to order a mix of nuts and dates. A large crowd
gathered and chattered effusively until I got dizzy listening.

"That's all I know in Arabic," I said. Their laughter expressed
approval for the attempt.

"Mohammed, bring Mohammed here. He knows English," said
the vendor. Every male was named Mohammed; it must be a ploy
to make the tax collector crazy. So between Mohammed, who really didn't know English (although we didn't let on), and a house-
wife who pointed out the best selection and kept a keen eye out for
heavy-handed tipping of the scale, we got a superb trail mix at a
super price.

As soon as we got our visas to Algeria, we left Rabat for Marrakech. Although it was in the opposite direction from Algeria, no
visit to Morocco was complete without a pilgrimage to that vener-
able desert town. Moroccans referred to Marrakech as the true
Arabia. Crosby, Stills, Nash, and Young immortalized it in the
minds of old hippies in their song "The Marrakech Express."

We were having no luck buying a train ticket to Marrakech
when Mohammed miraculously "showed up." He instantly accomplished what we hadn't been able to, then escorted us to the
departing train and entrusted us into the safekeeping of Rashid, a
friend who, by coincidence, was going in our direction. I was un-
easy about being passed along this way, but Rashid was so jocular
and articulate that I soon surrendered my suspicions and settled
back to watch the passing terrain. For eight hours we rumbled
through increasingly barren desert and tiny brown towns while I
pondered the mechanics of Moroccan hospitality.

We arrived in Marrakech twenty years too late. Its exotic
charms had given way to tawdry commercialization. From the
rooftop of the CTM Hotel on the Djemma El Fna, the frenetic
hub of activity, we watched the spectacle below. A fortified Club
Med squatted at the busiest corner of the *medina*. Its patrons were
protectively escorted past hucksters, hustlers, and haranguers,
who slouched inert under shop canopies until droves of buses deposited purse-clutching tourists. Snake charmers wailed on nasal-
toned flutes mesmerizing not only the writhing, defanged cobras,

but the coin-tossing tourists as well. Many tourists were relieved of their wallets. Grubby kids turned feeble cartwheels for *cadeau*, a gift. Cassette vendors blared their wares in discordant competition over tinny speakers. Old men in red knickers roamed the streets with necklaces of brass cups and goatskins of water. The more lucrative side of their business was posing for photos. Hustlers grabbed gawkers to press their guide services. "It is too dangerous alone," they would whisper.[2] Shopkeepers cornered browsers until they bought their way out. Horse-drawn carriages clomped the streets next to cars spewing suffocating exhaust fumes into an air already thick with burning charcoal.

The freaks in the Djemma yielded to food vendors at night. Each booth specialized in fish or meat brochettes, vegetables, couscous, and even roasted pig heads. One dollar bought a tantalizing buffet.

Marrakech was sensory overload. To be fair, maybe we had spent too much time in cities to appreciate its enchantment, but within twenty-four hours we were screaming for tranquility. We got out the map and traced a route to nearby Mt. Toubkal in the High Atlas Mountains. There we would surely find peaceful solitude.

The car park where we went to find a ride was a dust bowl of cars going every direction. "Yardboys" rounded up passengers for each destination with shouts and shoves. To Asni we were first quoted one hundred dirham each and extra for our backpacks, which had already been locked in a trunk. Several invaluable lessons were learned. Never give up your luggage until the deal is set, even if you have to sit on it. And don't let loud arguing intimidate you—meet the crescendo. Mild, laid-backed Robb got into and out of three taxis, shouted mouth-to-mouth with the yard bosses, and wrangled the fare to twenty dirham total. Ten of us squeezed together for the ride.

At Asni we changed cars for Imlil, with an abbreviated exchange of curses. No rebate was offered for our having to push the car uphill through deep mud puddles.

Imlil was the end of the dirt road. Under a cluster of eucalyptus trees, a few tiny shops, usually unattended even when open, attested to an unhurried pace of life. Mountain guides advertised their services on a board nailed to a tree, yet they admitted they were unnecessary if you stuck to the trails. Beyond the small town of Imlil loomed the snowy peak of Mt. Toubkal; at 13,655 feet it is the highest in North Africa. Reputedly, it would be a three-day, round-trip hike and an easy climb even for flatlanders from Florida. A refuge near the top provided shelter for $3.00 a night. Like the refuge in Imlil, it was built by the French Alpine Club. We would start our climb the next day.

The day we arrived in Imlil was idyllic and serene. The vibrant greens of lush, terraced gardens enticed lazy exploration of the valley. Berber villages clung to the surrounding sheer mountainsides. Like brown stalagmites, the villages looked like a creation of nature. Lachen, who had shared our taxis from Marrakech, invited us to his home, a honeycomb of dark, cool rooms and cows in Dovar Mzik. We sprawled on the roof amid drying corn and watched the rhythm of the valley while sipping tea and munching walnuts. The sky roamed wide and blue.

"When you return from the mountain this will be your room," Lachen said, indicating one with a panoramic view and piled with warm rugs. As corny as it sounds, my soul felt liberated for the first time since beginning our trip preparations.

A fickle drizzle in the early morning blessed our departure. A French couple, Bridgette and Patrick, experienced alpinists, accompanied us up the mountain trail that would lead to the first refuge in the six-hour hike. Patrick moved like a skilled climber. He set a steady pace, not unlike a donkey, and never slowed nor quickened. We puffed far behind and sniggered discreetly at two ski poles that he swung at his side like superfluous walking sticks.

Four hours later we were bent over low, hugging the mountainside to avoid being blown into a chasm by hurricane-force winds. With each increase in elevation, nature invented new tests of endurance. Raging rapids flooded what were supposed to be wading streams. Rain flowed down our necks, and cold permeated our bones.

"What should we do?" we asked. "Turn back?"

"The refuge is only two hours away."

"Let's keep going. The sun will come out tomorrow."

Three hours later we crawled on hands and knees up a stream that was once the trail. Hail pelted our downward-turned heads, and the wind howled death threats while lashing our rain parkas.

Patrick turned a sharp bend and quickly crawled back. His shouts were at first drowned by a new onslaught of hail, rain, and sleet.

"Impossible! It is impossible, the wind is too violent. We must turn back," he said. No one argued.

However, we were stuck. Mudslides and a swollen river blocked all retreat. The refuge above was unreachable. A smelly, dank donkey stable carved into the mountain offered sanctuary. We huddled there until we were discovered by Ali, a young Berber checking on his donkeys. Ali's age was hard to determine—he could have been twenty-two or sixteen. He was animated and recognized a good deal when he saw it. He invited us to his hut for twenty-two dirham, meals and tea included.

Ali's four-by-six-foot hut was as dark as the stable. It too was carved into the mountainside with wood beam supports. The shutters and door were barricaded with rocks and poles against the persistent wind and hail. The four of us stripped to our soggy long underwear, hung our drenched outerware from the roof beams, and huddled under blankets and wet sleeping bags. Although Ali kept a pot of tea or couscous steaming on the charcoal stove and candles lit, the damp and chill never burned off.

This was the first time we'd seen much more than the backs of our partners, Patrick and Bridgette. Stocking caps pulled to their eyebrows had hidden their faces. They were a handsome couple and cheerful company. Not one complaint was uttered in that haven. It would have done little good. Our French was as bad as their English, and Ali's Berber was better than his Arabic.

Ali was either more nervous from the storm than he let on, or he thought it the duty of a host to play his transistor radio full blast. Maybe he thought himself a deejay, because he narrated each song. He was distraught when the batteries died after eight hours of scratchy static. When none of us offered replacement batteries, he started to sing.

I suppose we all expected the storm to let up by night. When it didn't, we stopped trying to maintain our false attempts at bravado. There wasn't much to do except try to get some sleep. The cave-like room was so small that we laid back to back, with Ali curled around our feet. If one person turned, all had to turn. I gritted my teeth and listened to the storm. Avalanches cracked and roared, thunder boomed, wind battered the door, hail bombed the roof, and the river vibrated the ground.

Nightmarish memories stalked my wakefulness. I thought back to the time we pulled twisted bodies from a mud slide in Venezuela. I remembered earthquake victims in El Salvador placing the crushed bodies of their children in my arms, hoping I could save them. I remembered, as a child, watching horses tumble on thirty-foot waves when the Colorado River flooded. All the horror and fear of these visions caught up with me, and I began to shake as hard as the ground beneath us. I was afraid that realities of the past would become realities of the present. This storm was another sign that our trip was ill-begotten. We had been fools to come this far, and we would be fools if we went on to the Sahara. I swore to myself to return home if we ever got out of the hut alive.

Robb's clammy hand grasped mine with a squeeze. "Don't worry, we'll make it," he whispered. "We always have and will this time too." I could tell he wasn't at all sure. "Think of something else, let your mind take you to some place happy and safe."

The next day the storm did not let up. In fact, it intensified, if that was possible. But since we had already survived more than twenty-four hours of its fury, we were feeling rather complacent. Several times Patrick put on his wet clothes, dug through the snow drift that blocked the door, and scouted for a way down the mountain. He would return pronouncing it impossible, and we would sigh with resignation. In the late afternoon, we suddenly heard a man's voice outside the hut. It was the guardian of the climbers' refuge. "Get out! If you value your lives, leave immediately!" he shouted. Without pausing, he disappeared into the mist. His alarm ignited shivers of adrenalin among us, and fear struck the core of our false composure. Patrick could not see where the guardian had gone. He returned with a Berber. "This man will show us a safe spot to cross the river for one hundred dirham," Patrick said. A usurious amount. "I agreed to pay him so let's get out of here. Now!"

The guide pointed to a mountain covered in snow, "You'll have to climb that." *We can, just get us out of here.* But when he took us to the precipice of a thirty-foot waterfall and said, "Cross here!" I decided he was a sadist, a madman, a cruel prankster.

Patrick wobbled into the chest-deep turmoil. The wind caught his parka, wrapped it around his head and tugged him toward the cataract. Like a series of still frames, Patrick tossed the parka into the white water and regained his footing. One by one, we waded across using the now unfunny ski poles for balance.

The mountain snow camouflaged a sheet of ice which, in turn, camouflaged treacherous shale. Again, the ski poles saved each of us from plunging to the valley bottom on a sled of ice and shale. Our ascent was further slowed by a blinding ground blizzard. Only by scraping snow from the ground did we find the original trail. For the most part, the trail had been washed away or broken off in avalanches. So much for easy hikes.

Imlil was nearly destroyed. The entire valley was flooded. Terraced fields were submerged under ruthless river currents that swept trees tangled with vegetables into the lower floors of the hillside Berber villages. All that remained were the few shops clustered around the end of the road. The road into town was gone. Everyone said it was the worst storm in anyone's memory, and its destructive fury had not abated.

We were either minor celebrities or apparitions in Imlil. Stranded climbers crowded in the refuge snuck jealous, half-averted glances at us. A few others congratulated us—small consolation for frostbite and pneumonia. Safety was celebration enough for us.

The town wags guessed the 26 kilometer road to Asni wouldn't be restored for at least six weeks. Until then, all the overland trucks and cars of the climbers were stuck in Imlil. Unhappy campers shivered in the rain the next morning and morosely watched the four of us hike toward Asni. For them nothing was going right, and for us everything was going right, or so they said. Running away from the mountain held no shame for us. We admitted it was the only smart move we'd made. Just having survived the ordeal ignited in us a ripple of pride and even strength.

We had to climb into the mountains to circumvent the pounding river. Every now and then a chunk of hillside tumbled into the water. Rain made the day bleak and the tufted grass slippery. The wind, less fierce than the previous days, tossed me into rocks like a frisbee. For the first time I wished I were fat. Fat and heavy like a boulder. My wind-blown gymnastics were witnessed by a group of donkey drivers, one of whom stuck a tail in my hand and ordered,

"Hold on!" That donkey tried his hardest to rid himself of me by trotting over obstacles. I am sure the men laughed. I did.

In Asni the sun shone. But its effects were dampened by news that the road was wiped out for another 5 kilometers. Those 5 kilometers felt like 50 miles to our blistered feet. Sagging with exhaustion, we eventually reached a taxi stand. The drivers, however, were not the Red Cross. Instead, they were the type of entrepreneurs who exploit misfortune. Rates to Marrakech were 400 percent higher than normal. There was nothing to do but pay or stay.

Ah, warm, dry Marrakech! The city was still crazy, but it was more tolerable after our far-from-tranquil break in the country. We spent several days there recuperating. Rashid magically found us and nursed us with food and hot tea.

To get to Algeria we had to pass through Fes via the Middle Atlas Mountains. Once again the rain followed. "Robb, if it rains while we are on the Sahara I am going to hire my body out for drought relief work," I proclaimed.

Mohammed met us under a double rainbow. The mysterious Moroccan appearance act. I didn't mind this time—he was now like family. He bubbled with suggested activities and lessons to fill a week.

"We're only here for the night," we interrupted, "tomorrow we head for Algeria."

"Then tonight we will have a farewell dinner."

Ten of his friends, now our friends, attended the impromptu feast. We sat on the floor and dipped our hands into bowls of couscous, tajins, and fruit. Beer, wine, tea, and even hashish were passed around the jocular circle. Each guest stood and told a story. Mohammed's neighbor, a cop, confessed to being in the secret police. Great, that was comforting. Maybe he was the link to the magically appearing Moroccans. Somehow all our movements had been known and anticipated. A wave of uneasiness came over me.

"Tell us about your trip to Marrakech," they clamored. So I stood and recited the tale of our adventure on Mt. Toubkal—the only story I was sure they didn't know. They laughed at parts we didn't yet think were funny and nodded their heads over the sections we thought were. "And that's the end of the story," I said sitting down.

"You have learned well. It is as we suspected. Allah has chosen you to learn and to teach others. You are true Arabians."

Maybe they were being polite, but I felt a foolish pride.

The train to Oujda, on the Morocco/Algeria border, departed from the sooty Fes station in what now seemed to be perennial rain. Salem was there to welcome his mother. The coincidence no longer bothered me. We shrugged, "It's a small country." He verified our tickets and led us to our compartment. "*Ila likka, Salem.*" He'd put us on our first bus in Morocco so it was only fitting that he put us on our last train.

I peered through the window at a landscape that became increasingly oblivious to life and reviewed our trip so far. It was too soon to generalize, except to say that Morocco had treated us kindly. We had arrived so tired and whipped by the Western world that we had been leery of the new one. Morocco bent our will, severed our identity with home, and gave us new friends. Whatever else our new friends were—student hustlers or secret police—they had guided us well. And Mt. Toubkal? Well, it gave us courage. There was no turning back now. Things were just getting good.

- 3 -

Eastern Morocco

There are two open trans-Saharan routes, both through Algeria. The Route du Tansrouft follows the western border and enters Mali at Bordge. The more trafficked Route du Hoggar drops south from Algiers through In-Salah and Tamanrasset to Niger. We had not decided which we would take, but we needed visas to both Niger and Mali, which meant a trip to both of their embassies in Algiers. The more northerly of the two border crossings between Morocco and Algeria is at Oujda/Tlemcen. Unfortunately, the Algerian side is notorious for turning pedestrians back to Morocco, a wiltingly hot 12 kilometer hike each way.[1]

The big dilemma was whether to attempt crossing between the northerly points or head directly south on the Moroccan side to Figuig. Being denied entrance at Oujda/Tlemcen would add an extra day to the week detour through Figuig and up to Algiers.

It was already the end of October and mid-season for the an-

nual European migration south through the Sahara. We went to
the Algerian consulate in Oujda to check the status of the border
policy. Our French was purposefully so wretched that the consular official called the border post just to be rid of us. "I'm
sorry," he said after hanging up, "I cannot know what to tell you.
The military controls the border and they decide." Sometimes no
answer is still an answer.

Then Allah provided a Scottish couple with the latest edition of
Africa on A Shoestring, which stated that it was possible to pick
up visas for both Niger and Mali in Tamanrasset, along the Route
du Hoggar. We were looking for good omens, and this flimsy
piece of information seemed to be one. We boarded a bus to Figuig. We'd follow the Route du Hoggar.

The bus was thirty years old and tattered. Its springs had died
long ago, so every dip in the road was etched into our spines.
Boards were laid across the aisles to accommodate forty extra passengers, and more bodies and bundles were heaped on top of
those with seats. Every window was firmly shut. The combination
of heat, body odors, and stale air was so stifling that it would have
asphyxiated a camel. I opened a window, and someone immediately slammed it shut, almost mashing my nose. I opened it again
with an audible grumble. The other passengers won the battle of
the window, however, when sand and dust rushed in, instantly
clogging my nasal passages, eyes, and throat.

The Sahara began west of Oujda, but when traveling in an air-
conditioned train it was a theoretical environment framed through
windows. Now, on the bus, we became part of the desert, and the
familiar was jerked into raw, undisguised strangeness. Soon, nomad tents no bigger than pointy-headed boils sprouted on the
endless horizon. The desert really did look like an undulating sea.
Toward midday, I could no longer sustain reality against the more
powerful mirages. I turned my focus from the windows to the inside of the bus and the irritating flies.

Dress was definitely more conservative in the desert than in the
cities. The men's turbans constantly tumbled apart from the heat
and the jostling of the bus. The women were enormously hefty
and resembled pointy, white nomad tents with veils clenched in
their zippered teeth. The only patches of exposed skin were the
men's whiskered chins and the women's feet, which were decora-

tively tattooed or hennaed with intricate patterns of stripes and dots. Irritating, clinging black flies covered the interior of the bus like a carpet.

The heat stifled normal brain functions, and everyone dozed with their heads bouncing off one another's shoulders. Maybe the slowing of body functions was a physical adaptation to the discomfort of broken springs, communal dirt, and fetid sweat.

The bus jerked to sudden stops—sometimes to refill the transmission fluid, which was stored under our seat. Other times a person mystically materialized, starting out as a mere dot in 360 degrees of barren desolation, until he boarded and was transformed into another body seeking buttock space on the crowded benches. Other times I suspected the driver of braking to allow a mirage to cross the road.

"Are we crazy or what?" I said to Robb, whose mouth slacked open with sleep. "I can't believe we're doing this. What if we get to Tamanrasset and find out we have to go up to Algiers?" Maybe it was just as well that he slept through my worry session—he hates it when I worry. Eventually my jaw slackened in sleep too.

If it weren't a large military garrison, Figuig would be a pleasant oasis town, laced with disintegrating Roman ruins and green palms. Only sullen soldiers stalked the quiet, ghost-ridden streets. We had expected to meet travelers to pump for information, or a ride, but we were the only ones in town and the only guests in the one hotel, which sported a billiard table but not a restaurant and didn't have electricity or running water. We found figs and creamed cheese in the market and ate by candlelight. "You know, Robbie, all day I couldn't help but think that we must be crazier than hell," I said. I was off and running again and, unfortunately, he was awake this time.

PART II

Morocco, Algeria, Niger, and Mali

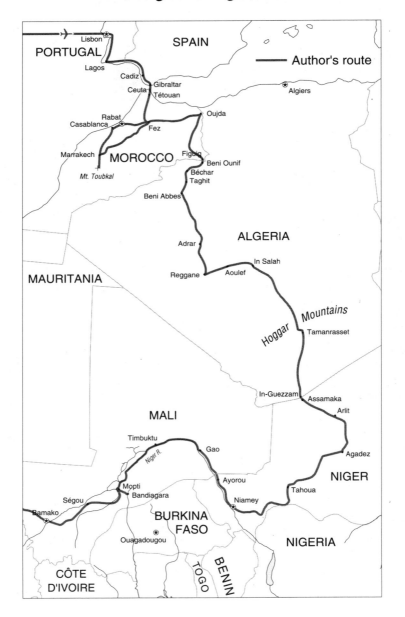

– 4 –
Algeria

"Impossible! You can't walk across the Sahara!" said the Algerian border official. A fly excavated the scowling furrows of his face. The murky room, no bigger than a double wide trailer, was vacant except for the official and his fly, and our two opened backpacks. Outside, mirages rippled the mute desert sand. Dry, 100-degree heat sucked from our tongue any French we might have known to explain for the fifth time that we did not have a car, that we had walked twelve miles to that desert outpost because no vehicle had rumbled past the entire morning. Red sand encrusted the long hem of my skirt and jacket cuffs: a testament to our claim.

"Until you show me your car, smuggled engines, and tires, I will not release you," he said. Robb and I agreeably settled into the coolness of the building's interior. It would be a long wait unless he could conjure up a vehicle. I hoped that he could.

The official stalked the exterior of the building in search of our stashed cache. We were disappointing prey. Without bribes or confiscations his family would munch dates for dinner. To him we were rich Europeans laden with gold, but nothing in our backpacks glinted of gold except a shiny peseta coin from Spain. *"Un cadeau pour moi,"* he said, making it disappear into a pocket of his crisp uniform.

Earlier, on the Moroccan side, the officials found $1.50 in dirham in our backpacks and ordered us back to Figuig to change it. We refused. It was our second hike to the border that morning. The first time we had been sent back to Figuig because we hadn't collected exit stamps from the police in our passport. "We'll give the money to a beggar," we protested. But none were around. Eventually, a captain had allowed us to keep the coins and released us to continue our hike into Algeria.

We rested contentedly in the office, away from the searing sun, while the Algerian searched for our hidden car. We were in no hurry to walk again, so we thought he gave up too quickly when he reluctantly stamped our passports, approved our money declaration form, and, with an impatient wave of his hand, told us to leave. For a long while he watched our slowly receding backs as we trudged the sand silted road to Beni Ounif, the first town in Algeria. He and his fly hoped to witness evidence of our treachery.

The treeless, mud-baked town of Beni Ounif was sealed tighter than a ziplock bag. Not a shop, souk, bank, or door was open. No djellaba-draped residents wafted down streets on the heels of errands. No money changers swept down on us to profit by a dinar or two. Not a vehicle rumbled through town, which was a desert crossroad judging by the paved road and stop sign. The silence was eerie.

Only time passed during that still afternoon in Beni Ounif. Our plan was to change money and catch a bus south, maybe to the city of Béchar. But not one vehicle passed all day. The bank, like the rest of the small town, was closed. We waited by the roadside and doodled in the sand. Late in the afternoon, we detected movement in a small corner restaurant. The restaurateur explained in laborious French that it was a day of celebration. Of what? Well maybe it was to commemorate liberation from the French in 1962, or the inauguration of their first elected president.

Shrug. He was certain however that the bank would reopen the next day. Until then we were stuck.

We checked into the Hotel Beni Ounif. A pretentious name for a squalid truckers' *hammam*—a male-only hostel. It was expensive—ten dollars for a room that had no electricity or water and was already occupied by many species of critters. But the shifty manager accepted us on a promise to pay. That night we nibbled leftover bread, sardines, and dates by the flicker of a stubby candle and were kept awake by scurrying vermin paws. Flutes, like the kind played by snake charmers, wailed until dawn over hundreds of speakers hidden in the minarets of the town's mosques. President Bendjedid broadcast his celebration in Algiers to the invisible populace of Beni Ounif.

The bank opened in the morning, and we changed our money. We then grabbed our bags and walked toward the crossroad eager to put the ghostly town behind us. We didn't get far before a trucker offered us a ride to Béchar. Algeria was rumored to be a hitchhiker's paradise, but this ride was our first confirmation of that rumor. The driver was comfortably friendly, and I soon dozed on Robb's shoulder.

Béchar was a big city, almost industrialized. The streets flowed with people, although most businesses were closed for the celebration. We could not find anything to hold us there, so we went to the bus station to squint at the schedule on the marquee.

"Do you know where we are going?" I asked Robb.

"South," he snapped impatiently.

"I mean, what city?" We didn't have a guidebook.

"I am looking for the first bus that goes south and arrives at its destination before dark. OK? Can you read those Arabic numbers?"

The schedule was irrelevant we learned when we stepped up to the counter to buy tickets: the celebration had delayed the buses, and they were all assuredly full. Finally, we got tickets (but not seats) on the bus to Beni-Abbes. It would leave sometime within the next six hours and arrive sometime around midnight.

"What's in Beni-Abbes?" I asked Robb.

"It's a town, which means it probably has a place to stay. You're getting cranky. Why don't you find something to eat and leave me alone?"

I found kefta sandwiches smothered in flies.

Once we fought our way onto the bus and it rumbled out of town, the terrain was stunning. The craggy mountains and shelves of flat rocks that had surrounded us since Oujda suddenly yielded to majestic, sweeping sand dunes. It was the beginning of the Grand Erg Occidental and what we had imagined the "true Sahara" to be. I leapt from my seat and shouted "Look!" The sight of three-hundred-foot-high dunes was breathtaking. Excitedly, Robb and I pressed our noses against the closed windows while the other passengers, who were accustomed to the scenery, merely looked at us. Our excitement grew when the bus detoured for a rest break in Taghit.

Taghit was a real oasis town with lacy date palm forests clustered on the banks of a meandering creek. We rushed from the bus and panted to the top of a dune to join a gaggle of children sliding down its face. The drudgery of the previous days lifted. Such moments make all the other discomforts of travel worthwhile. I wanted to stay in Taghit, but the bus beeped its horn and started creeping away with our luggage.

With nightfall, the indigo sky glowed like a gentle night-light. Although we could no longer recognize the contours of the earth, the crescent moon cradling Venus was no less spectacular. Sleepy passengers awoke, children sang, and adults chatted amiably. Faces and voices turned to us with curiosity. They laughed when we answered that we did not know where we were going.

As we disembarked into the darkness of Beni-Abbes, two shrouded women took my arm. "Come with us," they whispered from beneath their veils. We waited while Robb and their male companion retrieved our luggage. "We take you to our house." they said. We politely protested. The women giggled. "Our English is only a little bit. We take you to a hotel, but tomorrow you come to our house for tea."

We expected another squalid trucker's hamman. Instead they escorted us to a plush hotel. Persian rugs, recessed lights, a chandelier, and potted plants made Hotel Rym look like a sultan's palace. We did not even pause to close the room door before leaping into the shower. For five days we had eaten with our hands without water to wash them.

Dinner was a hot meal of soup and vegetables, fresh fruit, and water served in carafes like a fine wine. We knew then that kind deities smiled on us. Our spirits soared in response to this unexpected, but much needed, luxury.

When we awoke at dawn, Robb pulled aside the curtain to reveal a train of camels ambling up a burnished sea of sand dunes. "My god!" exclaimed Robb. "This is better than Taghit. It's better than Lawrence of Arabia. Quick! Let's follow them."

We tugged on clothes and scampered after the twitching camels' tails. We followed in the camels' footsteps until the town of Beni-Abbes disappeared behind a crested sea of sand, and the cloven prints of the camels were swept from history. The silence seduced our souls and consciousness with the lull of timelessness. The sun sequestered any shadow and melted east with west. Mirages enticed us onward. We were suddenly startled back into consciousness, as if by the bark of an alarmed dog. We were adrift on a wind-whipped ocean of sand. With eyes hooded against the sun, we hurriedly retraced our fading footprints.

Back at the hotel, we noticed for the first time a giant movie set erected against the dunes. A placard displayed the title, *The Sheltering Sky*. The British film team lounged in the hotel lobby while Bernardo Bertolucci, the director, morosely paced. Since the film crew stayed segregated from the town, we saw very little of them.

Later, the man from the bus appeared to take us to his home. Radjaa was his name, and he was a science teacher. He lived in government housing with his wife, child, and sister-in-law. The two women greeted us at the door, dressed not in the head-to-toe veils they had worn the night before, but in flimsy nightgowns!

We stayed in Beni-Abbes five days with Radjaa and his family before hitching a series of rides that took us south to Adrar and Reggane, east to Aoulef, and eventually across the trackless desert to In Salah, a city on the main north-south route through central Algeria. Maybe ten days passed in the interim. Time had lost all meaning.

The people who gave us rides invited us into their homes, fed us, and shared their family sleeping room. From Beni-Abbes through many small, mud-walled towns of the Grand Erg Occidental, we squatted cross-legged with village elders, teachers, and local policymakers. Discussions ranged from global political problems, technology, agriculture, and urban development, to the status of women in the United States and the Muslim fundamentalist movement in Algeria. We were regarded as both teachers and students.

Radjaa tutored us in French and Algerian Arabic, desert agriculture, and geology. With each new friend, the lessons escalated in their complexity. In Algeria the literacy rate is 80 percent, but oral tradition still prevails: lecture, recitation, memory drills, and quizzes. Frowns and even chiding corrections marked the failure of our tongues to wrap around awkward diphtong or our inability to correctly recall an earlier lesson in, say, subterranean irrigation. A constant a cappella of voices, hardly louder than the buzz of omnivorous flies, translated and retranslated English, French, Arabic, Berber, Tuareg. On rug-strewn floors we'd drift into restless dreams against the fragmented murmurs of conversations that continued until dawn.

Women rarely traveled or even walked down a street, and they never entered the ubiquitous tea salons. I self-consciously moved and talked in a world of men. I grew tired of their company.

Doors and veils segregated women from the exterior world. Inside the sanctity of the home, women lounged unveiled, in simple dress that exposed tribal tattoos and quick smiles. Many of them had never met a westerner, and they were as curious about us as we were about them. With the exception of the Radjaa sisters, who spoke English, we shared no common language. Under the shade of grape arbors we would talk, each in our own language, and with gestures to explain the meaning. Often we collapsed in laughter over our inability to communicate ideas or concepts. Why Robb and I had been elected for integration into family life, I'll never know. I was simply grateful for the company of my sisters.

The women sometimes sang for us in high-pitched ululations and often gave us bracelets stripped from their own arms.

The gracious Algerian hospitality led me to make a grave mistake in etiquette. I told the Radjaa sisters that it was the fifteenth anniversary of my marriage to Robb. Excitedly, they prepared a special feast for us. Embarrassed, Robb and I went to the market and brought home a pile of vegetables to add to the pot.

That night they presented us with a candle-lit cake and sang "Happy Birthday to You." They gave us gold-gilded chinaware, gem stones, and fossilized crystals to "remind us that the desert had once been an ocean." We protested against the extravagance, and they sucked in their breath and brought us pieces of furniture! We finally, begrudgingly, accepted a few fossilized rocks in return for my only pair of earrings.

Later Radjaa explained that our contribution of food to the feast had been an insult. By protesting their gifts we had behaved correctly, but we had protested too much. "Some people might think that you are unhappy with the gifts and desire something finer," he said. We learned it is improper to give a gift in return for a gift. Radjaa laughed—we were their "students" so we were forgiven. From then on we accepted their gifts with polite protestation.

Privacy was the most difficult resource to come by in the desert—it was only a polite illusion. Where the eye can see beyond the horizon, privacy was created in whispered conversations, by djellabas that concealed the identity of the person underneath, and by the outward pretense that the self didn't exist, that no one exists. We had no djellabas to hide us, and our hosts always hovered close by with tea and lessons. Our privacy came when the sun's mantle smothered everyone with afternoon sleep. Then we would wander alone in the quiet streets of the towns.

In the evening the towns would once again stir with activity. The grape arbors were tilled; gossip swapped over the well; buses chugged to life; and kids terrorized the streets with feisty screams, rock fights, and soccer balls made of wadded plastic. Food markets opened with vendors' wails of "You're cheating me! How can I feed my eight children if I let you pay so little for these tomatoes? *In sh'allah*, it is God's will. Only because you're my sister. One day, who knows? I might need a favor." The musty odor of roasting charcoal, smoldering fires, mint tea, and simmering tajins permeated the cooling desert winds.

At sunset townspeople filed up the dunes like cars to a drive-in theater. They sprawled in single lines along the crested sand to witness the instant that day became cobalt night, and the sun's orb was replaced by billions of stars. At that mystical moment, prayers reverberated from the sand-brown minarets in the towns. Just as the sun disappeared and the winds turned icy, we would all slide, jump, tumble, and giggle home to dinner.

From Adrar to In Salah is a short direct line, not quite an inch on a Michelin map, yet no road connects the two points. The road winds north to a junction near El-Golea north of In Salah. It would be a three-day trip from Adrar according to locals. We wanted the shortest, most direct route to catch up with the European migration across the Sahara.

"There must be a way to get across this roadless section," we asked.

Our host frowned over the map as scars on his forehead puckered. "See, you can get partway, to Aoulef, then the road ends. From there to In Salah it is only sand, but I've heard that it is sometimes possible to catch a ride."

"How long can it take?"

"I don't know. The rides are not regular. Maybe three days' wait or only one in Aoulef, *In sh'allah*, God willing. It is too difficult, much better for you to stay here in Adrar."

Long, florid speeches were polite expressions of gratitude for hospitality, however, as with protesting gifts, I could never figure out what was too much or too little. The long speech we made to justify our need to move on eventually elicited a smile of approval and a ride was arranged from Adrar through Reggane, and east to Aoulef.

After nearly two weeks of quiet towns, Reggane looked like a metropolis. Sand swirled from the feet of donkeys and people, music whined from tea salons, jeeps sagged under heavy grain sacks loaded from shop doors, and buses so crammed with people that turbans flowed from the doors and windows like banners creaked through the town.

East of Reggane we reentered desert flatland. The desert here was rocky and harsh and lacked the sensuality of the Grand Erg, yet it commanded attention. I tried to apply what I now knew about desert life to what I saw. But geological contours, vegetation, and tiny, isolated villages changed so rapidly that they defied permanent description. I gave up trying to classify what I saw and settled back to watch the endless diversity of the desert.

Aoulef was literally the end of the road. The hot tarmac suddenly stopped as if severed by a knife. Beyond loomed an expanse of tufted grass and rock-strewn sand. At least ten men crouched in the meager shadow of a building waiting for an onward ride.

We joined the men to wait for a ride. Occasionally, a Peugeot taxi would pull up and deposit more passengers among our ranks. The "waiters" besieged each car, shouting, waving money, elbowing to get inside the doors that the driver scrambled to lock. "No, go away. I won't go to In Salah. My car won't make it! Go away before I run you over. It will be your fault," the driver would shout.

"That's six more passengers for In Salah," I whispered to Robb. "We'll never make it."

"Don't you have something to read? Can't you relax? Why don't you go sit inside that little restaurant?"

"No, I feel awkward." I pouted.

"Then shut up and read. Christ! Go back home if you can't take it." Irritation mounted with the heat of the sun and the length of the wait.

Restlessly, I prowled the sleepy village. I met four men preparing to descend into a well with crampons and tethers. "For 1,300 kilometers all the wells are connected by underground tunnels that were constructed centuries ago," the men said. "We're going down to look for leaks. Please come, it is safe. The tunnels are very wonderful and ancient. We show you."

Well, maybe, I thought. I'd like to see the tunnels. But my curiosity quickly gave way to paranoia. "I must first ask permission from my husband," I said, begging out.

Then another desert taxi wheeled into town. Three more passengers tumbled out, the usual riot ensued, and the taxi rumbled away empty. After they'd brushed the red sand from their clothes and hair, a black man, a white man called Chris, and a big, burly Algerian who looked like a construction worker emerged. The Algerian nodded to something that Chris said, while his blue eyes counted the waiters.

The Algerian didn't sit, he stalked. He and I recognized the restlessness in each other. "Come, let us have tea," he said to me. Robb still read, and the big man's companions ignored us. Tea was an invitation to negotiation, and I was curious to see what Allah had up the sleeve of his djellaba.

"How long have you been waiting?" he asked. He and the tea shop owner had just exchanged cheek-to-cheek kisses and cassette tapes. I looked at my watch as if I hadn't kept a minute-by-minute log.

"Oh, about seven hours," I said, "but there are now twenty of us who have been waiting almost that long."

"Have more tea. That man is your husband?" he asked.

I nodded.

"We say here that the king of the desert is the taxi driver because he decides who goes and when."

"Nobody has gone anywhere, only arrived," I said between slurps of tea.

"Tell your husband to be ready. I will return in one hour with a car. I am the construction foreman for the new road between In Salah and Tamanrasset. I too decide who travels. Many taxi-kings owe me favors, and I will find one of them here."

True to his word, he returned with a Cadillac-class jeep. The other waiters pleaded for a ride but there was barely enough room for the driver and his friend, the Frenchman Chris and his Senegalese companion, the road builder, and us.

The driver brazened the sand, talking and twirling the steering wheel in circles that kept a mesa-like escarpment at our left shoulders. It is eighty miles from Aoulef to In Salah by a trackless desert so rough that we had to scrunch low in our seats and pad our heads to cushion their frequent beating against the roof of the jeep. The Senegalese man was knocked nearly unconscious when the driver spied a desert fox and gave chase.

A splendid swirl of reds and blues in the western sky announced the sunset prayer break. The Muslim men knelt in the sand three times, their intonations the only sound. Atop a hill, far from anyone, a man in a nightdress and striped cap crawled into a bed for the night. That was all, just this guy and his bed.

That evening we coasted into a palmerie on the outskirts of In Salah. The engine and headlights of the jeep were turned off in order to escape detection by "the thieving police patrols." It was eleven o'clock when we stumbled into a hotel so cheap it didn't have a sign. The bleary-eyed desk clerk slowly looked up from his tea. "What is your *beezneez*?" he asked.

"What's a *beezneez*?" we asked.

The clerk evaluated our backpacks disguised as piles of sand

and said, "This hotel isn't really a hotel. It is only for *L'Beez-neez*."

Chris chatted up the desk clerk in his most lyrical French, while Robb, the black Senegalese man, and I sagged into our sand heaps, too tired to listen.

Chris switched to English. "Hmmph! Come outside with me a minute. Look, I don't trust this guy. I don't know what he's talking about, hmmph, a hotel that isn't a hotel but a *beezneez*. He's trying to insult me with this idea. He says there is a real hotel down the street."

"If he has cheap rooms then I don't care what he calls this place," I said. "Let me talk to him." I trounced in again.

"Well, have you decided your *beezneez*?" The manager flashed a set of brown-stained teeth before wrapping his lips around a Hoggar cigarette. "Have some tea with me," he said.

The tea was tepid and loaded with brandy. I sipped with loud appreciation. "It is too late to go to a hotel," I said. "Since you've got rooms, let's pretend for tonight that we have one of these *beezneez* things, and we'll stay. We're tired. We just arrived from Adrar. We'll move to a real hotel tomorrow."

His eyebrow arched. "You came across the desert? Where's your vehicle?"

"We don't have one. It's been a very long, hard day. I need a shower. See, we're covered with sand."

"Across the desert without a vehicle...that's good, mon ami. Have another glass of tea while I get your rooms ready. Across the desert, bon! You are very strong."

"Thank you."

Chris griped all the way to his room. "Hmmph, I'm leaving tomorrow for Senegal. I won't spend another minute in this desert. This guy here, I don't like him insulting me with his *beezneez*."

We stayed three nights at the hotel that wasn't a hotel and never learned what *L'Beezneez* was in spite of drinking brandy-laced tea with the otherwise loquacious manager.

Chris claimed to be on sabbatical from a Parisian university where he taught literature. Intense and, at times, haughty, he was impatient to get to Dakar to exhume his childhood "roots."

"I swear I will be across this desert and in Senegal in two weeks," he said.

Robb and I were planning on two months.

"You see, I'm looking for this man who took care of me when I was young," Chris continued. He showed us a crinkled photo of an African boy cradling a chubby, white baby. "He will tell me who I really am. You see, he was just twelve then, but he taught me everything because my parents were busy with work. I haven't seen him in thirty years, but I will find him. I'll show his picture to everyone in Dakar until I do."

We were saddled with Chris after his Senegalese companion slipped away in a truck that smuggled undocumented people across borders. For two days, we tried to buy onto one of the overnight buses or trucks to Tamanrasset in southern Algeria, but seats were sold weeks in advance. Next, we went to the campground on the outskirts of In Salah to look for a ride. The only people there were those whose vehicles had broken down.

"Merde! I'm running out of time. I must get out of here." Chris pouted.

"Tomorrow morning we'll go to the edge of town and hitch a ride with a truck," suggested Robb.

"It will never work," argued Chris, "we must fly."

We accompanied Chris to Air Algiers just to keep his funk from ruining the day. Sure enough, the flights were as full as the buses.

"Don't give up, Chris, keep trying," we said as we steered him into the office again. After several glasses of tea with the office manager we got seats for $18 on an unscheduled, forty-passenger Fokker leaving the next morning. The rest of the day was spent filling out paperwork required of foreigners flying.

At first we were disappointed to be flying, but once in the air, we were struck with a profound awe. Until then the Sahara had been a yellow area on a map splashed across the upper third of the African continent. Maybe I, like Chris, had viewed it as a river to be crossed. Looking down on dunes more endless than eternity, I realized for the first time the enormity of it. We spent more time flying over a small scratch of sand than it takes to cross the Atlantic Ocean by jet.

The plane followed the Route du Tansrouft to the town of Bordge on the Mali border, where the plane rested three hours. There wasn't much to see but flies crawling into the gaping mouths of sleeping passengers.

A child with milky, oozing eyes sat on the lap of his black-draped mother. A fly fed on the infection, crawled through his nostrils, then flitted into his mouth. The child was oblivious to his parasite, but I wanted to kill that fly. I watched, horrified, until I noticed that my own shirt was a solid black canopy of flies. I swatted at them but they just resettled in the same places, no fewer for my assaults. No matter how I moved they stuck.

"What is the matter with you?" Robb hissed.

"It's these damn flies! How can you just sit there? Look, they're all over you too!" I slapped his chest as if I were beating a rug.

"Cut it out!" he hissed again. "Will you stop making a spectacle of yourself?" Every wakeful eye in the plane was watching my hysterical gyrations. Yet not one fly had fallen dead.

"Oh, sorry," I said meekly. I went back to watching the blind kid with only one fly. There was a lesson to be learned from him if I could just figure it out.

Tamanrasset, or Tam, as it is affectionately known, snuggles between the dramatic Hoggar Mountains to the north and a vast sea of sand to the east, west, and south. The plane swooped between columnar spirals of rock and weather-etched mesas illuminated by the late afternoon sun. At one point, I was sure the wing tips scraped the rock walls as the plane made an almost vertical maneuver through the crevasses.

Tam was a quirk in time and place. It was a city of striking contrasts: old and new architecture, residents and transients, cars and camels. Because it is the only city in the southern third of Algeria, it is a crossroad.

Tall Tuareg men swathed in indigo cloth and turbans piled high on their heads like minarets, shyly peeked from their face coverings and slunk in long-legged strides. These were the Blue Men of the Desert, so called because the dye from their clothing has rubbed into their skin. Descended from the earliest inhabitants of the desert, theirs is a matrilineal society in which men, not women, cover their faces.

Among the Tuaregs, black-draped Muslim women scurried almost unnoticed. Soft-spoken, black-skinned people from the south swayed in bold, bright prints. In contrast were the loud, white-skinned Europeans in khaki desert fashions. The Europeans swaggered, demanding space and attention. They roared through town in expensively outfitted jeeps and motorcycles.

Tamanrasset is the business center of the Route du Hoggar. Everything was available and for sale there, from day-old U.S. and European newspapers to Nouas beer and wine; from friendly advice to opportunistic lies. Souvenir boutiques catered to the tourists. Back alley stores stocked dusty cans of sardines on empty shelves. Black market dinar, *"L'Change"*, was furtively exchanged at a rate twice that of the bank.

There was no place better to hitch a ride to Arlit, the first town in Niger, than at *L'Camping* on the northern outskirts of Tam. We headed there immediately and checked into a *zerib*, a cane stalk shanty lined with plastic, but deceptively comfy.

Here, within the walls of *L'Camping*, was a European enclave bustling with excitement and purposeful activity. The boisterous laughter of men and, yes, even women mingled together openly! Several pairs of shoes jutted from underneath engines or transmissions of every vehicle there. The air reverberated with the clanking of wrenches against motors and expletives uttered in a hundred different languages. By night the tinkering went on by the flickering light of campfires and flashlights. Cooking pots clanged and neighbors met to trade car parts, jab at maps, smoke cigarettes, and brag.

The only alteration to this routine occurred nightly between 5:30 and 6:00, when water flowed from the spigots, and grease-streaked campers lined up at the communal cold water showers with water jugs and heaps of laundry.

That first night Chris cavorted through the shower with two blonde men. His professorial sulk was replaced by juvenile giggles.

"Hey, Chris, how goes it?" I called out.

"I've got a ride," he sang, "I'm leaving tonight!"

"No! Really? Who are you going with?"

"Ha, ha! I told you that I'd be across this fockin' desert in two weeks. Ha! I go tonight with compatriots...the marvelous French!" He leaned over the short wall, his eyes arrogant with knowledge, and said, "They're in *L'Beezneez.*"

He'd meant to sting me, and he did. I searched for politeness,

"Well, good luck to you, Chris." But he was singing the French anthem and didn't hear.

The overriding concern for us, however, was visas. Without one for either Niger or Mali we could go nowhere but north to the embassies in Algiers. Upon our first inquiries in town we were told that only Senegal was represented in Tam.

We worried until we found the Mali and Niger consulates almost side by side. By running back and forth between the two and juggling documents we got visas within twenty-four hours.[1] Meanwhile, we'd set in motion the serious business of finding rides.

Maybe it's a peculiarity of a Virgo to be finicky, to choose common sense survival over reckless adventure, but I didn't see a vehicle that I'd ride across town in. Mercedes and Peugeots literally sagged, broken by the road and the weight of provisions and passengers. Axles were tied in rope slings and engines clanked from sand-engorged mechanisms.

Nor did I meet a person with whom I wanted to spend five days alone in the desert. The camp broke down into three types of people: European *beezneez* men going south to sell dilapidated vehicles (I had since learned this was the mysterious *L'Beezneez*), the overlanders who bought seats out of London on refurbished garbage trucks for three- to six-month adventure tours of Africa, and the loners.

The *beezneez* men were typically paunchy and crusty in oil-stained jeans, creaky leather jackets, and gold chains. They kept to themselves, reticent, and competitively jealous of their market secrets. They were conscious of vehicle weight and sneered at hitchhikers. The overlanders swaggered. They tried to look and act tough like imagined movie idols. "Hey, look at me, I'm a real adventure man!" they seemed to say. The loners usually traveled by motorcycle. On the fringe of this melee were the few hitchhikers, the roving hopefuls. As diverse as it was, it was an interdependent group. The very real dangers of the desert lurked just south of the Tamanrasset city limits, and survival depended on mutual assistance.

Out of approximately ninety travelers, at least twenty moped about the campground dashed by a gruesome experience: A car and motorcycle caravan had been besieged by a sudden sandstorm. When it cleared one of the cyclists was missing. Two days later they found his body just a few hundred yards from the *piste*, the sand tracks. Another motorcyclist, James, witnessed his companion hit a sand bog and flip into unconsciousness. It took a week to get his comatose friend to the hospital in Tam, where he almost died from "secondary complications" before he could be flown to a hospital in Britain. James went out to the desert to collect their gear and it had all been stolen. He said, "I don't have the willpower to go on but there is nothing for me if I return home." He, like us, had sold everything to pay for his trip.

Many travelers in *L'Camping* were trying to prove their manhood, to find themselves, or were running away from something. One Dutch overlander confessed, "I'm here because I am afraid of nature, and I'm learning to trust those who are more competent than me, like our drivers." Later, his drivers told me it was their first time to cross the Sahara and their first time to run an organized tour. Three times they started out of Tam and three times they broke down.

David, a manic-depressive, rationed the medication that controlled his illness. His moods vacillated after his passport and money were stolen in a bread riot in the Tam souk. "I've been stuck here for over a month and still have no ride. I guess it's my fault because I don't trust anyone now."

There were however some "normal" people at *L'Camping*. Gary, a German, was newly graduated from medical school and was driving a Peugeot to his first assignment in South Africa. Two other Germans transported a load of pharmaceuticals to Mali to sell so they could pay for studying Sahelian music. A group of Swiss were delivering ambulances to a sister town in Mali. Some enterprising Australians stuffed their trunk with dates destined for sub-Saharan markets. Monica, a German motorcyclist, waited for a caravan to link up with because she could not upright her bike alone. And Golo, a student from Berlin, hitchhiked with Martin, a hypochondriac.

The longer we stayed at *L'Camping* the more discouraged I became. "We're never going to get a ride if we just sit around and wait," I said to Robb. "I don't know if I can listen to any more stories. We need another plan."

"O.K. If we don't have a ride by next Monday, we'll go out to the police station and hitch a ride on an Algerian truck," Robb bargained.

"Great! At least the Algerian drivers know what they're doing, unlike some of these people."

With no public transportation across the desert, the only two ways to go were with the Europeans or in the big Algerian trucks.

"I want to try one other thing—a notice to hang in the restaurant. I haven't seen anyone else do it, but it's worked for us before." It said:

> AMERICAN COUPLE
> WANTS RIDE TO ARLIT
> WILL PAY
> ZERIB 12

I had it translated into French and German, the two most commonly spoken languages besides English—the *lingua franc* of the road. That done, we started our preparations.

Trans-Saharan travelers are each responsible for their own provisions. It is a rule of the road. Another rule is that each person needs a minimum of seven liters of water for each day. I don't know who computed that magic figure, because I'm sure it should be more. Still, water was so scarce that it took two days to store our minimum allotment.

Food was selected on the basis of availability, ease of preparation, and nutritional value. We chose food that could be eaten hot or cold. The desert is so arid that all moisture is leeched from everything upon contact with the air, preserving it for an indefinite period. For power food that met all criteria, we packed dates and nuts, carrots, peppers, tomatoes, onions, oranges, sardines, soup mix, bread, and sweet cookies.

Our poster attracted attention to our plight but not a ride. When luck came I didn't recognize it. One morning the manager of *L'Camping*, a chubby, stylishly dressed Algerian, approached me and said, "We're driving to In'Guezzam this afternoon and you and your husband can come with us." In'Guezzam is the Algerian border post with Niger—416 kilometers to the south.

"We need a ride to Arlit. We could get stuck at the border."

"If you don't find a ride you can come back with us this evening."

This did not add up. It's impossible to go to In'Guezzam and back in less than four days let alone in an afternoon foray. I said as much.

"Ha! We know a secret route that only takes three hours. It's the same one used by the military police," he responded

I scrutinized the manager and his Parisian fashions. Impossible. There was no other way. It was a trick. I declined.

"*In sh'allah.* I offered," he said. Within an hour he careened out of *L'Camping* in a jeep filled with boys whose laughter rang out like that of kids just released from school. At the time I didn't feel the incident was worth mentioning to Robb.

Soon afterward Robb trotted up. "We're faking a vacation. Pack a few things. We're going into the Hoggar mountains, to Assekrem!"

A rather loosely organized group from the campground had gotten together and negotiated a discounted price for a three-day excursion with jeeps and drivers to Pere Foucald's 1920s hermitage in Assekrem. His name is sung in these parts with reverence. To the Tuaregs, Pere Foucald was a visionary who first translated their language. But to the French, the monk was a demigod. To us the excursion was a chance to get out of Tam and to shirk the shroud of gloom overhanging *L'Camping.*

Golo rode in our jeep that was driven by a Tuareg, named—surprise—Mohammed. It was the supply jeep and as Mohammed pointed out, "We've got all the food for the refuge, ha, ha, we can go anywhere we want! We don't even have to go there! Ha!" We arrived at Assekrem after nightfall, long after everyone else. As a result, we had to sleep and eat with the drivers. One hundred forty-three other tourists had staked out seats and the musty mattresses before us. It did not matter. With Mohammed's independent spirit and Golo's cheerfulness as company, we roamed the Hoggar. We got stuck and we got lost—many times.

The Hoggar was spectacular with lunar-like buttes, box canyons, nomad families scratching the sand for subterranean springs, thirty-thousand-year-old lava fields, and rock etchings, "made some time after the volcanic explosion." Mohammed animated the region with legend and Tuareg music called Taherdente.

"It is the women and old people who sing and clap to make the rhythm," he explained. "Our songs are about love, happiness, and magic. This is different from Muslim songs, which are prayers to Allah. Now listen. . . . Two women sit on opposite sides of a board stretched across a tinde, a large drum. They rock back and forth, up and down. The men stand on the camel saddles and move in a circle around the women. Over this ravine is where the Atakar of the Hoggar divides from the other three regions, let's go."

At one point Golo commented, "I suppose the jeep has replaced the camel." And Mohammed replied, "Not any more than the airplane has replaced the car."

Two of the greatest events in the Hoggar were sunrise and sunset among the bizarre mountain formations. We would climb to the top of a peak, huddle together for warmth, and watch Mother Nature paint the sky.

We returned to Tam re-energized from the holiday. Golo boldly begged a ride with Gary, the German doctor. "There is room for only one person or I would invite your company. I must also leave Martin, and we started this trip together. Clearly I hate to tell him, he is already depressed." Dorky, goofy-looking Martin had been dumped by rides three times already.

"Begging is the only way to survive here," said Golo. "I'm learning to be hard and to live without pride. I am so confused by myself, by what is right and wrong. I do not understand anything."

He left in search of Martin but a few minutes later returned. His body twitched with excitement.

"You will not believe what I just heard on the radio! What a day this is!" He bounced onto the bed and smacked his forehead, knocking his glasses askew. "I must be dreaming. I must return to Germany at once."

"What happened?"

"Here I sit in the middle of this desert, and I'm missing the most important event in my lifetime!" He leapt up and paced.

"Tell us!"

"The Berlin Wall is coming down! East and West Germany will reunify! Never did I think this thing possible."

"What? You're kidding us."

"I don't know this word 'kidding' but I hear this news just now on the shortwave. Can you imagine? One Germany!"

"This is astounding, but is it true? What will happen? What do you think it will mean?" we asked.

"Yes, I think it is true. If I wait to go home I'll never get a job, everyone from the east will come to take them all. The university will be full. Everything will be more expensive. But it might be easier to get an apartment in the east side...."

"What do you think it will mean politically?"

"That, too, I don't know. I'm not sure it is a good thing. I don't trust us to be one nation again. You see why I must leave?"

"You just got a ride, you can't leave now."

"You're right," he said, riffling his hair with his hand. "I must be hard. Have you seen Martin? I must tell him, and I have to help prepare the car. What a day! I'm too young to be confused."

Several messages awaited us when we returned to our *zerib*. Some of the would-be rides had departed already. After checking other leads, we decided instead to hitch the next day with the Algerian trucks.

David, the manic-depressive, caught the rumor of our departure and came to our *zerib*. "Pardon me, I know I'm behaving rather boldly and rash. This is embarrassing to beg, but you know my circumstances, may I accompany you tomorrow?" We did not want his company, but it was a public road, so we accepted David with our fate.

The three of us went out on the town that night. Newspapers had not yet arrived, so we had no more news on Germany. Nor were there any letters for us at *poste restante*. I started worrying about Mom, but Robb aborted my ruminations with a bottle of wine from the black market.

"Let's celebrate! I've always dreamed of crossing the Sahara and now we're doing it. Toast success," Robb said.

David said, "Yes, and good riddance to this Tamanrasset. Yesterday I visited with a magistrate, a family friend, who told me of his official investigation into the bizarre death of a Belgian family. According to the police report, they got lost in The Forbidden Zone while in route to Arlit. After two days the Belgians ran out of food and water so they burned their car to attract help. It didn't, but without protection, the baby died from exposure and dehydration, so they ate him to keep the other child alive. When that child died, they ate him too, still hoping for rescue. The husband later cut his wrists and told his wife to drink his blood, 'If there is a chance that one of us might live I want it to be you,' the chap said. No, don't laugh. This is a true story. The police know what happened out there because the woman kept a journal until she died. Now get this, her last entry went, 'I have no regrets for what we have done. My only disappointment in life is that I didn't live long enough to see the movie *Rambo III*."

"Aw, come on, David, that's got to be a joke," we said. Now we were rocking the bench with mirth.

"I swear to you it's true. The magistrate is a very busy, serious man. He doesn't joke." David pouted. Ominous clouds of depression swirled over his head.

I looked at my watch. "Shall we walk home now? We've got a big adventure tomorrow."

The stars were the only lights in town at 5:00 A.M. when we met David at the front gate to *L'Camping* the next morning. The air was cold and still, like a frozen food locker. We hopped and jiggled to get warm while waiting for the ride to the police station that David had arranged. The police station was where we would hitch a ride with the trucks. Half an hour later, a car creaked over the corrugated ravines and coughed to a stop in front of our mound of food, water, and backpacks.

The sleepy officer at the frontier police station said it was too early for traffic. "The trucks come at eight o'clock. Wait in front by the road. It will be easy to get a ride because they must all stop here to register."

We moved our provisions to the road and scrunched down to wait. After a while I noticed Robb was rolled into a tight ball and grimacing.

"What's wrong?"

"Nothing."

"What's wrong? You're grimacing."

"I have a pain in my lower back."

"Where? Maybe you pulled a muscle. Let me rub it."

"No. Don't touch me. It hurts too much. Aagh. Shit. Maybe if I just walk around."

Robb walked until he disappeared over a dune on the far side of the road. I ran after him.

"How do you feel?" I called, launching an avalanche of sand onto his crumpled body. He laid fetal-like in a culvert.

"Horrible. In fact, I've never felt so much pain."

"Maybe if you let me help you back into town..."

"No, go away. It's probably just gas and I don't want anyone around when it lets loose. I just need to get up and walk some more."

He staggered upright and, clutching his side, started up another dune. I was chasing him further into the desert, so I retreated to the road. When the sun poked over Libya to the east, I snuck back to check on him. His moans were like a beacon. Robb was white, cradled in his own arms, and rocking in a little hole that he'd spooned out. Enough, I thought. I ran back to the police station.

"You have to help me. Something is wrong with my husband, he can't move."

"Where is he?" the policeman asked.

"Over there about a kilometer."

He blew a whistle, and about ten more policeman ran out tucking shirts into rumpled brown pants. They slung Robb's body between them and carried him back to the road where the officer flagged down a passing car.

"Take these people to the hospital!" he said.

"I'll go with you," David offered half-heartedly.

"No, you go on without us," I said. "We don't know what is wrong, and we don't want you to get stuck again." Stuffed into the car with four men I whispered to Robb, "Hee, hee, good trick. You can sit up now that we got rid of him."

The driver of the car blared the horn like a mock siren. "What is wrong? I take you to the hospital, non?"

"No, no, please take us to *L'Camping*," I said. "Do you know where it is?" We wanted to avoid the hospital. With luck, we'd find Gary still at the campground.

"*L'Camping*? I know this place but this man is very sick so we go to the hospital."

"Aaagh. Please take me to *L'Camping*," croaked Robb. The others in the car shook their heads in protest and argued vehemently among themselves but took us to *L'Camping*.

"*In sh'allah*," they said when they dropped us off.

"I'll go find Gary," I said, helping Robb back into our *zerib*. He convulsed with dry heaves at every step.

"Pami, I've never felt such pain in my life. I'm worried....aaagh."

"Don't worry. If Gary has left or can't help, we'll get the first plane to Algiers, then up to Europe. No big deal. This is what we agreed to do if there was a medical emergency." We were both thinking that the trip wasn't going well. Once again it looked as if our trip was headed for a premature end, if not a disastrous one.

Gary emerged from the *zerib* about thirty minutes later. "I'm not sure. You see, he is my first patient, and I do not have diagnostic instruments, but I think he has a kidney stone." The symptoms fit—an excruciating pain starting in the back and spreading to the lower abdomen. "But he said he has no history of the kidney stone, so I think it may be dehydration," Gary continued.

"He drinks plenty of water, how could he be dehydrated?" I asked.

"Hmmm, not enough. It is the sun. Too hot. I'll go now to look at the pharmaceuticals the other Germans bring in their car. I think I saw just the right medication. Make him walk and drink."

Robb alternated between hobbling, vomiting the water that he forced down, and lying scrunched up in a ball moaning. "I am so sorry to ruin your trip like this," he panted.

"Don't worry about that. This is part of the adventure. I just wish you didn't hurt so bad."

"Oh, it is the worse pain in my life. I think Gary is right about it being a kidney stone. Shit, shit. I feel like I could die. I'm glad we didn't go to the Tam hospital, though, and that Gary hadn't left."

Gary was gone for days getting the medication, or so it seemed. When he finally returned he said, "Give him forty drops of this now," something called Baralgin. "And twenty in another hour. It will make him sleep."

"Then he'll be fine?"

"Hmmm, maybe with luck. Without luck he has a big problem. He should pass it in four or five hours. If not, go to Algiers."

Robb slept, and I fretted with my journal. "If all things happen for the best, then we can be thankful this didn't flair up while on the back of a truck. At least we have a *zerib* and a doctor. Robbie is otherwise strong and healthy, so I'm optimistically counting on him passing the stone quickly. Nevertheless, I'm certain Robb should rest here a few days more. I don't mind the 'setback' as he called it. It couldn't have happened in a better place." I assiduously avoided dwelling on the negative outcomes that were all too obvious.

I nervously consumed many cups of mint tea, fruit juice, and nasty cola while I waited in the shadows of the campground restaurant. Robb snored on. Then, suddenly, he stood before me, holding onto the edge of the table for balance, his skin almost translucent, his eyes unfocused, and his beard and hair rumpled from bed.

"We got a ride across the Sahara!" he said."We're leaving tonight!"

Who was this madman? What hallucinations had visited his drugged sleep?

"What are you doing here? How do you feel?" I asked astonished. "What do you mean we're leaving tonight? With whom? Sit down."

"I was asleep when I heard someone at the door. At first I thought it was a dream, but the voice continued so I got up to look. Miraculously, I felt no pain. Sure, a little soreness, but the real pain was gone. Anyway, some guy was standing there and he said, 'I saw your sign,' the poster he meant, 'we're leaving tonight to cross the Sahara. You and your wife can come with us if you talk to our chef,' I think he meant chief. 'Come at five o'clock.' Then he went away, and I came here looking for you. We have to get ready."

"Who was he?"

"I don't know. Someone. I think he was familiar."

"Yeah. But who was he? I mean, where are we supposed to meet him?"

"I don't know. Somewhere here. They are driving Mercedes vans. I was asleep, then I was awake, but awake without pain. I've passed the stone! We can leave tonight!"

"No, we won't. You're resting for several days. Robb, a person doesn't just go through what you have then get up and cross the desert. No way. We're staying here."

"What? And get stuck again? I swear to you I'm fine. Now go find these people before they leave."

"They're probably in junky cars."

"No. This guy was different. You'll see."

I was miffed. I was not convinced Robb was recovered enough to travel. I hoped not to be able to find the "familiar guy" and his vans, but they were alone in the field: three schoolbus-yellow vans that I'd never seen before. The windshields were intact, the bumpers hung in the right places, and I couldn't detect any tell-tale sagging under the frames. I almost skipped them. This was madness, folly to consider leaving that night. Yet if I returned without arranging the ride, Robb would be furious.

"Are you leaving tonight for the Sahara?" I asked.

"Yah."

"Did one of you talk to my husband about a ride?"

The clanging on the vans stopped. Three greasy faces replaced six dirty feet. A fourth man stepped around the bumper of a van. "I did." he said.

"Who is the head cook? I'd like to talk with him." I winced under their glares. "The chef, the chief?" I quickly tried to correct my mistranslation of French.

A slightly pudgy guy with rosy cheeks and tennis shoes, an All-American collegiate type, stepped forward. "I'm the chef."

For an hour we laboriously interrogated each other. None of us spoke good French, the chief spoke little English, and I spoke no Austrian. What are your supplies? Condition of your vehicles? What do you expect? What is your experience? Eye-for-eye mutual distrust was exchanged. Payment of $10 per day was discussed. I wanted to find something objectionable about these guys or their vehicles. Instead, I was grudgingly impressed by their preparedness.

"Where is your husband?"

That was a good question. How to field it was an even better question. I couldn't tell the truth without blowing the ride.

"Oh, he went into town to change money. He'll return shortly."

Then the chief drew his chest up in a big huff of air and said, "I cannot be responsible for you, your food, or water, and I cannot make you any guarantees. Anything can happen out there. It is not safe. You are small, and the work will be great."

He meant a kind warning, but his paltry English made the words sound gruff. I was insulted. Nothing churns my blood faster than to be told I can't do something or the implication that I am not capable. I heard myself proclaiming loudly and all too boldly, "We are not afraid!"

The chief blinked, startled by the force of my statement. The three other men translated my statement among themselves.

"The others are equal partners so we must discuss this decision among ourselves," the chief said. "Please wait over there."

There was still hope that they could find against us. Oh, why did I say such a stupid thing as we are not afraid? What if Robbie developed another kidney stone out there?

"We've made a decision," said the chief. The four confronted me. Not a friendly face among them. "We do not need passengers, and we don't need the money because it is nothing for the responsibility. I don't know why we do this. We like you perhaps. You may come with us if you can be ready by nine o'clock tonight."

"Really?"

"It is true. But you must be ready with your own food and water. We will not wait."

"We'll be ready."

"And we want to meet your husband first," the chief added.

"No problem. As soon as he returns from town I will bring him to you. Thanks."

As I turned away the guy who had admitted to calling at our *zerib* caught my eye with a wink and a thumbs-up.

"Well, did you find them? What happened?" Robb greeted me from bed. He was still fetal and pale, looking not much hardier than earlier in the morning. If anything he was more haggard, his eyeballs dully set in black sockets.

"Let me sit down," I said. "I'm not sure what happened."

"Just tell me. Do we have a ride or not?"

"Of all the stupid things, I told them that we weren't afraid."

"Get on with it. Was it the guy I told you? Did you recognize him?"

"No, I didn't recognize him. They only arrived this afternoon. Don't ever do this again! Are you absolutely, positively sure that you passed that stone and that you're feeling better?"

"Yeah, yeah. Just tell me what happened. Did we get a ride?"

"Comb your hair, do something to yourself because I have to take you to meet them. We're leaving tonight at nine."

"Yes! Alright! I knew this was the one." He sprang from the bed and started moving the backpacks around. "Get moving, we have to get ready. Where did you put the food?"

"Robbie. Come here, please. I need to hug you." We slung our arms over each others' shoulders and absently patted one another on the back. Soothingly, like old friends who might wipe a tear from the other's eye. "This is the stupidest thing we've ever done," I said.

― 5 ―

Digging Across the Sahara

We left Tam like smugglers, in the blackness of night. But, unlike smugglers, we stopped for *Le Formalite*: All people traveling across the Sahara must first register with the frontier police.[1] Supposedly, registration assured search and rescue intervention if we didn't arrive at the Algerian border when we were scheduled to: four days later. However *Le Formalite* was a joke with no more credibility than the term implied: a formality.

A paved road extended from Tam for a distance not much longer than a Concord runway. Where the road ended we camped. Robb and I scraped thorns from under an acacia tree and laid back to stare at heaven. Gnarly branches stabbed Orion's glittering belt and scratched the moon's full face. With the tumble of events that had occurred that day, I could not believe we were actually under way. Only a few hours earlier, a medical emergency poised us on the brink of abandoning the trip altogether. And now we laid under an acacia tree in the Sahara! It was a reckless act of defiance. I hoped it wouldn't backfire on us. We prayed that this ride signaled a change of luck and that the kidney stone would stay our secret.

In the early light of morning, the drivers revved the engines of their vans. One of the engines didn't sound right. A water pump had frozen! Robb and I exchanged "uh-oh" looks; bad luck stuck to us like dung on a shoe.

Fat Eugene and little Hans stripped down the engine, bolt by bolt, while Helmut and Walter paced and sucked on Marlboros like pacifiers. In the distance, trucks rumbled through the post-dawn chill. If not for Robb's kidney stone yesterday, we could have been on one of those safe trucks. Instead, we were stuck with strangers and a broken vehicle.

Our newfound confidence disintegrated. The desolation of the terrain intertwined with my spirit. I kicked at it. "Go away. Think constructively." Eventually, the last engine bolt twisted into place and the four engines impatiently ignited.

Almost immediately Eugene's van quagmired in a sandfield—our first. A nearby camel disdainfully chewed his cud like a rude pronouncement on our technology. We set to work digging the van out. Our tools were shovels, sand ladders, muscle power, and a giant jack mounted on a cumbersome board, which the Austrians phonetically called a "hatcheck." We dug the sand, raised the wheels, and slid the sand ladders, really just heavy boards, underneath. Then everyone pushed the vehicle a few feet forward, moved the boards again, and so on until we reached firm ground. The procedure was quickly memorized through repetition but not so quickly executed.

The vans were all identical in year and maintenance, which meant their parts were interchangeable with the spare engine stowed in one of the vans along with a replacement engine for the Peugeot, which the chief drove. The vans were stocked with two fifty-five gallon drums of water, three drums of diesel, and one drum of gasoline for the Peugeot; oil, eight spare tires mounted and inflated, the gigantic "hatcheck," shovels, flares, and home-made sand ladders—several lengths of three-by-eight-inch boards cut to the dimensions of the wheel base.[2]

We crossed 30 kilometers or 18 miles of desert that first day. Not exactly a record for the Paris-Dakar Rally. Night came suddenly and brought frigid temperatures. Light from the full moon was as cold and distant as the stars. I shivered and for a few moments snuggled with warm thoughts of home.

The vehicles were attended to first, just like herds are attended to first by the shepherds who depend on them for survival. Fuel and water, filters, cables, and tubes were all checked, replaced or refilled. Little energy was left for our cold supper. Exhaustion, isolation, and the silence of the Sahara wrapped us in pensiveness.

Robb and I were assigned to ride in different vans to better distribute weight. When we finally wriggled into our sleeping bags, with our voices to the wind, he assured me that, although sore, he felt great. "All my life I've dreamed of doing this," he said, "never though did I imagine it would be so beautiful. I love it here, I feel so lucky, and I like these guys too. They are all characters."

Bulbous-bellied Eugene had been dubbed "Sableman" because of his habit of sinking into sandfields. The only French he knew was *sable*, sand, which he interspersed frequently in an outpour of Austrian swearwords. Eugene was a kind person who exhibited a rough boastful exterior. He was a weekend warrior, and the trip was one long weekend for him.

"I've been on public dole for two years," he said, his hands laced behind his head like a man in a hammock, "because my wife doesn't want me to work. It's the only way she can keep me at home. As soon as I get money in my pocket I take off traveling. I once applied for a job, but she begged them not to give it to me. She'd rather work herself knowing that I crawl back into bed with the cat than let me work." Six years earlier he and Helmut made this same trip. "My wife hasn't let me go anywhere since then," he said with a wink and a conspiratorial laugh.

Helmut, the chief, was crossing the Sahara for the fourth time. "When you are here in the desert, you think you are crazy and that you'll never come back again. Then, after you are home for a few months, you start thinking and talking about it again. You feel you must come back. It is strong, forceful. I cannot escape it," he said in jumbled French, English, and Austrian. He was the organizer, the brains of the enterprise. "We'll sell the vehicles wherever we get the best price. I don't need the money, I do this for adventure. It is for Hans and Eugene that I try to make a profit. They own nothing but these cars."

Helmut, in the Peugeot 305, led the caravan to test the sand for firmness. When his wheels whirled without gripping the sand, the vans would circle back, then with the accelerator floored, try to fly across the soft bed of sand...if we were lucky. Sometimes the vans would sink, submerged to the doors, as happened four times on the first day. It was a new style of driving, and the learning curve was steep and circular for all of us. Especially Eugene.

Robb rode with Hans who, at twenty-eight, was balding with tufts of blonde hair around his ears. He was slight of build and bustled with quick, darting movements that reminded me of a squirrel. He awoke at dawn and heated coffee before the rest of us groaned greetings to the day. Hans was away from his mother, wife, and children for the first time in his life. "My village is so small that there is not a street. My children know nothing about cars." Robb and Hans quickly developed a communication based on sensitivity and gestures more than language. Hans knew one word of English, "firewater." Each night he unveiled a bottle of home brew and meted out a half-shot to each of us. As we choked and stomped our feet from the killer liquor, he would grin mischievously.

Walter drove the van I rode in. He was a gypsy of sorts who worked intermittently as a welder or an electrician to finance his travel caprices. In fact, he was a hired driver for the trip. "It was a cheap way to Africa. A friend told me about these guys, I called them, and the next day I was on my way." He was a voracious reader, quiet, and spoke five languages delivered with dry wit. Walter was thirty-five, with a handsome, lean face and a single earring symbolizing his renegade spirit. Because he was a loner and an impromptu adventurer, I was somewhat surprised when he told me he was married. "After we sell the cars, I'll go to Ghana where my wife will join me in January. We hope to find a place to settle down for a while."

The next day we averaged three miles per hour. The going was desperately difficult. It was a day of looping back on our tracks and progressing only a few meters before being stopped by another sandfield.

Long discussions accompanied each entrapment. I suspected it was an excuse to rest. While the Austrians argued the best strategy, Robb would dart across the sandfield testing for firmness and a probable path of escape. He came close to running across the Sahara. His path-finding efforts were invaluable, however, and he was informally promoted.

I dragged the shovels, hatcheck, and heavy sand ladders from spot to spot, van to van, but otherwise my status remained that of congenial company and the chronicler of the adventure.

At one point, we lost the *piste*, the tracks in the desert sand, and strayed into The Forbidden Zone. The *piste* was laced with tire tracks left from previous vehicles that circled as we did. "The Way" was denoted by occasional kilometer markers, a stack of rocks or car wreckage strewn like grim tombs to unknown soldiers. They were of little use as path markers; the entire 360 degree panorama was littered with these foreboding tombstones. They usually signaled a desert form of quicksand so we gave them wide berth. But sand shifted and new bogs continually developed.

The Forbidden Zone lies within eyesight of the piste but when you're in it, the piste is not within eyesight. It earned its name the same way other deathtraps—Dead Man's Gulch, Place With No Way Out—have earned theirs.

That morning we confronted an expansive sea of soft sand. Tire tracks split in all directions. Abandoned cars covered acres. We tried for hours to find a way through the field and finally backtracked and struck a course that was supposed to be a wide arc. Helmut led as usual. When our tires gripped a hard surface we picked up speed.

We were careless, and the vans separated beyond line of sight from each other. Still, we sped on, lulled by the movement and the breeze through the windows. Another basic mistake was distributing provisions according to weight. Walter and I carried all the water, but no food or fuel. Separated and alone, none of us had a chance.

Helmut doubled back in search of the others while Walter and I waited with our despair and Saharan hallucinations. "Damn that Helmut! Damn, damn, damn!" Walter slammed his fist against the steering wheel. Helmut had not said so but we knew we were lost in The Forbidden Zone. Enough time passed that Walter and

I both got maudlin about our lives. I said that I didn't want to die
without Robb, then we both cried.

We could hear them arguing before the roofs of the yellow vans
peaked the horizon. Everyone was cursing Helmut. Although
united, with slightly improved chances of survival, we were not yet
saved.

Hans peered through binoculars without finding a hint of the
piste. Helmut scouted in the Peugeot and returned shaking his
head. We might have backtracked if we had known where we had
strayed.

The sun glared from its zenith. The chicanerous heat shimmered off the earth's sloped back and distorted the real and imagined. The temperature hovered over 100 degrees Fahrenheit, and
the dry air sucked all moisture from our bodies. We had to drink
water, although we were acutely aware of the need to ration. We
were totally alone—even the dead cars were absent from the
sandscape. The only witnesses to our unspoken fears were an occasional fly and a solitary dung beetle on stilt legs.

A cement *oblisque* was spied after four hours of searching. It
was a kilometer marker set along the piste. What a relief to have
found our way out of The Forbidden Zone. Helmut estimated that
we had strayed 43 kilometers from the route. The experience af-
fected each of us so profoundly that we never talked about it
again.

Nights were a welcome respite. They brought rest, food, coolness, and a marvelous, star-filled sky that was so silent and still
that the only movement was that of the earth. The Sahara may be
unforgiving, but it is a place of incredibly dynamic beauty. Maybe
it was our emotional response to its indifference that made it seem
so dynamic. Each new sandfield was a challenge, and, even
though we were fatigued from digging, we felt glory when we
eventually extricated ourselves. We felt loneliness in the desert's
immensity and camaraderie in our teamwork. The night sky gave
us welcomed shelter from the sun that, in its turn, warmed us
from the night.

Promptly at nine o'clock each night, a soft breeze swept clean
the sand. Robb and I slept on the ground in mummy bags. We
learned after the first night to aim our feet toward the wind to prevent sand from filling our sleeping bags. Nevertheless, we awoke

each morning with a half-inch of fine grains weighing our eyelids shut.

Day three was like all the preceding days except for two events. First, a sandstorm almost buried us. In the distance, the enormous black cloud looked like a thunderstorm. We were nearly dug out of a sand bog when it pelted down on us, clogging our lungs and blowing the mounds of shoveled sand back under the vehicles.

Then we arrived at an escarpment, or rock bluff, that we couldn't see around or over. Robb trotted past the steep boulder field to direct us to the pinnacle. And there, parked in front of us, was a caravan of trucks and jeeps. The passengers were picnicking under the full midday sun. Among them was David.

I barely glimpsed his red bandanna and sun-splintered lips. We waved and hooted without stopping. While glad to see he was surviving, I was thankful for the kidney stone that had delivered us from both David and the trucks.

The small town of In Guzzeman blocked the way to the border. Our vans rocked through the pot-holed street of In Guzzeman past several blocks of oil-blackened mechanic's shops. Beyond town rose a series of high, mushy sand dunes and stuck vehicles. Robb scouted a route through the field, but from the top of a towering dune he ran back waving his arms "no." Walter jumped the accelerator anyway. We literally took flight and then rammed a culvert of sand. The front of the van crumpled under impact as did my consciousness. I awoke to a groggy vision of Gary, the doctor, and Golo peering through the cracked windshield.

Their car was stuck in the same dune only a few feet away, and next to them were the other Germans, carrying the pharmaceuticals. All had departed Tam while Robb was still writhing in pain. "We never thought we'd see you alive!" they exclaimed boisterously while pounding Robb's back. The secret of the kidney stone was out. Walter, who had gone to the *zerib* with the invitation, giggled.

"Wow, and I thought Robb was on drugs—stoned," Walter said. "Because of that I thought you would make good traveling companions."

Helmut was perturbed by our deception, but that too passed by the time all the vehicles were towed out of the sand (that is, all the vehicles but one big bus that had been stuck four days). Our circle of camaraderie expanded among the Austrians and Germans.

Helmut declined an invitation to camp with the others and led us the last remaining kilometers to the border post. We camped outside the fenced perimeter of the border guard's barracks. Helmut quelled our complaints over our location: "Border formalities here and in Niger are very difficult and can take a long time. Our only chance to reach Arlit tomorrow is if we are first through in the morning."

A border guard squatted with us for the evening. "I want to show you something," he said, "Come with me. See these cars?" He pointed to a row of Peugeots, Mercedes and trucks. "These cars belonged to Europeans who died in The Forbidden Zone over the last year." They were macabre monuments to the fine line between good and bad luck. I tried not to listen to his tales of searches that always ended in descriptions of death. It was too real and our escape from The Forbidden Zone too recent.

The soldier then whispered, "There is another route that takes only three hours from Tamanrasset. It is much safer but is restricted to military use."

"Robbie, there is something I didn't tell you. Remember when we were advertising for a ride? Well, the manager of *L'Camping* offered us one."

"So?"

"Well, it was to here only and that's why I turned it down. But he said he could drive from Tamanrasset to the border in three hours. That's what this soldier said too."

"I don't buy it. It's impossible. If there was another way, don't you think the Algerian truckers would use it?"

"That's what he said. And that makes two people who said the same thing."

"I still don't buy it." When a person has his mind so set, there is no way to convince him of something that you know little about. I could not verify the alternate Sahara route, although evidence suggested its existence. The boys from *L'Camping* claimed to make frequent use of the road.

The moon was still full that night and the wind blew furiously. On the police side of the compound fires sparkled, voices laughed, and mongrels growled and yipped as if fighting over a carcass. "Civilization" was noisy.

The sergeant in charge of the border didn't arrive from Tam until 9 A.M. Meanwhile, vehicles backed up on both sides. Drivers paced and waved documents to stake out their order of passage. Robb and I nervously reviewed our money declaration. We'd lost a receipt and were worried.[3] While fretting, a tattered line of army dudes slunk past. The last in line turned and flicked a sign to me, a slowly descending eyelid.

"Do you know him?" asked Robb.

"Yeah, and I'm surprised you don't recognize him. He was the chief police officer at Tam who carried you out of the desert."

Suddenly, we were waved into the hot, steamy interrogation room. The sergeant glared a yellow eyeball at us. He wanted something and would find it. The policeman from Tam then appeared and intercepted our outstretched papers. He stamped them. A lazy eyelid signaled his complicity.

To call Assemaka, the Niger border post, a town, would confer on it a dignity it did not deserve. Nevertheless, a stand of eight palms, several mud-brick buildings, scrawny chickens, and maybe a hundred people sprawled in the dust gave Assemaka an aura of permanency. Large, fiber-wrapped bundles baked in the sand. They had been unloaded from trucks for customs inspection. The flatbed trucks had stood so long without movement that brightly colored cloth canopies had sprouted from the wheel hubs. Under them bony, brown-skinned mothers breast fed babies while hordes of flies rested on their sweat-glistened skin. Assemaka was as listless as a malnourished leper colony. As the gateway to black Africa, it was as different from Algeria as Antarctica is from Martinique. It was different not only in its casual decrepitness and resigned hopelessness of the people, but in the scorching, wind-abandoned heat. The 35 kilometers between borders was like crossing into another world.

Scrawny border police with scarred cheeks and dark glasses swooped like crows on each new arrival.

"Stop! Stop here! Don't move. Put everything in the sand!" they cawed.

What they were really saying was, "They're mine! I saw them first!"

They pecked and squabbled over every item in our possession, from toothpaste to the spare motors and tires, until a pregnant-looking chief swaggered over, beat the scavengers with a stick and ordered us to The Formalities. Our paperwork was then shuffled from building to building, back and forth between offices like a slow-moving pendulum. The border would close at noon and it was already after eleven. We hustled to beat the clock.

If anything was purposeful about the system it was to extort bribes. The drivers had to present *carnets*, titles, licenses, insurance, etc.[4] A tourist tax of CFA 1000 (Central Franc African), was levied against each of us. Luckily, Helmut had enough to pick up the tab.

But sure enough, just as we lined up in front of immigration to retrieve our passports, the door slammed shut. Five men and one undocumented woman were inside. When Helmut persisted in knocking at the locked door, it was finally opened by a man whose face clearly read, "This interruption better be worth my while." Unscathed by the threatening glare, Helmut furtively revealed a bottle of cognac wrapped in a towel. The scowl faded, and we were impatiently handed our passports.

With great whoops we ran to the vans before another pretense detained us. Meanwhile, the Germans had arrived. They were stuck in the waiting void. "Ha, Ha!" We shouted, rather obnoxiously, "We're showering tonight in Arlit!" The Germans had that hopeless look of permanency about them as we sped off into the desert.

One incident at Assemaka nearly earned me residency. During the paperwork shuffle I sat under the palms with my journal. A cop pounced down and "arrested" me as a spy. I disclaimed any understanding of French and made him labor to tell me that writing at the border was prohibited. I bluffed a laugh, "It is only a letter to my mother. See?" I said. While he ranted, I scribbled "Dear Mom" across the top of the page. "Mama," I said. It worked. But it taught me to always carry a folded piece of paper, a start of a letter to Mama.[5]

Two days later we chugged into Arlit. All the tires were flat, the Peugeot was in tow, the last of the food and water had been given to the passengers of a stranded truck, and Walter ranted, "I hate adventures!" Between Assemaka and Arlit we got mired in the deepest sandfields of the entire crossing. In one ocean of soft sand we dug six hours before extricating the first vehicle, and we still had four vehicles to go. The heat was steamy and intense and the labor slowed by our declining spirits.

Arlit was announced with a fringe oasis and a yellow flume of clouds from a French/German/Nigerian joint-owned uranium plant. During the 1970s, the price of uranium had been high, and Niger's skewed GNP had been one of the most prosperous in Africa. Since then the world demand for uranium had plummeted and so had the per capita income in Niger, making it one of the poorest nations in Africa. The plant still employed several hundred people and spewed noxious pollution into the air.

The campground was on that same nasty side of town. As we rolled through the gates, we were besieged by dusty Tuaregs waving souvenir swords. It was a barren and filthy place but it had a shower. And semi-cold beer.

– 6 –
Niger

The town of Arlit was the most poverty-stricken place east of Haiti. Plastic bags and burlap scraps formed quilted lean-tos for drought-deposed Tuareg families. Arlit was bereft of animation except for us. Still riding high on Western vitamins and the adrenalin of victory, our good health alone was enough to make me feel uncomfortably like a crass multimillionaire.

The Austrians dismissed our debt for the ride because we (Robb) had worked so hard. They also offered us a free onward ride as long as they had the vans. Helmut, however, wanted to spend several days in Arlit.trying to sell them there. We were soon to learn it was not a place to linger.

Grudgingly, we surrendered our passports at the police station according to law,[1] and changed money at the bank. One American dollar equalled CFA 275, and in that desert outpost, it converted into buying power as $2.50 for instant coffee, $1.00 for a coke,

$20.00 for a plate of goat with rock-pitted rice, and $10.00 each to sleep in the filthy dirt of the campground.

The only good deal was sixty cents for a large bottle of beer. We drank plenty of them in the scrub-shaded courtyard of the Hotel Tamesna, where a drunk smashed empty bottles against the wall as if he were playing a polite game of darts. Along the courtyard walls sat a row of aloof aristocrats in flowing robes. Nubile boys buffed their manicures and pedicures as if they were shining shoes.

We were pegged to our chairs by sniveling souvenir salesmen, by the fear of the flying bottles, and by an alcoholic stupor. Hans alternated between drunken weeping and railing at Helmut. "I hate this place, and I hate you for bringing me here." We had looked forward to our arrival in Arlit, but the town was so dismal that the thrill had washed off in the showers. In comparison to the desert solitude, Arlit was hell. Even digging was more fun.

Robb dragged a chair next to Hans and patted his hand until his anger dissipated to a whimper. "Culture shock," Robb whispered.

That night Helmut collided with another vehicle. Since he had forged all his documents, including insurance, Helmut quickly and loudly accused the other driver of all blame. The event attracted a crowd and the fracas caused so much confusion that no one could reconstruct culpability. The squeaky wheel, Helmut, was paid CFA 10,000 to shut up before the police arrived.

The Germans strolled into town then. After much backslapping, we decided to celebrate our survival with dinner at the one restaurant in town—the Tamesna. Goat with rice or goat with spaghetti were the only entrees for the night.

When we descended from the second floor restaurant into the courtyard, a lair of prostitutes ambushed the nine men. At least twenty-one women locked them in a groin wrap and, like a mutant centipede, propelled us to tables. Flight was made impossible by entwined legs, and bared nipples stifled protestations. A hand waving, "Go away!" was grabbed and clutched to a gyrating pelvis. "Fuckee, fuckee!" the women sang like a war chant. Clearly, protest sweetened the game.

Actually, I enjoyed the women's uninhibited teasing and the men's reluctant embarrassment. It was a sort of female revenge after months of male company. Robb's elbow sharply dug my side, "Will you do something about Hans?" he urged.

A voluptuous dark-skinned woman had his balding head in a vice grip between her breasts. Hans wept, "I love my wife, leave me alone."

"I love dis lil man," the woman sang.

"He's my husband," I said.

The woman's eyes routed my lie to the core.

"No, dis mon is your husband," she said, pointing to Robb. He was the only unmolested man in the patio. I don't know how the women divined our relationship except by intuition or African radar. I thought our behavior had passed for purely platonic.

She slid into my chair, which, at least, gave Hans a break. Her body was billowy soft and her dark skin cool. It was the first softness I'd felt since we left home. Maybe because of that, she reminded me of my mother.

She told me her name was Sepina and that she loved me too. As we talked she stripped bracelets from her arm and slid them on mine. Soon several other women nudged onto our chair. They were from Ghana, Nigeria, and Benin. Abandoned by husbands, widowed, or sold by their fathers, they were smuggled north to the Muslim strongholds for six weeks of economic opportunity. A chance to earn enough money to feed their children or to eventually reach Europe, where "I'll never haf to lie with anudder mon again."

They didn't have travel documents and were often caught by the police. "It's no problem," said Sepina. "They rub the body all over and stick their bone between the legs over and over again. I must make my mind accept this because it makes my way. I haf only my body to give."

A local drunkard came behind her as she talked and he rubbed his bone against her shoulder.

"Go away. Dis is my friend I sit with. Go." When he didn't move, she swung at him with her open hand. "The mens is always takee, takee. They must show respect. After all, I am a tourist here too," she said with a sniff of pride.

Only Eugene openly enjoyed the lusty attention. He grasped and sucked at every inch of female flesh that he could hold in his lap at one time. He ultimately disappeared with three women. I

guess at CFA 1000, the same price as to sleep in the dirt of the
campground, he got a deal for his money. To everyone else it
earned him the status of pariah and prayers for his wife. More
than 8.3 million people in sub-Sahara are infected with AIDS.[2]

The Tamesna closed up, and a late-night bar next door opened.
The prostitutes moved us over there, where we stayed until our
eyelids stuck shut with sleep. Joan, Golo's new devotee, refused to
surrender him. She ripped her dress in lamentation and spilled
tears over our knees. "I will kill myself!" she wailed. Suicidal
Joan had to be shoved out of the car. All of us felt inhumane by
the scene. Golo, though, took it to heart. He mourned her death
and his role in causing it.

The vans didn't sell in Arlit. The price was too low. "Many vehicles come now," the buyers said. What did sell was the spare engines, jerry cans, tires, tools, hatcheck, empty barrels, and a ton
of used children's clothes. Gas, however, was not for sale so the
Peugeot was towed another 192 kilometers to Agadez on the
paved "Uranium Road."

In Agadez, the first stop was the police station to register. Our
arrival was greeted with an alarm—more like a shriek—and a
bristling hedgerow of rifle barrels. The screeching was so rapa-
cious that several minutes passed before I realized they were pointing to a soda that Eugene was drinking.

"Eugene," I said, "slowly take the Coke bottle to the van. They
think it's a Molotov cocktail."

While that solved the immediate problem, others lurked. Paranoid schizophrenics were in charge. As Walter said later, "It was a
question of nerves."

The stench of composting urine and feces burned our nostrils.
In the windowless anteroom of the police station, twenty women
and sixty rickety, swollen-bellied babies camped, cooking for their
husbands whose black hands jutted through a small, barred window high in the door. They eloquently beat the air beseeching
help.

Two police officers slept at a table. Gently, Walter jostled one
awake. "You must heal my hand," said the sleepy cop holding a
finger like a swollen plantain. Walter replied, "I am not a doctor."
The cop snapped, "Fix it!"

"We are here to register," Walter persisted. But the cop laid his head down again. "Look, start our passports, and when our chief gets here he'll take care of your hand. He's a doctor."

That did it. They woke up. "Line up!" the healthy one shouted. "What do you want? Why are you here? Are you spies? Where will you go?" The heavy interrogation came just short of rubber hose beatings. My knees went wobbly, and I grasped Robb's arm for support. The heat, odor, and threatening intimidation besieged my muscles. Our position was tenuous. The jailed hands waved. Eugene, Hans, and Walter were held against the wall at gun point and body frisked. Then the police turned to us.

I wore a Hausa gris-gris, a necklace of African charms—shells, swatches of hair wrapped in multi-colored leather pouches—made by a witchdoctor in Arlit for protection against everything. The cop suddenly saw it.

"You have gris-gris," he said. "Uhm, that is good."

They were either Hausa, or the gris-gris worked because they stamped our passports without question before resuming their harassment of the Austrians.

"Don't move! Don't talk! We'll kill you!" the police shouted at them.

"Here's the doctor!" Walter said suddenly. "Doctor, this man has a bad hand. You must heal it."

Helmut assessed the scene quickly. "I can heal it," he said, "but not until all the passports are returned."

Grudgingly it was done. Helmut turned the swollen hand, with a display of serious concern.

"Go to the car and bring my saw," he ordered all of us. "Hurry, we have no time." We fled on cue. Behind us, Helmut explained, "I must cut your entire hand off. It is the only way."

"No, no, patron, I need it," the cop pleaded.

A few seconds later Helmut casually sauntered out. "Get the hell out of here. Fast!" he whispered.

We ran. We ran like we did from the border of Assemaka after Helmut sold a car radio to one of the customs police. "It doesn't work. Before he finds out, lets get out of here!" he had told us.

Helmut set up shop at the Hotel Sahara, a brothel, restaurant, and meeting place for *L'Beezneez*. The vehicles were parked in front like billboards advertising a used car exchange. While choking down a meal of couscous and beef (sun-rotted camel), the dealers showed up. First came the front men to check out the scene. Then the principals filtered in—the men with money. Their luxuriantly soft robes and gold nuggets swathing their necks proclaimed their importance.

Meanwhile, Walter, Golo, Robb, and I were left to fend off the Tuareg souvenir salesmen who surrounded our table. To get our attention they plunked "genuine Tuareg wooden door locks," "the famous iron cross of Agadez," and "authentic swords" right into our plates of couscous. Like rapists, they rationalized "no" meant "yes."

"If one more person touches me, I will kill," murmured Walter. Yet when the next one touched him, he said calmly, "I want to talk with you. Just talk, do you understand?"

The man said yes and showed another cross. "Pure silver, patron. Good price for you."

"No, you don't understand." said Walter sadly, "I want you to tell me about your life, where do you live? What do you think?"

"What's your price? You give me your price and I say yes."

Walter kicked over his chair and yelled, "Don't you have a single brain in your head? Don't you think? Does anyone in this fucking country care about anything but money?"

Agadez has been described as exotic, a worthwhile tourist pilgrimage. I guess it depends on what it is being compared to—where you last came from. The last vestige of Agadez' mightiness fell with the great droughts of 1973-1974 and 1983-1984. The droughts wiped out more than 60 percent of all livestock, mostly cattle, and the last of the camel and the salt trade. Since the sixteenth century, Agadez hosted numerous desert enterprises, including caravans transporting gold and slaves. Now, ravaged of their sustenance and past glory, the Tuaregs of Agadez have sadly turned to fake antiques and begging.

Many factors made us edgy: the loss of privacy after the desert, the new cultures, the police, and the constant and now dominant business of selling. But what upset us most, perhaps, was the loss of history, nomadic lifestyles, and pride.

We went to the Sunday camel market. I wandered among the great "ships of the desert," and knelt by a few. Somehow a camel lying on its side didn't look any more right than a car without an engine. "Are you asleep?" I cooed prodding a bony belly. It was dead. One-third of the camels at the market were dead. Sombrero-shaped pillars of salt, once the basis of war and trade, stood un-licked and unsold. The one-time cattle and camel barons now sold spoiled meat and photo opportunities.

. Helmut, Eugene, and Hans moved into the Hotel Sahara to be closer to *L'Beezneez*. The best offer for the vehicles was Ghana grass. "Now what am I going to do with a ton of that? The market is ruined," Helmut lamented. "This is my last trip. We won't even get out the money we put in."

In Agadez, posters of General Ali Saibou, head of state, frowned over rows of canned olive oil, a gift from Italy; wheat and rice, gifts from America; and other gifts from Belgium and Japan...all for sale. We were angered to see all of our foreign aid, "charitable gifts to the drought-stricken and starving," being sold instead of reaching the people the gifts were sent to help. I priced some of the goods and found them to be more costly than what I paid at home. The people who truly needed them would not be able to afford them. No wonder everyone talked about money all the time. Someone was making fast bucks on international aid, and it wasn't necessarily these poor shopkeepers either. I decided I would ask questions of the aid community and stay alert to future evidence of aid fraud.

At the campground, Tuaregs and Bororos hounded us. They even followed us into the bucket shower with displays of jewelry fashioned from dental silver imported from Amsterdam. The Bororos looked like a costume designer's idea of Scheherazade—tall with long faces painted abstractly in many colors and wearing graceful, long robes belted in silver. Their effeminate movements were like the grand dame transvestites of New Orleans.

Still their conversation did not stray from commerce. It was as if abstract concepts had never formed in their vocabulary. Surely they must have a way to express hope, uncertainty, the future, the cosmos. That's when I put my book aside and sat down in the dust with the Tuareg salesmen to watch. If there was a language in movement, I would learn it.

Golo found his friend Martin, and David found us. His ban-danna was tied around gray stubby hair, his fair skin peeling like the pages of a warped telephone book. Clutching his trousers to bony hips, he asked us for a ride. Pathos aside, David was manic.

At that moment Helmut drove into the campground. "Hurry!" he said, wildly scooping clothes into the van. "We sold a van. We have to leave now! Sableman and Hans are at the police station signing over the papers. Quick!" When the door slammed shut, I was dismayed to see that Martin and David had tossed their bodies in with ours.

Thirty kilometers out of Agadez, Helmut waved us over.

"Someone has to drive my car, I've got a fever," he said.

Golo was nominated driver, and David and Martin his passengers. Martin hyperventilated with his latest terminal disease, and David's manic-high irritated our heat-sopped nerves.

Helmut stood with his head cocked, listening. "Look, we've got to hurry...if the police catch us...We substituted the good van for one with sand in the transmission. They'll find out soon after they drive it. We might have an hour head start so hurry!" Damn straight we'd hurry. Agadez prison! Odd thing about Helmut—he was a cherubically nice guy to hang around, but his habit of leaving towns in a hurry was worrisome.

David wailed from the car, "Oh, my God, I'm a criminal. I should have stayed with the Belgians." We thought so too.

How we all lost each other on the straight road to Niamey, I don't know exactly, but we didn't meet again until one o'clock in the morning. Walter got lost on the Nigerian border. And Golo stopped to mediate a fist fight between Martin and David, who had cut back on his medication and was totally berserk.

Our passports were filled with police signatures. It reminded me of an autograph book or a dance card. The police checkpoints were usually located near a well, where lines of sullen, bony women and girls waited to fill their buckets and gourds. Men lounged in the shade. Walter asked a man why he didn't help and was told, "Men's work is to make sure the women work. I have four wives and watching them keeps me busy."

Several times women or children were offered to us. "Take one home with you, no problem."

"What is the price of a woman?" we asked.

"Not much. A small *cadeau*—a gift. You can even take a strong one."

We didn't buy any of the women offered to us. The ethics of it were painful. Buy one and encourage the system? Buy her only to set her loose on the streets of Niamey, to be sold again? Separated from her tribe? My male travel companions were angry. They could not understand my silence. But the truth was, my heart was broken. I felt humiliated, and anger tied my tongue.

Women were sold every day and not just at roadside wells. The prostitutes told of being sold for sex as children when the harvest was mean and resold again into marriage. The issues were complex. The custom of multiple wives and twelve children for each wife seemed irrational. With immunizations, more children lived to die of malnutrition. Several women told me privately that they would be content with one, maybe two children.

These same women adamantly defended polygamy. A Peace Corps volunteer summed it up: "You first have to understand that women do all the work. They herd, carry water from the well, give birth to twelve children, breast feed each one until he's two, walk miles collecting firewood, pound the *manioc*, cook, grow gardens and take the products to market. For one woman alone it is too much work. Maybe the kindest thing that could happen to her is to share the burden with three other wives."

It was a strange dichotomy that a woman could be sold for less than the cost of a plate of noodles and goat meat in a restaurant, and yet slavery was supposedly abolished in Niger. The term "slave" did not apply to women. When people spoke of slavery in Niger, they often referred to the Hausa—a large Nigerian tribe who had migrated through several regions of west Africa.

Niger was the last West African state to officially abolish slavery. The Tuaregs resisted acquiescence until the French put the clamps on them in 1921. But not until the economic devastation of the last decades were the Tuareg's Hausa "servants" cut loose. One USAID director, who had been in Niger twenty years, blamed the social and economic disintegration of the country on the severance of this symbiotic relationship. "The problem now is Tuaregs need to work and they don't know how, and the Hausa want to work but need someone to tell them what to do."

There is probably truth in that statement, but its simplicity obscures other realities. According to other West Africans, the Hausa *were* working and allegedly controlled much of Niger's trade. "The resident tribes of Niger resent them. They are like the Lebanese or Indians, they're business people. And the truth is that nothing would move into, out, or through Niger if it weren't for the Hausa traders."

The first sign that we were emerging from the desert was a river. Boy, was that a delightful sight! The fluvial rice fields and grass-tufted rolling hills looked like a jungle after the sand and rock of the past six weeks. Children no longer had to beg drinking water from passing vehicles; here they bathed in it. Even houses changed from mud-daubed and grass-peaked huts to rectangular, brick compounds.

We reached Niamey from Agadez after thirty-two hours, and not the six that Helmut had projected. After a long wait at the police/customs checkpoint at the outskirts of the city, we were admitted to the city with orders to report immediately to Surete to register.[3]

Niamey was a city alive! Our heads cranked side to side on our shoulders. So many streets, people, so much activity....

Helmut, Hans, and Eugene took up residency at Hotel Rivoli. The rest of us moved to the cheaper Hotel Mustache, a brothel with such rapid turnover that its address elicited snickers throughout town. Robb was repeatedly assured that, "You can have two wives, one can be temporary." Even I was propositioned. We scrubbed the room and everything we owned, including sleeping bags and backpacks. Stains penetrated the mattresses, and the ubiquitous sand had penetrated our cameras despite their having been sealed in plastic bags.

My first impression of Niamey was tainted by the rotten odor of uncovered sewers, which crisscrossed every street. Like The Forbidden Zone they portended "No Way Out." An ignominious death would surely follow a misstep.

Yet flowering trees almost gave Niamey the aura of a lush garden. Supposedly beggars and thieves were barred from the city. No one hassled us to buy, sell, or "give a *cadeau*." We walked unhampered day and night with complete safety (sewers excluded). Vendors in the street and *Grand Marche* bantered with good humor. When Walter dabbed a red "spice" on his tongue, the vendors rocked with laughter. "That's henna! It's what the women use to paint their feet!" they exclaimed.

A man slipped me a white envelope. Stenciled on the front was a guy with a giant erect penis. "Give this to your husband tonight.

It will make him strong." We never could figure out how the powdered leaves in the packet were supposed to be used.

Fried, crispy grasshoppers proved a tasty snack until we learned they probably contained megatons of pesticides. Locusts were a major obstacle to agricultural development, so one USAID project was to bombard them regularly with pesticides.

The real attraction in Niamey was the Niger River, which bent through town like a flat, brown ribbon. It was a visual salve on sand-burnt eyes. Small dugouts paddled against its current, and fishermen tossed nets into the dusk as if trying to lasso the sinking sun. Crocodiles slithered past. Male launderers spread clothes in the trees to dry. In other coves, obscured by green bushy banks, women bathed and washed their underwear. Hippo sentinels signaled retreat.

In the evening we enjoyed all-night dancing at the Tokoulakoye or Niamey Bar. Bodies swayed in deep gyrations, hip-to-hip, along the walls and tables. Prostitutes heaped hopeful attention on the rich white men. On the crowded dance floor, men danced with men and women with women—salsa style, with hips swinging sideways and shoulders opposite to the Zairian band. It was the collective rhythm that has long oscillated between Africa and the Caribbean.

"I know this dancing!" I said and jumped up to publicly unleash everything I'd repressed. I am Latin, and I knew the beat as the one that paced my heart in the womb. The women circled around me. I taught them what I knew, and they taught me even more frenzied movements.

There were many "good" restaurants in Niamey, and, like the SCORE supermarket, they tantalized us. But they were too expensive. Luckily, street food was excellent. For a dollar we filled our bowls with rice, sauce, vegetables, and meat brochettes. Small wooden benches provided al fresco dining. Children hung in the background, not begging, but waiting for leftovers from the "kitchen." We soon learned to order a little extra, and, like the Nigerians, we pushed it aside first for the kids to eat later. Thanksgiving Day we thus feasted from street vendors—a kind of progressive supper with desserts of pineapple, bananas, coconut, chocolate, fresh yogurt, and melon.

I greeted each morning at the Mustache with a pep talk.

Roaches crawled across our pillows and not even a cold shower could drown orgasmic moans from adjacent rooms. Thanksgiving was an excuse to treat ourselves. We went to the Hotel Gaweye to call home and to swim. Golo said it made him feel guilty for being "rich enough" to afford CFA 1,500 for a day at the pool complete with padded chaise lounges; clean, fluffy blue towels; and hot showers! Robb and I felt no guilt for buying a day in heaven.

The switchboard staff was helpful. The operators tried throughout the day to place our calls, but with absolutely no success. Eventually, we sent telegrams and languished for news from home. Later we met a Bostonian from the embassy who explained why we hadn't been able to get a call through. The telecommunication satellite did not recognize area codes that had changed several years earlier. Ironically, both our mothers lived in those unreachable zones.

Niger had the second highest number of Peace Corps volunteers in the continent, so meeting them was inevitable. Several volunteers on medical rehabilitation invited us to swim at the ambassador's pool. When they spoke of their "undiagnosable diseases," Robb was convinced they suffered from depression. Their symptoms were bracketed with unhappiness. The women had gained weight on the local diet, and, because they were non-diplomatic staff, they were soon to lose their privileges at the American recreation center and at the Thursday night movies at the Marine House.

One afternoon the ambassador's wife, a born-again Christian, strolled down to the pool. The Peace Corps volunteers were in underwear, so I intercepted her tight-bunned hair and disapproving glare and interviewed her on the current topic of health while the others got decent and Christian-like. She told me vitamin deficiency was the major health problem and that Niger spent the least on health care of any African nation. I wondered if these same problems weren't reflected among U.S. personnel.

We spent ten days in Niamey for one reason or another. During that time, I practiced Tae Kwon Do at the B and M Gym behind the Hotel Terminus. The U.S. Embassy Marine guards who were my sparring partners invited us to Thursday movie night at the Marine House. It was like a cultural lifeline: cold American beer, hot dogs, popcorn, and movies that would not have attracted our dollar at home. I am not overtly patriotic, but after that touch with home, I would have carried an American flag through the streets of Niamey.

We ran into a few old friends in Niamey. It was like finding out how a misplaced book ended. The tall Dutch guy from Tam who was afraid of nature but not of riding an overland truck was decked out like a hideous, imitation hippie. Bangles smothered his wrists and neck.

"I fly home tomorrow," he said, toking a cigarette. "Let's just say that I never got along with nature, and no one got along with me."

Many overland groups had reached Niamey from Tam. Fractious quibbling had split several, and in one group a driver was fired and replaced by a passenger.

Chris came to the Mustache one evening with his French friends. They spun on their heels and left. "This place is disgusting," they exclaimed. We met them later. Chris had given up Senegal for *L'Beezneez*. They hinted at big deals, yet hadn't had any luck selling their vehicles for the asking price. "We French know trade secrets. After all, we started this business forty years ago. The others are too stupid, so don't think we're going to help anyone by telling about our deals," Chris said. I didn't want to be around him anymore.

Our caring group fell apart. Helmut, Hans, and Eugene came to the Mustache early one morning. Hans had a whisky belly and acted like a smaller clone of Eugene. Helmut, cheerful as always, said they were in a hurry to leave for Ouagadougou. They had sold the vans for $1,850 each, not $6,000 as they expected. They did not break even after cost, paint, and repairs. "We have to hurry," said Helmut again, "we found so much sand in the transmissions they won't last long."

Golo's friend Martin suffered from a swollen face. It looked uncomfortable, but was no more serious than teenage acne. His days were spent in clinics or moaning about his "imminent death." Finally, he flew home "to die."

Without his medication, David sank off the deep end of depression. He refused to leave his room or to eat. Walter and Golo tricked him onto a bus for Burkina Faso by telling him they were all leaving. David needed help, and it wasn't available in Niamey.

Gary flew to South Africa because he was late for his contract date there. He and the other Germans lost money on their car sales too. The two with the pharmaceuticals gave up their dream of music studies and signed up with Golo and Walter to go to Burkina and Ghana. Robb and I would not waver from our plan to go to Mali.

We all sniffled when we separated. Walter and Golo had filled our days with laughter, long discussions on the "meaning of it all," and compatible silences. The camaraderie of the road is an amazing life force. We knew we'd pick it up again; yet, it would be a long time before our affections for these friends would be replaced. They were those rare people that you travel the world to meet.

So here in Niamey, a chapter ended for Robb and me. We were on our own again after a month with the Europeans. Friends aside, we suspected that their presence had shielded us from a Niger experience. We regretted the loss. On the other hand, no story of Africa is complete without an encounter with *L'Beezneez*—it was an integral part of Africa's history.

– 7 –

Back into the Desert

From Niamey to Gao, Mali, the road hugged the banks of the Niger River. The *piste* was rugged, even tougher than the Sahara. The bus lurched dangerously through deep *wadis*—dried river beds. The road winded north from the sub-Sahara into the sand-blown Sahara. The dust was worse than at any time in our travels. It coated windows, clothes, hair, and lungs.

The heat increased with the barrenness of the landscape. A narrow green ribbon marked the banks of the Niger river that sprang from the Guinea highlands and flowed two thousand miles north and then south into the Gulf of Guinea. Small towns carved from brown mud looked poised to slide into the river. Other than the right angles of the walls, the towns were almost indistinguishable from the terrain. Permanent ladders, like porcupine quills, jutted from spires. Rain spouts accentuated the pitch of the roofs.

Women wore their dresses slung low over their shoulders and

gaping on the sides, for air flow. Men wrapped their faces like mummies, which was a concession to the sand more than style. Our envy of their dress grew with our own discomfort.

Children were distributed freely to every lap. Robb and I were given two who slept with innocent trust. Twelve foreigners rode in the back of the crowded bus—a few French, but mostly Dutch, a group of friends who would travel up the Niger River in a large canoe they bought the previous year. They transported boat engines and supplies to Gao, where the expedition would begin.

At every stop, Neti, one of the Dutch, gleefully passed out handfuls of pens to the greedy cries of the kids, *"Donnez moi un Bic."* She must have read about it in a book. For us, we'd come to hate the screeching for Bics, and we started hating Neti equally for perpetrating the nuisance. By mid-afternoon she zipped her pouch closed with finality. "I am beginning to hate these little bastards," she said. Neti was more astute than I thought.

We were dreading the border crossing: it was rumored to be the most ruthlessly corrupt in West Africa. We were also told to expect fifteen police checks between Niamey and the border. I counted only four. Nevertheless, most travelers avoided the Niamey to Gao route for these reasons. We were learning that something always goes wrong at border/police checks.

On the Mali side of immigration, soft drink, tea, and food stands twinkled by kerosene lamps like a cozy oasis in the dark night. They were run by the families of the police, so plenty of time was allowed for everyone to buy. One little urchin bobbed in my face until I wanted to smack him. "Madame, take my photo with flash! Good souvenir!" he chanted.

The engine of the bus roared and lurched forward. Then, suddenly, the chief of police arrested the whole bus. We were corralled into groups: the French and the Dutch were kept together, Robb and I were taken to headquarters, and the Africans were left to meander. During our interrogation, we noticed that Robb's passport hadn't been stamped. It was our fault, they said, it was a trick to make them look bad. We eventually got properly stamped and released to join the Africans. The other foreigners were held until the "spy" among them confessed.

The Africans said the police had accused one of the foreigners of taking a flash photo of the border. No one had seen anyone with a camera. Harassment swelled into intimidation, and finally the police ordered the foreigners to pick four who would be formally arrested as spies, or the bus would be held as a hostage. Four volunteered, and the bus was released to the customs post a few hundred yards down the road.

At customs, everything was impounded, including the clothing and bedding on the roof. It was cold, and we were hungry. One man opened his home to us. He offered a kind of maggoty spaghetti, two moth-eaten mats, a filthy sheet, and the company of his dogs in the compound. It was an unhappy event. The night air was frigid and the mosquitos thick. We huddled together for warmth, but the greedy Sahara sucked that from our bodies too. Only by shivering did we circulate blood until dawn.

In the morning, the interrogation resumed with the four arrestees claiming innocence. The passengers backed them up. The police, however, wanted something for their trouble.

"Give us your cameras," said the chief, "and we will let you go."

On principle, the four refused. "Take the cameras and you take us with them."

Spitting angry, the chief announced he would bring the regional chief of police from Gao to settle the matter.

The sun ascended, burning holes into our heads and stooped shoulders. No one was allowed near the truck. Then at 11:00 A.M., seven hours into the day, the four foreigners appeared over the rise toting their cameras and smiling. The regional chief had released them because none of them had a flash attachment.

The customs formalities began then. The Dutch transported the biggest bundles, so they were called first into customs and levied with a $300 import duty. Two market women, *commercantes*, paid another $275 between them for pails, tubs, and plastic ware. The customs men were in a jovial mood over their windfall and, lucky for the rest of us, they paid scant attention to our meager belongings.

Meanwhile, an Exodus overland truck cruised into the customs yard. White faces gleamed from the air-cooled, open truck. Wow, were they going to get it, we thought. The driver disappeared with the chief, sauntered out three minutes later, then sprayed us with sand and exhaust as the truck peeled out and onward.

"How can that be?" I wondered, and I was not alone in my resentment. Every other face in our group contorted in some level of hatred.

"It's not fair," everyone mumbled. "It's discrimination because they're white and rich. We have to pay their way."

Finally, our bus was released from customs inspection. It took another hour and a half to repack the bundles before we could hit the road again.

Many sweaty hours later, a rumble of contentious voices broke out in the bus. It started with a single speech delivered by the largest market mammy on the bus. She took up three hundred pounds of space. A few other men stood and spoke after her. Then almost everyone was yelling. They spoke in local languages, so we watched their unusually demonstrative behavior with curiosity but without comprehension.

When the argument simmered down some, a man was elected to translate to the foreigners.

"A very big customs post comes soon, and we think they will make us take everything out of the bus again," he said. "It will take six hours, maybe another night, and cost a lot of money. Some people say the white people in the truck paid a big bribe, and we should try it too. If we each pay CFA 500 ($1.50) we will make a bribe. Other people say the bribe won't work, and we could lose our money. Some people do not have money, and others say they won't pay because they aren't carrying anything. They say this is a way for the *commercantes* to put their burden on others. All of us are tired and want to go home so we will try the bribe. You must decide what you will do. Those who can't pay or won't, well, it is their business."

All heads at the front of the bus twisted around to watch our response. Our anger over how easily the Exodus truck had made it through the last customs post still irritated us like sand in an oozing wound. Either because of their whiteness or because of their bribe, they had been let free. No one wanted another six-hour delay or another night on the cold ground. We foreigners were as split as the rest of the passengers on what to do. But we could also afford the CFA 500.

"This is the most incredible scene," said Robb. "I never thought I'd see them organize against abuse. Yet, here they are doing just that. I don't know if it'll work, but I think it's worth backing their decision. I vote for it."

The money was collected by the speaker, counted, then deposited in the bosom of the three-hundred-pound *commercante* who would be in charge of the bribe. Names were not taken of who had paid, but each face was memorized like a receipt. Ultimately, CFA 8,000 was collected—four thousand short of the amount projected as workable.

At the customs station we disembarked silently, nervously. Mothers crouched in the hot shade of the bus to breast-feed. We milled as the police eyeballed the fat bundles on the roof. The market mammy stood unobtrusively to the side. Every eye was on her. When and how would she make her move?

A half hour passed, then forty minutes. Then, without notice, passengers began embarking. Not far down the road, a victory yell cracked the sand veneer of a hundred throats. Congratulatory eye contacts passed around the bus like handshakes.

Robb whispered, "Whether you know it or not, you've witnessed the first step toward democracy."

"Humph, a bribe is a bribe," I snorted. "That doesn't change anything, it perpetrates it. I bet Niger and Mali could feed their people if they didn't have all these police checks with tolls. By the time they pay for the article, internal tariffs, bribes, transportation, and their own expense nothing is left for profit. They will never compete on the world market if they can't move their products to internal markets. I think it's sick." Admittedly, I can be sanctimonious after the fact.

"You're still missing the point," said Robb. "From the way the conversation sounded, I would guess this is the first time a group of unrelated people organized to effect their fate. I think it is exciting."

"Yeah, and why did we pay? Because this is an African bus. Exodus got through because they are white. That's why. This country is as racially biased as the United States—without any of the advantages. None of us should have paid anything. You may call it democracy, I still call it a bribe."

"Well, it was worth it from my point of view just to have seen it in action. Now that the Berlin wall is coming down, well, you just wait and see, I predict big changes here in Africa."

"Personally, I don't see that what happens in Berlin will have any impact on what happens here. People are too subservient to authority to change."

"Well, just wait and see."

In Gao the bus was impounded for another night. No one could take anything out of it. "So they can determine value by full light," we were told. The passengers, empowered from our last collective success, protested. Not until the police swung their batons did we move out of the yard grumbling displeasure. The Africans slunk across the soccer field to friends or family. We went to the Hotel Atlantide. The hotel was expensive—CFA 6,850 for a barren room without running water; a torn, blood-spotted mosquito net; and a contingent of parasitic hustlers. But without sleeping bags, the campground several miles out of town was out of the question.

I hated the inconvenience of having our belongings confiscated yet another night so I hated Gao. I hated Mali. I hated depressing desert towns. I hated the kids screeching for *cadeaux*. I hated registering at the police station and paying another CFA 500 in tourist tax.[1] Ill humor settled over me like a black cloud.

Our plan was to take a river boat up the Niger River from Gao to Mopti. It would be a minimum six-day trip over water instead of dusty, rutted roads. I was looking forward to that. As soon as we got our belongings from customs the next morning (we were charged nothing, but the Dutch had to pay another $150 for their marine engines), we went to the harbor office to check the boat schedule. It indicated that the river boat should have arrived two days earlier. The harbor master said he didn't know when it would come in. The rumor in town was that the water was too low for the boat to come at all. My patience plummeted like a mudslide— we were captives.

I bitched at Robb as if all of it was somehow his fault. I might have made Gao unbearably miserable for him and me if it hadn't been for the invulnerable high spirits of Hans and Neti, a couple from the Dutch group. They invited us to a grand dinner at the restaurant of the family who had kept their boat. It was a joyous reunion. Gifts were presented: blinking Christmas lights and a boom box for the restaurant, and toys for the runny-faced kids.

Half the population of Gao, or so it seemed, escorted us to the

river for the unveiling of the *pinasse*—a large *pirogue*. Hans had
sent money for its repair and maintenance, and he was as anxious
to see it as Ali, the restaurant owner/caretaker, was to show it.
Ali, his nephew, wives, and children all beamed like beacons. The
railings and prow were carved magnificently like totems, and
brightly painted geometrics covered every inch. Without a doubt,
it was the most magnificent pirogue on the river. Everyone knew
it. The community pride was at least as magnificent as the boat itself.

No less than thirty people packed it to the gunwales for the
maiden cruise. Dancing and music on shore blessed the launch.
We stayed out until after dark, poking through the myriad islands
dotted with the stilt homes of the fishing Bozo tribe, taking passengers to their homes, and climbing the great dunes whose feet
dipped into the river itself. We ran laughing and flung ourselves
down the face of a dune as the sun set. In that setting, and among
that company, life was grand and magical.

By the time the pinasse returned to Gao, I was racked with chills
and fever. I bypassed the jubilant celebration and crawled into a
back room of the restaurant where it was dark but heated by
kitchen fires. A hundred roaches scampered over the supplies for
the expedition. Sweating, I cuddled among them not caring what
happened to me. Two wives came to sit by me. I wanted desperately to be able to talk to them. Staring at the henna tattoos on
their feet, I hallucinated.

Later, Robb crept into the storeroom with news that Hans had
invited us to join the *pinasse* expedition. There were four Dutch in
the expedition and they figured they had plenty of room for us
too. They would spend two weeks traveling up the Niger to Mopti.
Robb was excited. Then his eyes adjusted to the dark scene. "Are
you okay?" he asked.

I drooled. What did he think? How did I look? My fever soared
higher than the temperature outside. "Robb, I need to throw up,"
I said. "Can you help me outside to a sewer?" He helped me back
to the hotel.

"It's so cold," I said, shaking. Robb piled all the clothing from
the backpacks on top of me like insulating bricks. "Please go
away," I said, not wanting to spoil his happiness. As soon as the
door closed behind him, I crawled to the toilet hole and vomited

until black and green chunks of my lungs fell out, then I passed out.

Sometime after midnight Robb came back into the sweat-stenched room and said something about the river boat being in. "What do you want to do?" he asked.

"I want to go with Neti and Hans on the pinasse."

"They're leaving tomorrow. I've checked around and there isn't a doctor here. Look, you're in no shape to travel, and I don't want to risk taking you on the pinasse; there won't be any shade and if you got sicker we couldn't get help. I already told them to go on without us. We'll stay here until you are well."

"In Gao?" I asked.

His nod was blurry.

"This is the last river boat until next August?"

He nodded again.

"I want to go now," I said wanly, "on the river boat." I did not want to stay in Gao.

I vaguely remembered riding on his back, slung like a sack of aid wheat, down a long street with lights at the end of it. An iron cot sagged beneath me. A door clanged shut. I shivered.

– 8 –

Cruising the Niger River

"Do you want some food?" Robb asked, his face fading in and out of focus. He held a platter of something unappetizing under my nose. "The captain asked for you, and I told him you were sick so he had the cook make this up for you."

"Jesus, take it away from me. Do you have any water? Where are we?" I asked.

"We are on the river boat on our way to Mopti."

"Good."

"It's Sunday morning. You've been asleep since Friday. How do you feel? Do you remember me carrying you here?"

"No, only vaguely." I remembered the sound of flip-flops shuffling past the door. I felt better, although weak. "Geez, I don't know what hit me."

"I wanted to take you to the doctor but you refused. I was really worried. I'm glad our antibiotics are working. You'll have to stay on them for at least a week." He caressed my hand. "First I got sick and now you. Aren't we a pair?

"Why don't you come up on the deck—fresh air will make you feel better. You should see it! There are huge sand dunes on both sides, fishermen in canoes, birds, and the boat! It's real old, kinda reminds me of a paddle-wheel boat without a paddle. There are three decks, not counting the roof, and the whole lower one is a market. It's magnificent! Come on."

"I don't want to move."

"I'll help you out. Just to look."

"Maybe if you take that food away from me. Thank the captain, and the cook."

I leaned on Robb and the boat railing. It was truly magnificent. Towering dunes, like those at Beni-Abbes and outside Gao, reminded me of healthier, happier times. Brown-walled compounds slipped toward the water, and the green stubble of rice paddies intertwined like braided ribbon with the blue of the Niger River.

"Didn't I tell you it was beautiful!" said Robb with a sigh.

I turned my head from him to hide tears of exhaustion. I didn't want them construed as tears of self-pity. I wasn't yet strong enough for that.

Robb moved a stool under my wobbly legs. "Thank you, I'll be fine here for a while."

Next to me, at the railing, leaned a chocolate-colored woman with neat coils of hair wrapped around her head. Her eyes asked, "Are you healthy?" I willed mine to answer, "Yes, I will be." She helped me back inside to my bed.

The river boat to Mopti from Gao took five and a half days. I was strong enough by Monday to explore the 150-foot boat, the *General Soumare*; eat rice in the captain's dining room; and make short forays into the towns where the boat stopped. I needed a lot of rest between jaunts, so I often sat on the stool outside our door where I could watch everything. The chocolate-skinned woman who shared the cabin next to ours with her husband, sat alongside me.

It was mainly through gestures, eyes, and watching that we communicated. I regained my strength with the momentum of her stories. It was as I suspected in Agadez: the secret of communication was in movement. The verbs, nouns, and adjectives of movement were as eloquent as the most descriptive literature.

Here is her story: "I am traveling with my new husband from my village to his, where I will live with a new tribe, and his one other wife. I do not know him yet. He is a rich merchant and is very kind. He paid my father a lot. I don't know how much, how many goats and cloth, but now my father is wealthy too. It is told that his first wife does not work hard and she dresses richly. So I am lucky. This is the first time that I am away from my mother or my father's family, and it seems to me that I will live too far from my home among strangers. I am scared. I don't know how his other wife will accept me. Because she has no babies yet and they have been married over two years, I must have babies for him. This too scares me. I am afraid to do this thing. He is a stranger who puts his body on mine. I must have the babies that I know will hurt, and I will be alone in this, although he is kind. It is important that I am with a child when we arrive at his village; it will make him richer and give me importance too. His first wife will hate me otherwise, and she will make me feel unwanted."

Four times a day her husband silently led her into their cabin. He would nod, almost bow, to me in passage. Afterward, she would sit again on her stool by my side.

As I got healthier, I became more curious and aware. The scratched steel walls of the tiny, first-class cabin now resembled a jail. The sound of plastic thongs shuffling on the deck filled the day and night with noise, motion, and even gossip. The steady beat was louder and more reliable than the engine. Like drums, the feet shuffled in rhythmic motion telling the tale of the boat: "There is water in the first-class showers so I go there to bathe and to wash my children's clothes. The sun is high and it is time to hang the clothes on the railing to dry. A baby is sick in third class. The white tourists might have medicine. We are nearing a village and must prepare our wares. A big official is coming on board and we will dance tonight in the captain's dining room."

When the big official came on board, the recreation officer hosted a big dance for all twenty passengers in first class, and anyone else who would pay.

"Come with me to the party," said Robb. "It'll be fun."

"I would love to but I would be no fun. Give me a few more

days rest, and I'll follow you anywhere. I want you to go, though, and tell me about it." Now Robb isn't a dancer, and without me he isn't a mixer. So it took a lot of encouragement, but he went.

"Very interesting," he reported later. "No one came."

"What do you mean no one came? I've been listening to music all night."

"No one came! The bigwig and his four wives came on board. In fact to make room for them they kicked the French out of their cabin. The recreation officer preened in a suit and tie—he's the one with the limp—and the captain fluttered around a lot. There was nothing to drink—no coke or beer. Three women came and the bigwig tried to feel one of them up while dancing. The doors were locked so the women couldn't escape. I let them out. Then there were about thirty men sitting around looking at each other. We left too. It was hysterical! I did get this coke for you though. It's hot, but it might be the last one on the boat."

When the boat left Gao, maybe two hundred people were on board. By the third day, several hundred more people crowded the three decks, the roof, and the aisles with charcoal stoves, babies, laundry, sleeping mats, livestock, and bundles of wares. Space was traded like any other commodity on the small riverboat. It was a microcosm of all the regional tribes, each with their individual clothing styles and favorite prints, tribal scars, tattoos, skin tones, facial structure, nose rings, turbans, hairstyles, and languages.

At each sizeable town, Bourem, Bamba, Gourma-Rharous, Dire, Tonka, music was piped over the public address system to announce the boat's arrival. In a carnival-like atmosphere, the market mammies rushed down the gang-plank to meet the village traders for a frenzied swapping of glassware and pottery, cassava, fruit, cigarettes, candies, kettles, and woven mats. What was purchased in one town would be resold further up the river at the next town. Each market venue allowed time for idle exploration of the streets, mosques, and daily markets. As I regained strength, I accompanied Robb on excursions more frequently and for longer periods. In dusty bins, we found antique trading beads and brass bracelets, sticks of chalk that women eat when pregnant, and the black stone that draws the venom from snake bites.

A bull toot of the ship's horn announced when the boat was about to depart. Displays snapped shut and vendors elbowed each other up the gang-plank. Only once did someone fall. Her merchandise sunk with the help of bathers who planned to retrieve it later for themselves. The distraught *commercante* dove after what little she could reach while the *Soumare* pulled away. The horn swallowed the distress cries of every onlooker. On shore, the police tugged the urchin thieves onto land. Then, ever so slowly, the boat nudged back to shore, and the sodden merchant with her salvaged wares was hauled on board. Such a cheer I'd never heard before. It was one of those moments that makes everyone feel good.

Fabled Timbuktu was little more than a 2:00 A.M. whistle stop. Because of the gradual shift of the river and sand, the town was isolated twelve miles inland. A midnight curfew capped any movement into the city, yet the foreigners all prepared to leave the ship until the boarding passengers waved them back. They told of being stuck there while prices increased daily. "The city is dead, worse than Gao," they hollered. "It is ruled by unethical hucksters." Their description of Timbuktu was so bleak that no one disembarked.

Meals with the captain were always lively with conversation and tasty food: fresh fruit deserts, soups, and stews with vegetables. The Malian bigwigs and their seductively quiet wives presided over the table. A French couple nostalgically referred to the glory days of French colonization. Soon no one spoke to them. Karl, a German geographer who had traveled the Sahara since the early 1950s, captivated all of us with tales of camel caravans over now lost routes and with informal lectures on the impact of water management on village organization.

Aside, he secretly confided in us, "This is my last trip. I will never come here again because I cannot live with the pain of watching these magnificent people and their civilization die with their land. You cannot believe seeing what you see now how these tribes were once proud and even rich."

Karl wiped his glasses. "I don't know any way it can be saved. You see, the Sahara advances twelve miles a year, but that is not the only problem. New Saharas are being created in pockets far south of here and are spreading outward. Overpopulation is the basic problem. The animals have all been hunted and the forests chopped for firewood. Population will never be curbed because every man or woman wants twelve to twenty children; it is no longer a question of economic necessity but of religion and social esteem. The worst thing that ever happened to them besides religion was aid programs. We sold it to them because it expanded our markets, our surplus, our expired products or harmful ones. So when we made it more economical for them to accept our rice than to produce it, the fields dried up. Now they're aid-dependent. Their religions and societies don't encourage initiative but, rather, acceptance. We send in experts to correct problems; I am an expert, and I tell you we are botching things up worse than ever. It's a downward spiral with every conceivable, inherent reason for this continent to be dead in another ten years."

Karl certainly had the experience and knowledge to make such a dire prediction. Already in our short travels we had seen what he spoke of. The excitement of traveling among these ancient cultures was fragmented by sadness for the collapse of their civilizations. What we were seeing was not the beginning of the end, it was something worse, because there didn't seem to be a way out of the "downward spiral" that Karl described. At times, I felt like a voyeur at a funeral fete.

Shipboard life, with its loud music and activity, had cast a spell of unreality on us all. One Dutch passenger commented, "I sometimes think I am dreaming this and none of it is real. I can no longer tell the difference." A somberness settled in the gayest of hearts as we approached Mopti—the end of the boat trip, the end of illusions.

– 9 –
The Dogon Myths of Mali

Mopti was exotic from the river view. The harmattan haze shrouded it in a mist of sand, penetrated by the spires of the large mosque on the hill. French colonial buildings and trees promenaded along the bank. Only up close could you see the peeling paint on the doors and window shutters, and balconies sagging from disuse. Goats and chickens wandered through the empty buildings as if they were inferior stables. The houses were a legacy abandoned, avoided as if diseased, ignored as if useless.

In the old part of town, the pre-colonial Mopti, the busy waterfront market and the area behind the huge mosque teemed with life. Soothing, soft shade undulated with the soft curves of sculpted mud walls. The lines of doorways and stairways were sensual, gentle, and congenial with human rhythms, unlike the hard right angles of the French buildings. In the afternoons when life seemed to nap, compound courtyards pulsated. There, spices were measured into smaller bundles, hair was plaited, sisters danced, plastic bags were folded and stored for reuse, children scrubbed in tubs, and millet was pounded for dinner.

Along the waterfront, *pirogues* and *pinasses* puttered day and night with passengers and products. New hulls, as big as arks, were carved from scarce lumber. Shaped like the tablets of Moses, salt was displayed alongside tie-dye cloth precut to wrap around a woman's waist. Nose rings, earrings, plastic grain sacks, vegetables, and fruit were piled along the road. Barber shops advertised the latest styles: the cocaine cut and the Mike Tyson cut. A funeral arrived by pirogue. Four men shouldered a small, cloth-draped body on a board—a child old enough to have been named. Goats were shampooed, and laundry washed. By night small fires winked in earthly imitation of the heavens.

Until greeted the Malian people look through you without expression. *"Ca va?"* opened conversations, transactions, doors, and friendships. The greetings were repetitious, with singsong inflections denoting the context: "How does it go? It goes well. How does it go with you? Do your family, your goats go well? You go well. Yes, and you." The unhurried exchange, in its most polite form, is a mutual acknowledgment of life.

Handshakes were elaborate and ritualistic. Palms slid to fingertips, a twist and grasp of knuckles, then thumbs topped one another. The women held onto my hand playfully and pulled me to sit among them, to share their meal. We teased each other, the joke flashing in the eyes until everyone was laughing, caught up in the game of facial expressions and hand movements.

We stayed at Bar Mali; at CFA 3,000 it was a budget bottom hotel and bare as a vulture's banquet. It was a whorehouse, like many hotels, but it emanated the kind of homeyness unknown in more posh places. Someone was always cooking on the small balcony or in the hallway with an open invitation to dip a handful.

Time seemed to idle, and, before we knew it, we had spent four days in Mopti. It deserved more time, but my pocket calendar showed only seventeen days before Christmas. We wanted to be on the coast—in Dakar, Senegal—by then. We would have to move fast to make it, especially since we wanted to go to the "Dogon Land" south of Mopti.

In our survey study of African art, we had learned that the Dogon people are known prominently for their architecture, wood carvings, and metal work. They are also known as the most accomplished farmers on the continent and adhere to "pure" animism.

From Mopti, the two most commonly used gateways into Dogon Land are either through the town of Songha or the town of Bandiagara. Songha, although further from Mopti than Bandiagara, is more heavily trafficked because it is near the escarpment, the mountain ridge where Dogon villages are clustered. We chose to go to Bandiagara and hike 21 kilometers to the escarpment.

The straight-line travel time to Bandiagara, thirty-six miles away, was supposedly one hour. We strolled into the car park at Mopti and boarded a bush taxi—a Toyota pickup truck with wood benches around the bed—that was full and ready to leave. It didn't actually depart until nine hours later. On the way to Bandiagara, the truck overheated three times, two tires blew out, and we were detained at a police checkpoint over an irregularity in someone's documents. The trip took twelve hours!

In Bandiagara, a horde of hustlers scrapped over our bodies and backpacks. Each kid in town claimed to be a SMERT guide, and each claimed a better deal than the others. Like auctioneers, they shouted out increasingly higher prices, as if they had learned to add but not subtract.[1] They argued among themselves over who would get the finder's fee from our hotel room and food. We pushed through them saying, "Later, later." Too tired to haggle, we headed for the Kansaye—a legendary hikers' hostel owned by Mamadou, a ninety-two-year-old war veteran. It was late, but Mamadou scraped some rice and sauce from the bottom of the pot and found us a couple of warm beers.

The next day the guides again harassed us. "You can't go alone, SMERT doesn't permit it. You don't know the ways of the Dogon, they won't let you into their villages; if you offend them, they might kill you. It happens to tourists each year. I will guide you for only $10, $25 each person each day. Cheap price. It is too far to walk (approximately 26 kilometers), and it is not permitted. You must take a moped, only $10 a day, maybe less, if you pay for mine too. No? then I will get you a donkey cart then. Only $12 for each of us or $40 each way."

At 6 A.M. the few other travelers were up and hopping onto whiny mopeds with their guides. Robb and I struck out on our own to the baleful warnings of the guides. "It is illegal what you are doing. You will be arrested. You cannot go alone."

A lanky, semi-toothless, sixteen-year-old loped along behind us like a puppy. "I am your guide," he insisted with tremulous determination. His eyes implored. Something unspoken, but important to him was at stake.

"Do you understand that we want to walk?" we asked him.

"Yes, yes," he said.

"Do you understand that we don't want a guide, that we want to walk alone?"

"Yes, yes."

Unwanted or not, he would tag along. "We will pay you ten dollars to walk with a quiet mouth."

"Yes, yes," he agreed, hopping from foot to foot. My name is Abdoulaye. I am called Ali the Guide."

For a few minutes we felt right with karma. Not two hundred feet of stubbled fields had passed under our feet when Ali sat down. "You know, it is too far to walk to the *falaise*. Much better to ride a moped." Ali eventually caught up with us.

By 8:30 A.M. the sun had heated the flat bushland, and there wasn't a leaf of shade in sight. We passed groups of women balancing enormous bundles of sticks on their heads. Babies swung from milk-swollen breasts. An entourage of naked, swollen-bellied children scampered behind them. If one woman stopped to readjust her load, it took three more to help her. A few times Robb heaved the wood onto their heads, much to their utter amazement.

We got a short ride with the German equivalent of a Peace Corps volunteer. Ali grinned blissfully. Then we stumbled onward for countless oppressive hours until we were picked up by French doctors delivering an ambulance to Djuiguibambo, the first of the Dogon villages on the escarpment.

The famous carved doors depicting elongated ancestors such as Nommo, the god of water, in apposition to Yourougou, the god of drought and fire, surrounded the village. Round houses with peaked grass roofs that looked like hand twisted, dry spaghetti, and granaries and chicken coops that looked like miniatures of the houses wound up, down, and around narrow passageways.

The village was celebrating a harvest festival. Circles of women danced with a hypnotic shuffle as men swayed on the perimeter, hanging back like wallflowers waiting for an invitation. Teenage girls or boys, together but never with the opposite sex, held hands with whispered intrigues.

An all-male city council deliberated at the *togu na*, a kind of city hall, then invited us to stay for the festivities. Some men said masks would be worn on the seventh day, and others said not at all. Also a dance with muskets would be held some time. Meanwhile we could rest at the house of the chief who sold colas and beer.

Ensconced in a chieftain's chair was a smug Swiss guy, Christen, reenacting the white man's discovery of Africa. To block him out, I drowsed on a shaded mat on the chief's veranda. The chief offered to show us the ceremonial collection, a preview of the celebration. One dark room was filled with items for sale; the "sacred objects" were in an adjoining room. There was a "small charge" to see those, but he showed them to us anyway.

For three days we hiked through and around the neat Dogon fields on the perimeter of the 200-kilometer plateau. In addition to being the most accomplished agriculturalists in Africa, the Dogon are also successful herdsmen. Each village had healthy looking cattle, horses, donkeys, goats, chickens, and even horses. Well water was carried to the fields in gourds balanced on the head. Men passed us carrying muskets with crudely shaped stocks hewn with an adze and homemade barrels. We labored up and across the escarpment, or *falaise*, on ancient, twisting trails etched in deep crevasses. The trails were so disguised that only by mentally measuring approximately fifteen inches could the next foothold be found.

The steep wall of the escarpment is spotted with miniature clay cities that resemble the Cliff Dwellers of southern Colorado. Magnificent in their mystery, stories abound about their origin and purpose. The most common tale is that they were homes of the Pygmies who lived in that region until five hundred years ago. Some Dogon say they are granaries that are no longer used. White people hypothesize that they are burial houses for the Dogon, and that is why no one is allowed to explore the sacred mountain cities. This is not altogether true, however, because permission to explore the cities can be bought. In our case, we simply went and were never stopped. I have read several treatises on the subject, yet I haven't found anything definitive. If Pygmies did live there, then they were a smaller version of their contemporaries. The doorways looked too short. As for being granaries, we couldn't find much evidence—no millet or relics. Whatever the truth of their origin, the cities are magical to behold.

Another story says the Dogon are pure practitioners of animism—the belief that inanimate objects contain souls. Supposedly, they were the last tribe to resist conversion to any other religion. The animistic totems, rocks, trees, etc., were so ubiquitous that tourists could not travel this region alone. Only a Dogon guide could avert the disaster of stepping on an ancestral soul.

It was a lovely story and very likely true before tourists arrived with money. Throughout these Sahelian countries, Islam officially counts some 90 percent of the population as adherents. Unofficially 100 percent of the population practices some form of animism. In reality, the religions have all been mixed. Where one begins and ends is difficult to know. If the Dogon were unspoiled practitioners of animism, then why did we see a mosque in nearly every village? Nor did we meet a resident who warned us from our path, from climbing hills or strange rock outcroppings, or from resting under a tree. I suspect the religion has been corrupted and the myth propagated by guides and other people who make money from making adventure look dangerous.

Because of respect for animistic objects, photos were supposedly forbidden. Etiquette required that photo permission be obtained from the chief and a fee paid based on the inherent sacredness of the object to be photographed. Another story was that ten U.S. dollars must be paid to each chief of each village for permission to cross his territory. And still another story was that there was no way into Dogon Land except by foot, which necessitated a guide. Yet, this story was also false, because in one remote village we met a western woman crippled by polio who had reached Dogon Land by road.

The Dogon was a land of myth and legend. It was charming, intriguing, bastardized, and exploited. Hikers paid for guides and mopeds because they thought it forbidden to walk alone. They paid the $10 village fees to their guide, who supposedly gave it to the chiefs. They were stopped from walking into the escarpment or to far-flung villages because they were sacred. And, they paid their guide to take a photo of a baobab tree!

We paid our guide, sullen toothless Ali, who walked along behind us, and we paid for soft drinks, food, and a rooftop to sleep on. No one else asked for money. Our guide did not guide us. He sulked behind and never once hindered our movement. Stories abounded in Dogon, and one was about Abdoulaye, our guide. His teeth were kicked out by a Japanese tourist who, after hiring him to hike, tired of listening to Ali moan and complain. In my opinion, it was excessive punishment for a clash of different work ethics. He was embarrassed when the story was told laughingly as a joke on his "luck."

Another story was told about us. We heard it from the Swiss guy, Christen, who paid a guide $60 a day for everything. The story went that when we got out of the bush taxi in Bandiagara we said, "I hate these fucking niggers." Because we were supposedly racists, the guides would have nothing to do with us. In fact, that was why we were made to walk. The village chiefs did not collect money from us, hoping instead we would go away.

"If we are racist," we asked Christen, "what are we doing here? Why did we sell our house and leave our jobs?"

He crossed his arms in righteousness and lectured on our attitude. "You don't know these people like I do," he said. "They are simple, poor, and honest. They have no reason to lie. So if my guide said that you said this thing, then I believe him."

This was the first time in Africa we'd encountered racism and the first time we were made to feel our whiteness so acutely. Ironically, it came from another white man. We had been challenged more as foreigners than as two whites among millions of blacks. What we couldn't understand was what Christen gained by promulgating the lie. People believe whatever benefits them most.

Despite this, though, our time with the Dogon passed well. In the villages, we stayed in family compounds and slept on rooftops. Neighbors came to visit, tell stories, show off their children, cloth, or metal work. We joined the chicken roundup, swooping in on the fattest one until someone would snap its neck.

Sauce and a lump of millet pounded with a large wood mortar and pestle was the mainstay of the diet, so chicken was a treat. The thump-thump of the mortar and pestle was one of the sounds of Africa, along with the shuffle of feet heard from pre-dawn until late at night. The beat of the two mimicked the slow beat of the heart, constant as waves on a beach.

The women were strong in the shoulders. Their lats and deltoids bulged from thumping the huge wood mortar into the pestle of grain. I thought myself in fairly good condition until I joined the Dogon women at work. Twenty slams of the pestle and my shoulders cramped with a burn I'd never before felt. They thought it funny when a small girl replaced me at the mill.

I stood in line at the well with them before sunrise. Each woman or girl took a turn hoisting the bucket—a stitched tire pouch—from the depths to fill the next waiting gourd in line. The women joked and laughed softly among themselves about the night before. And about me, too, judging by their glances and giggles. I would have laughed at me too. When it was my turn at the well, I realized the well was much deeper than I had thought—maybe two miles deep. I thought my lungs would burst. Only pride sustained my work.

I could not balance the gourd of water on my head so I clutched it between my arms and walked gently over rocks and gullies I was sure weren't there before. It was only a few hundred yards, but I spilled three-fourths of my load. The women laughed when they showed me their full gourds. "I'll do it better this time," I said, but they diverted me into tasks less wasteful than spilling precious water along the path.

The men hitched donkeys onto a large wooden tooth to draw water for the fields. I couldn't fathom why men used animals for their work and women didn't, except to say that the Dogon men, although they did work—they hunted, they worked in the fields beside their wives, they wove cloth or worked metal, they even helped with the children—they didn't work as hard as the women who were the first up and the last to go to bed. For the women, the well was a meeting place, a place to exchange news. It was not to be hurried by a donkey. Only more work awaited them anyway.

From Bandiagara we caught a bush taxi to Severe on the east/

west highway just south of Mopti. We were determined to hitch-
hike a bush taxi or bus from Severe to Bamako.

Nothing cruised the highway but a few government jeeps and a
pedestrian who plagued us to go into Mopti. He crouched alongside until we moved further down the road, then he would follow.

"Sister, you do not understand," he said, "you cannot get a ride
from here. I speak true. Do you know me?"

"No, my brother, I do not," I said. After the hustlers of Bandiagara, we were leery of knowing anyone.

"How did you arrive here?" he asked.

"Ici? Here? By the Sahara." I replied.

"In Tamanrasset there was a Swiss man called Andy in a green
Volkswagen bus?"

"Yes . . . ?"

"He brought me here to my family. Andy wanted to take your
husband and you but was worried for the weight. Because I am
only one person, he took me. I try to help you because I remember, but you do not understand me when I say that you cannot get
a ride from Severe."

"I am sorry that we do not remember. We are tired because the
way of life is new to us."

He nodded. Once again, I was embarrassed by my judgmental
temper.

"My cousin goes to Bamako, maybe today. I go ask him to take
you. You must wait here until I come back."

An hour later we were speeding down the paved road toward
Bamako, the capital of Mali. We smiled with our good fortune.
Alas, the jeep blew a few tires and broke down in Teni, a roadside
strip of garages. Our driver borrowed another car from a
"cousin" who lived in Teni and delivered us to the car park in San.
He apologized profusely for not taking us all the way to Bamako.

At the San car park, the yard boss tried to bully us into hiring a
private station wagon. Ultimately, I wish we had. We waited two
hours for twenty-three passengers to amass, then took off for Bamako scrunched on a wooden bench in a pick-up truck.

Before the ride was over, thirty-eight people, babies excluded,
were mashed into the back of the taxi *brousse*. Bony hips rubbed
unmercifully into the sciatic nerve of their neighbors. At first it

just hurt, then burned, then throbbed, then went dead. Permanent nerve damage, I am sure.

At midnight, we stopped at Segou. No one got out because there was no way we would get in again. The driver ordered us to make room for six more people—one man with his four wives and a buddy carrying a musket. The wives obediently tried to climb in, but turned around saying, "It is impossible." We knew that. They tried again with the men pushing their asses over the transom.

Inside, everyone whimpered from the pain of moving numb limbs. The driver stuck his head under the tarp and ordered us to sit on each other's laps, which we were doing anyway. He struck the women sitting nearest the door. "You are hiding space!" he shouted.

Robb flew into a rage, "You will not put one more person in here!" he shouted. He shook with the agony of movement and anger. "We are too many!" Robb blocked the doorway and when the driver tried to push past him Robb, grabbed him in a collar lock, "I said, do not touch us! We are too many! I will report you to the police."

The women added their voices from the darkness, parroting Robb's. "Yes, this man is right. We pay money for these seats, and we do not have seats! You make us suffer this pain. The police will see."

The boss backed down, and it seemed that the rebellion had succeeded. A quarter hour later, the six newcomers were added to our corporal mass anyway. Without food or water, we were too weak to fight any longer. It was easy to see how slavery had flourished. Over our laps and on our feet, bodies hugged our knees. A bare breast flapped over Robb's thigh. The woman looked up at him, like an apology. She could not extricate an arm or hand to retrieve it back into her dress.

The excruciating pain again snuggled into our bones. I felt tears rolling down my cheek. Indeed, tears and whimpers accompanied us all the way to Bamako.

The only escape was to dream. I dreamed of transmigrating the passengers onto a European bus, each of us with our own cushy seat. I dreamed of hot food served by a stewardess, a movie, and air conditioning. The driver would ride tied to the muffler. I must have giggled out loud because Robb looked at me as if I were mad.

The night was dark. Passengers cried out. We tried hard to accommodate each others' need to shift weight from butt cheek to cheek, but the slightest twitch unsettled all thirty-eight people. The only thing in my knowledge I could equate it with was theoretical: a slave galley, chained together, no food or water, and our bodies and minds beaten into submission.

I couldn't tolerate it one second longer. I wanted to escape, and I wanted to kill the driver, but only after prolonged torture. If I'd had a gun, I think I could have blown his head off and smiled, watching it fragment into a thousand pieces.

We reached Bamako, the capital of Mali, at 4:45 A.M., much too early for cheap taxis. We waited in the car park with mugs of coffee until sunrise, when fares dropped. A hundred more people slept on the floor of the transient room, each wrapped in his own dreamland.

I wanted to short shrift Bamako. It was filthy from dirt roads, too many people, thousands of charcoal stoves, and mopeds. If you hiked to one of the hills overlooking the city, all you would see would be a dusty haze. Coughing was endemic and epidemic. Although the Niger River flowed through the city, it cleansed nothing. Unlike Niamey, nothing was built on its banks.

In Bamako, we met several international aid workers and American Embassy people. They bragged about their extravagant living allowance because Bamako was a hardship post. They also showed us their cellars filled with tax-free, duty-exempt food, and name brand products, shampoos, and toothpaste, from home. "Thank God, we've got everything we need," they said, "and we don't have to deal with the local population." This was their badge of courage.

Robb and I found a balcony to sleep on at Hotel Djoliba. For only $18 a night we got a torn mosquito net and a straw cot among a row of other travelers—mostly Africans migrating to their homelands after five to eight years of working mines or roads. They, too, complained, "Bamako is more expensive than Abidjan [reputedly the most expensive city in Africa]. I must hurry or I will spend all the money I've saved for my family." Even street food was expensive, so we pooled our money for shared meals prepared on the balcony porch.

One night we went with our African friends from the hotel to an open-air theater to see the premier of the movie *Finzan*. The movie was funded by UNIFEM, UNICEF, and the governments of Mali and France. It was in locally spoken Bambara with French captions and was about a Bambara woman who resisted female circumcision and another who refused to marry her brother-in-law after her husband's death. Both women were kidnapped after attempting to flee. The one woman was forcefully circumcised with a shard of glass, and the other forced to marry. Sight gags portrayed the men as lazy and incompetent. The audience, mostly affluent Bambara couples, laughed at the comedy and were thoughtfully quiet through the dramatic struggle of tradition versus change. Tradition won, but it was portrayed with such ugliness that you wanted it to lose. Our friends were men of different tribes. They explained that as men they had no right to an opinion on the customs of women. "It is women's business," they said. For me, I got my first insight into the power of the women's organizations and the prevalence of female circumcision.

Two express trains run the Bamako/Dakar route. One is a Malian train. Nothing more, really, than a string of cattle cars that haul people—shades of the holocaust. We booked passage on the other, a Senegalese train. It was called the best train in West Africa. In fact, it was one of the only trains in West Africa.

Soot and embers blew in the windows, singed eyeballs and clothes, and burned holes in lungs. It was blistering hot. A zillion people jammed into the aisles and the spaces between cars. The odor of sticky sweat choked the cabins. Metal bars divided the first-class seats. They were bothersome relics of the white man's rule, when individual space was a valued commodity. Now, they are instruments of torture under the African reign of communal property/communal space. Our little space quickly filled with neighbors' purses, bundles, and babies. It was the strangest thing: almost every woman in our compartment deposited her belongings on our laps whenever she went for a walk. The drop-off and pick-ups were done without a word of explanation. We felt like a baggage counter.

Our African bunkmates from Bamako traveled second class, by far the best accommodations on the train. They made the forty-two-hour ride to Dakar endurable by relieving us occasionally and obtaining Castel beer when the bar "ran out." They said the women trusted us not to steal and that is why they left their bundles and babies with us. We would not understand for at least another month why the women trusted us and not their travel mates.

After immigration on the Senegalese side, sleep was impossible. Ticket takers and police checked passports every forty-five minutes or so. Our eyes, bleary with soot and sleeplessness, gazed with relief at the outskirts of Dakar.

Dakar sprawled over the flat land like a flood. Its population eddied out to meet the train almost two hours before arriving at the station. It looked mean, anonymous, and urban.

PART III

The Gold Coast from Senegal to Nigeria

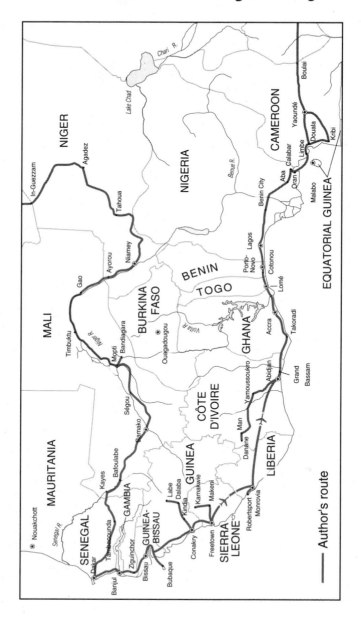

- 10 -
The Gambia

Dakar, Senegal. Since fifth grade geography, the name has conjured dreams of exoticism, foreign ports, and pirates. The more immediate significance of Dakar, for us, was the ocean and beaches, a place to cleanse ourselves from three months on the desert, a Christmas haven, and mail from home.

The Dakar of our dreams and the Dakar that we found were very different. It was the biggest city we had seen since Seville. More than a million people contributed to an atmosphere of tension caused by high prices, unemployment, crime, and strained relations with Mauritania and The Gambia.[1]

Mauritanian traders, who controlled much of the commerce, had just been sent back north to Mauritania. Some people said it was a racial dispute; others said the Senegalese were jealous of the Mauritanians' economic strength so they had them evicted as a way to take over their businesses. Instead, shortages and soaring prices occurred, and the two countries continued to war along their shared border.

A month earlier, The Gambia, which is surrounded by Senegal, broke from the Senegambia Confederacy, a pact of mutual assistance between the two countries. The Gambian ambassador to Senegal told us that Senegal had exploited The Gambia economically, and The Gambia wanted more independence. He chuckled when he said, "Now they find out. We don't send them any of our food."

Senegal was still a one-crop country—groundnuts, or peanuts. Yet, so many countries produced groundnuts for export that the market was glutted. Senegal was not only in an economic stalemate, it was losing ground.

I was hungry for European-style food and was tantalized by odors wafting from the Lebanese-owned restaurants. But when we were charged seven dollars for a cup of espresso and a slice of toast, I had to give up my dreams of European food and drip coffee. We went back to native "cuisine" and instant coffee. Each morning we joined the stevedores on the docks where, for a dollar, water was scooped from bubbling cauldrons, then stirred with heaping teaspoons of instant coffee and powdered cream. The steaming plastic mugs were split from heat and stained by years of lips and other coffee.

The center of Dakar was a fortress of elaborate (in)security systems. It was full of tall, fortified walls, private guards at every doorpost.

Members of the aggressive Wolof tribe were the acclaimed ninja vendors of the continent—the "If you do not buy from me, I will knife you" type of thing. And, indeed, several people showed us scars attributed to the Wolof knife.

We encountered a gauntlet of Wolof pickpockets who thought everyone dumber than they. I guess the odds were in their favor, since Dakar at Christmas was crammed with tourists—many in their sixties with passports and travelers checks flapping from shirt pockets, or money-stuffed purses looped over arthritic arms.

"Buy this shirt," said a man shoving a polyester rag in Robb's face. He walked clumsily as if to trip Robb, but he suddenly bent down and grabbed Robb's leg. The strategy was obvious: two guys coming from behind would snatch Robb's wallet during the melee. The only problem was we didn't carry a wallet. They targeted Robb and ignored me trailing behind narrating their movements. "Three o'clock, one is approaching at three o'clock," I yelled at Robb. Robb spun and knocked him over. I kicked him into his friends, and they fell like bowling pins. Robb screamed loudly, "Thief! Thief!" and they ran into the gathering crowd. Stupidly they tried again the next night, and the night after that. The fourth night no one bothered us. The lesson was finally learned.

There wasn't much pleasure in winning a few rounds while the battle for the streets still raged. We didn't lose anything except the joy of freely wandering the streets. I wanted to stay in our room with the door locked. Robb insisted, however, that a few inept thieves would not ruin Dakar for us.

Arches of Christmas lights blinked over the main boulevards. At the SCORE supermarket, a skinny Santa Claus clanged a bell, and a few little fir trees scented the air with memories of home and family. I guess more than anything they reminded us of what Dakar lacked—friendliness and a sense of belonging.

No mail awaited us at American Express. Had we been forgotten? We felt abandoned by the people we missed and disappointed by Dakar. In the desert, thoughts of mail and days on the beach had spurred us on—we found neither in Dakar.

Because Dakar was foremost a port, the beaches were nasty with oil slicks, floating debris, and rocks. Bathing was no more possible here than in the mirages of the Sahara. North of Dakar and on Goree Island, the nearest palm-treed isle, beaches were supposedly nice. So, after three days without touching a toe to the water, we clambered onto the Goree Island ferry.

Goree Island lies at the mouth of the port like a green fried egg floating in a blue sea. It was pretty, with red bougainvillaea cascading over white walls, and quaint, with a sort of poky resort ambiance. An old fort had been picturesquely converted by one-time hippies into a sort of artists' commune; a renovated slave pen jolted me from fantasy island back into Goree Island's grim past. The only swimming beach was the same used by the ferry and fishing boats. Little Goree was no more our Christmas isle than big Dakar had been. We didn't know much about The Gambia, but we did know we didn't want to stay in northern Senegal. So we

packed and left Dakar on a whim. A bush taxi took us south from
Dakar to Barrajabe, where a ferry crossed to Banjul, the capital of
The Gambia. Between the two nations flowed the coveted Gam-
bia River—a mercantile lifeline and a protector of sovereignty.

We took a motorized *pirogue* to Banjul. They ran more frequently than the ferry and were cheaper although less steady and
more leaky. Dolphins played alongside the pirogue and sea birds
swooped in our wake. Clear, blue waves broke at the inlet to the
river with promises of clean beaches. This time, the Atlantic
Ocean was not an untouchable mirage. Even before the pirogue
nudged into the Banjul beach, we knew that The Gambia would
be our holiday paradise.

Banjul was a likable shantytown. It was smallish for a capital, it
offered few amenities, and had a deteriorating atmosphere about
it as if termites, not people, had migrated into its colonial wood-
work.

The roads were torn up in and around Banjul in a mad attempt
to pave them before Queen Elizabeth's arrival for their independence celebration. The construction heightened the atmosphere
of shambled temporariness. Even the bus stand moved from day
to day. Beggars were deposed from their usual seats along the park
by earth-moving machines. Not to be outdone by engine and construction noise, several beggars wailed their spiel over bullhorns.

"I like it," said Robb, "It's probably a UN project—Bullhorns
for Beggars."

The only place we could find to stay in Banjul was the Teranga
Hotel. It was the most graphic of all the whorehouses we'd stayed
in thus far. Sleep was robbed by loud, dark arguments and fists
thudding the soft flesh of whimpering women. I suppose we could
have waited for a vacancy in one of the more upscale whorehouses. However, our bodies and minds yearned for the pristine
ocean waves we had seen from the pirogue.

The next day we moved to Bakau Beach, eleven miles south of
Banjul, not counting the detours and construction delays. The
bus inched past a prison with amusingly stylized statues of a stern
black guard at the entrance, and a white colonizer tipping his safari hat at the exit. We also passed lush gardens with signs proclaiming them women's cooperatives with co-op funded
vocational schools under construction. Another portion of

profits from the co-ops was made available to women as business loans. Because women were not property owners, they could not otherwise access funds, although 70 percent of the GNP was attributed to women's productivity.

Bakau was a typical beach resort community—one busy grocery store, sunburnt northern Europeans, a handicraft market, and miles of fancy, walled resort hotels. Our hearts and hopes drooped slightly at the sight of so much tourism development. It was "high season" and room rates carried price tags of $50 a night minimum. We were hoofing it south to the edge of town, in search of more modest accommodations, when a British couple referred us to a guest house they were vacating.

The Atlantic Guest House ($18) was set back on a beach cliff at the end of a winding drive of trees and vegetable gardens. The room was big with two clean and firm beds; expansive windows flowed with sunlight and fresh ocean air. After so many sordid dark rooms, this one was like a Christmas gift.

Electricity was erratic and the guest house did not have a generator, but candles worked well; nor was there any water, unless we wanted to pull it from the well where I did the laundry. That was fine too. Next door, at a big resort, we found an outdoor shower. The Gambian staff there were confederates in our duplicity. They even snuck us free pots of coffee and tidbits from the breakfast buffet. I think they felt sorry for us.

I hadn't realized what a toll the past months had taken on us until then. We had each lost about twenty pounds. We were haggard and pale and had chronic coughs from sand-clogged lungs. Hearing English for the first time in months, we were almost tongue-tied. Our vocabulary had atrophied, and our ears were accustomed to interpreting smatterings of conversation and silences. We felt like butterflies emerging from cocoons.

The first afternoon in town we were hustled frequently. They were good-natured, lazy pitches to sell batiks [hand-printed cloths], guides, taxis, and friendship. We were hardened by now and kept on walking, verbally rebuffing their offers with another convenient lie: "We live here, brother. We are not tourists," we would say. "Do you see us walking?"

"Yes, sister."

"Do you see tourists walk?"

"No, sister. They do not walk."

"Then we are not tourists. Go find a rich tourist who will pay you."

"Yes, thank you."

"Go well."

"Yes. And you go well."

It was a tiresome afternoon. The conversation was repeated too many times to count. The African grapevine was faster than a lightning bolt and more comprehensive than a scandal tabloid. If we were to live in peace with the "Gambi" community, we had to establish who we were, what we were doing there, and never waver in our behavior. Within hours our biography circulated town, and never again were we bothered by a hustler or charged the tourist's tax.[2]

Walking kindled other relationships. The strangest one was a man who worked at the British medical research station. He came to the guest house and asked to speak to me.

"I see you walk," he said, "I want you to be my partner in a restaurant. I have the land, but I need money. You give the money, and I will do all the work, if you like. The tourists spend big-big, and you will earn your money back quickly. You can ask anyone after me and they tell you that I am honest."

I explained that we had no money to make a business. "I will give you my address," he said, "and when you go to America ask the people, who wants to be my partner."

Christmas and the 1990 New Year rolled into one wonderful celebration. We had left home, Florida, at the beginning of August, and now it was December 24. In terms of days and months, it seemed a short time. In terms of distance and experiences, it was eons. I had made one short emergency trip home from Spain in September; we had received no news from home since then.

Our Christmas present to each other was a phone call home from The Gambia.[3] Robb's mother was so startled to hear our voices that she wasn't sure it was us and started to hang up! "Ma, it's me, Robb! I'm in The Gambia!" he shouted. Ma was seventy-eight and a stalwartly independent New Englander. We knew she would profess to be well even if she wasn't. Ma practiced positive thinking like a religion, complete with daily incantations to absolve creeping negativism. Confronted with her power, trivial complaints were blasphemous. Miraculously, our harmattan coughs cleared up while speaking to her. She said that she had sent audio tapes to Dakar. (Because we left forwarding addresses with American Express in Dakar, the tapes caught up with us later.) We were not forgotten.

We were nervous about calling my mother. We first discussed the possibility of having to make another emergency flight home. Mom answered the phone speaking with an electric larynx, a device she held to her throat that transformed vibrations of air into words. Unaccustomed to the sound, we found it agonizingly difficult to understand. Then again, we all cried so much that it hardly made any difference. Mom told me she couldn't taste anything. My bossy-yet-generous little sister and she bickered. Mom had cataracts and couldn't see, but would go to a clinic to have them removed. The uplifting news was that she was regaining strength, and we could pursue our trip without the omnipresent fear and worry. But the real joy of Christmas was the news that a contingent of NASA and Lockheed employees was coming to The Gambia for a shuttle launch. Mom would arrange a mail exchange through them!

It seemed The Gambia was an alternate landing spot for American space shuttles. In case of an early abortion, a landing at the Banjul international airstrip would be attempted. Big metal nets were to be strung across the runway in an attempt to stop the shuttle's possibly unfettered velocity. According to team members, the nets had never been tested, and no one knew if they would work. Worse, the NASA contractors feared the possibility of exploding rocket fuel. We hoped the mail would arrive first.

Altogether we spent three weeks in The Gambia and Bakau Beach areas waiting for the NASA team, processing visas, and resting. From Bakau, we roamed the beaches twenty miles in either direction, skipping across boulders, dunking in private coves, and treading the cliff paths. We strolled the streets of town sniffing flavors wafting from myriad restaurants serving fresh shrimp and fish for under two dollars.

The resorts were crammed with Scandinavian and British tourists. During the day, they had their hair braided on the beach, so by night they were festooned à la tourist. Guides escorted them to the souvenir market for Christmas shopping while the really adventuresome (many women) cruised the beaches to snuggle naked in coves with fine young Gambian flesh.

The grand hotels flung Christmas and New Year's parties for their pre-paid guests. The parties and the guests were uncountable. We all looked alike, so Robb and I crashed the parties for free champagne and hors d'oeuvres, cocktail party talk, swimming pools, and the shows. The shows were spectaculars with choreographed dancing and fire-eaters that resorts and glitzy dinner theaters call cultural or native folklore.

After the resort shows, the performers washed the paint from their faces, removed the spangles and baubles, and played in the local, dirt-floored bars. Then the drums would roll all night. Other musicians would hoist in their drums large and small, until maybe twenty jammed together. Men danced together in fevered competition. The women were more inhibited, for these were male fetes. They shuffled in the shadows between tugs on beer.

Few tourists followed the drumming to these places; from the moment of their arrival by charter plane until their departure, they were warned against walking in town. The resorts boomed because guests were too frightened to venture from the parking lot. The independent local businessperson was stung by the myth and reaped little from the tourist influx.

Enterprising hustlers and taxi drivers perpetrated the legend of crime. "You cannot walk alone, better a taxi. Last week two dead tourists were found robbed in this same spot," they warned curious wanderers. It was a sad conspiracy to lure the tourist dollar; one that will haunt future tourism.

We were on the lookout for the NASA team. We thought we'd found them when we spied a group of raucous people chugging American beer on the beach. Before we could ask, a short blonde woman said perfunctorily, "You are Americans."

"Why yes." we said. "Are you with NASA?"

"Do you know how I knew you were Americans?" She wanted to be heard out. "Because no other nationality in the world would walk directly up to a group of strangers unless they were Gambian hustlers. We see very few Americans here. Please sit down, have a beer, tell us what you are doing in this godforsaken place."

They weren't NASA. She was the wife of the U.S. charge d'affaires, the acting U.S. Ambassador who, at that moment, was preoccupied with spying on topless women. The other couple was British. The man had trained the Gambian army after independence from England in 1970.

Nancy showed us around town as if we were baubles, playthings. She took us to The Fajara Club where she was president. "These are American travelers riding around Africa on trucks with the locals. Can you imagine such a thing?"

"Frankly, I'd rather not," replied a British commissioner of some sort after our introduction. "The locals are a scruffy lot. I prefer to stay on my side of the fence with a full bottle of gin." Nevertheless, we were to be Nancy's guests at the club for the duration of our stay. She even invited us to her home for New Year's eve. "I'll have my driver deliver your invitation, and pick you up for the party, too, if you wish."

Things were cozy with Nancy for a while, and we enjoyed eavesdropping on the expatriate alcoholic confessions and sexual innuendos. When Nancy insisted on driving us home, the coziness came to an abrupt end.

As we pulled up to our guest house, the owner, a Muslim, was out front serving tea to her veiled friends. Nancy suddenly slammed on the brakes, almost tossing us through the window.

"Oh, my God! It's the PLO spy place! Get out! Get out! Now!" she screeched.

She leaned across us, flung open the door, and almost pushed us to the ground. With the door still flapping open, Nancy spun a circle and tore out of the driveway. Somehow, we suspected we would never hear or see her again, and we were right.

A Peace Corps volunteer from Sierra Leone told us that the west African coastal countries were crawling with spies. "Everybody is there, the PLO, CIA, KGB, Mossad, El Fatah. You'll see what I mean when you get there. You can spot them in a minute." Normally, we were instinctively accurate at identifying the world's secret operatives, but our guest house family certainly didn't fit any of the usual characteristics. PLO spies? They were Muslim and Lebanese. The sons were a little strange, but they made an honest living from wood sculpturing and painting. The yard had an unused exercise course, but that didn't make them spies.

Intrigued, we snooped. There was a story about a brother shot in Lebanon. Another son collected guns and had spent a year in prison during a coup attempt for having one. He also had been imprisoned in Sweden for stabbing a policeman. Their mother bemoaned the folly of her sons as mothers do everywhere. We did not uncover any proof that they were practicing spies of any kind, nor affiliated with the PLO.

Meanwhile, NASA invaded the plush Senegambia Hotel on Fajara Beach. Among their possessions were fifteen letters from home! Santa had arrived! And he even had a hot shower! We pawed through our mail and divvied them up according to return address. Robb opened his immediately. I saved my letters to caress in private.

The Senegambia Hotel was impersonal and uncomfortable to us, so Robb and I quickly prepared to disappear back into the bush, to Bakau. Our hosts protested because "thugs lurked in bushes, as well as coiled cobras and locals with communicable diseases."

They insisted on driving us the ten miles back home. Never in Africa do you turn down food or a free ride. The NASA truck, with the good ol' boys from home and a cooler of beer, careened along palm-scrub-lined dirt roads. With tendrils of Spanish moss illuminated in the headlights like tinsel on a Christmas tree and our companions talking in space lingo, we momentarily traversed the ocean...to Florida, the old Florida I grew up with. For a few minutes I understood why people traveled away from home just to be closer to home.

The festivities were over. Bakau had been a blissful interlude. For the first time in five months, we slept in the same beds for more than four nights. Our bellies were fattened, the sand cleared from our lungs, and our skin glowed a healthy brown. We had mentally caught up with our movement.

Still, we were as far from understanding our journey as if we were still at home. If anything, we were more confused. We consoled ourselves with mutual assurances that it was too soon to know anything.

As for Robb and me personally, well, our relationship was tighter than ever. That worried me.

"I sometimes feel like we are the same person," I said to him, "that 'I and me' has assumed the plural of 'us and we.' I feel like I lost my individuality somewhere on the Sahara. Look at how we dote on each other. I am not knocking how we took care of each other when we were ill, but . . . ."

Robb clasped my hand in a rare demonstrative gesture. "There is only one way that we'll survive this in good health and that is together. So, we've got a good relationship. We are fulfilling a dream. What's so bad about that?"

"It's unnatural. We should hate each other."

"Don't worry. That will come. We still haven't reached the sixth-month crisis in the life of every long-distance traveler."

The next morning we caught a truck to the Casamance in southern Senegal.

– 11 –

The Casamance

The south of Senegal, the Casamance, is more like The Gambia than northern Senegal in that the Casamance rebelled against Dakar's "exploitation" and claimed independence. Several times in the history of the Casamance, secession uprisings were quelled by troops sent from Dakar. Shattered bank windows attested to the most recent unrest. The openly talkative people attributed the schism to jealousy. The fecund south produced the bulk of Senegal's agricultural output and attracted the majority of Senegal's tourists, yet, "Dakar gives us nothing in return."

An innovative system of "campements" was partially the reason the Casamance was successful in attracting tourists. Campements sometimes resembled hotels or campgrounds but the philosophy behind their placement, their *raison d'etre*, made them unique. Some eight campements thrived on the outskirts of as many different villages. Theoretically, the campements were kept separate from the villages to buffer the lifestyle of the village while giving the traveler a place to stay that replicated the village life. Many were operated as village cooperatives, so the villagers had no stake in fleecing the tourist, and the tourist had no reason to disrupt village harmony in search of a bed, a kettle of food, or a beer.

Campements were so popular that in Ziguinchor, the "capital city" of the Casamance, all cheap hotels claimed to be campements. We stayed in one where we renewed an old acquaintanceship with Christen, the Swiss explorer we had met in the Dogon Land of Mali. He still puffed with his exploits and one-upmanship.

"I stayed a month in a campement run by a French hippie," he said. "It was an authentic experience, not like Gambia...a tourist resort." He chuckled derisively. "You know nothing of the true Africa like I do."

"Haven't you got over that yet?" we asked.

"I am a true traveler," he said. "I stay with the local people and make them my friends. You don't know anything about traveling."

Then he became pensively silent. We waited, watching his jaw line crunch his teeth; his last pronouncement deserved no reply.

"I want to talk to you," he said. "I have learned a lot that I don't understand, and I need to tell someone. Will you come to my room? Everyone here knows the story, but I don't want them to hear me tell you." He behaved in an uncharacteristically humble way. He looked down and lowered his voice to the ground, "You cannot trust anyone. You cannot trust the natives in particular."

We passed several African families on the way to his room. Along the way, I greeted the women at the stone laundry trough where I would soon join them. Christen hissed at me, "I told you, don't talk to the natives. It isn't safe!"

Inside the room, he drew tight the drapery over the screened windows, then waved us into the bathroom. He whispered, "I think we are fairly safe here. I do not believe the staff had anything to do with what I am about to tell you, but I am not sure. Have you ever heard of juju?"

"Sure, it's what we call voodoo—magic."

"Do you believe in it?" he asked with arching eyebrows and soul-beseeching eyes. "Because if you don't, you'd better."

"Sure, we believe in it," I said, showing him my gris-gris. A gris-gris is an amulet or potent. I had asked the juju doctor in Arlit for protection against everything and anything, and he had given me this gris-gris necklace of leather pouches with potions, shells, and tufts of hair. So far, it had worked well.

Christen ignored me. "Let me tell you what happened to me. I was staying here around New Year's before going up country. One morning I walked over there past the gazebo. A man was sitting in it and he started talking to me. He asked me if I had a visa for Guinea-Conakry and I told him that I planned to get it soon. He said he would take me to get it, that he was once the ambassador to Guinea-Bissau so 'They'll give it to you,' is what he said.

"This man then said, 'you have something hanging from your nose.' He wasn't looking at my nose though, he kept staring intensely into my eyes. I wiped my nose. 'You still didn't get it,' and I wiped my nose again. Then suddenly he leaned across the table and plucked a hair from my nose. I was startled. It hurt. He kept talking as if nothing strange had happened.

"I wanted to get up and leave then, but I couldn't make myself move. It was very strange, as if I had no power over myself. The man said, 'You will go to your room and I will go with you.' We came to this very same room and he said, 'You must give me the money for the taxi.' I could not stop myself from what I did next. I gave him four hundred dollars although I could calculate in my head that it was too much. I gave it to him anyway. It was as if part of me wanted to give him the money.

"We got into the taxi together. Then, over by the market he said he wanted to buy a pack of cigarettes and that I should wait. As soon as the car door shut behind him I knew I would never see him or my money again. It was as if the noise of the door closing awakened me from the nightmare.

"I went to the police immediately. They said the man controlled me with juju. The police all wear these things, called gris-gris under their clothes for protection against the juju. Each man opened his shirt to show them to me. They say you have to be very careful, especially of hair. To make juju work they have to get something from you, like hair and that is why this man plucked the hair from my nostril. Even in the barber shops people take their hair away with them so no one can use it.

"The police looked but couldn't find him. So this is why I came back to Zig—to help the police find this man."

His face pleaded sincerity. "I hope you do not laugh at me. I had to talk to someone about it. I am confused, embarrassed, and angry. But I tell you, I could not stop myself, I could not go against him. This juju is very strong. Who would believe this impossible story? I tell you because you know me. You know how I was in the Dogon. I thought I knew everything about these people. Remember when I told you that you were racists, that I believed that you made that statement? Well, I believed it because my guide told me. I found out later that he was a liar. He lied about everything, and he cheated me too. I have changed. I am a different person. Now I do not trust these people. Maybe I am a racist now. This juju is very strong, but I must find this man, it is as if he stole a part of me, my soul, not just my money."

Christen had changed. The initial vengeful glee I felt at his misfortune softened with his humbled confession. With his prior arrogance now stripped away, he was a much nicer person to be around. We were not surprised he had fallen prey to scam artists. Pride had made him vulnerable.

When we returned to Ziguinchor, a week later, Christen was still at the Campement N'Dary Kassoum, but he was preparing to leave—for home.

"I found the man," he said, his face aglow. "I finally saw him one day in the market. He looked different. He had shaved his head, grown a beard, and was dressed in Muslim robes, but I recognized him. The police arrested him and interrogated him. It was awful, they beat him bloody to make him confess. Then all of us went to his apartment to search for the money, and we found part of it, but you would not believe what else. His room had an altar-type thing and all sorts of paraphernalia that the police said is used for juju. They confiscated everything so that he could not use it again. They also found that his identity papers were forged. They claim him to be his brother, who is the consul for Conakry in Bissau. He is in prison now, badly hurt from the beatings. They say they will keep him in prison for two years. Oh, it's a lot of stuff, but I fear for him; they are being hard on him. I am going to hang around here a few days more to see what happens. Then, I think, I'll go home. I've had enough."

Juju aside, Ziguinchor—indeed, the Casamance—was seductively gentle. The Casamance River flows through the province to the ocean, feeding deltas rich with vegetation and fish. Maybe the land, sea, and tourist dollar were kind to the people. An almost loose, happy atmosphere prevailed.

The people talked non-stop, and they loved to lecture. After a month of English, we barely recognized the French sounds. This didn't inhibit the speakers at all. One long lecture covered the major tribes of the region: the Bayrounka, Jiola, Mandinka, Pulh, Maujak, Ouolef, Mankagne, Babauta, and the Sarakifole. My "teacher" told me about the tribes' migration histories and gave me detailed descriptions of identifying marks, clothing styles, and traditional vocations. I wore out before he did, so I had to prod myself to stay attentive.

From Ziguinchor we took a taxi *brousse* to the town of Elinkine, near the mouth of the Casamance River, where we eventually found a pirogue destined for the delta islands. It was past sunset before its cargo of dried fish was unloaded and a new cargo loaded on: fifty sacks of salt, several fifty-five gallon drums, lumber, and passengers. We wanted to make an unusual circuit of islands via fishing *pirogues,* then hike across a swampy peninsula. Unfortunately, Robb cut his foot quite badly while wading onto shore at Karabane island, so we forfeited our plan to care for Robb's injury. Unattended wounds, even small ones, can prevent travelers from completing their trip. We did not want to suffer that fate.

The island town of Karabane was small and devoid of tourists, unlike the southern beaches of Cap Skiring, which local hype compares to Cannes. The one hotel, the Hotel de Karabane, was a value deal. It was basic, but the staff did everything but put chocolates on the pillow at night. It was vacant with the exception of a vacationing Senegalese family and Mousa, a radio technician who operated the island radio station. He guided the big Dakar boats into and out of the Casamance River.

"Yes, it is a big station," Mousa told us with self-importance. Several men from town sat around the table and nodded their agreement. "I can talk with the whole world."

"Can you talk to anyone?" I asked thinking of our ham friends who were hoping to intercept a radio call from us one day.

"Yes, my sister, we can talk a long way."

"Can you talk to America?"

"Yes, yes. I told you that I can talk to anyone. Do you see the big antenna by the station?" We had seen rams battering their heads to bloody pulps, women at the well, an eighteenth-century cemetery divided into Christian and Moslem sections. We had browsed island trails through hibiscus, cannas, and mangroves; explored a Breton church; played in the ruins of a French reform school painted with native graffiti; poked at rusted pieces of machinery; and drank local beer in the village compounds with big-bellied babies clinging to our legs. But we had not seen an antenna.

"Tomorrow I show you the radio station," said Mousa.

At 6:00 A.M. the next day, the village men who were not out fishing were gathered at the hotel restaurant. Mousa made a big deal of making them wait while he ordered extra cups of coffee and an enormous breakfast. He laughed boisterously. I guess showing us the radio station was a big event for them. Mousa and the islanders were proud of their technology, and they were proud to show it off.

The station was a small room on the back side of the hotel. Maybe sixty of us admired the big antenna, then all sixty of us squeezed into the little room to see The Radio. Air was sucked up before the moment of unveiling. "Patron, this is The Radio!" The crowd parted so we could see it. It was a CB hitched by raw wires to a six volt battery! It could maybe skip twenty miles across the water on a clear day.

The island town held their breath waiting for our pronouncement.

"This is the most fantastic radio we've ever seen!" we lied.

Yes, the sixty men nodded their heads in agreement.

"You can talk to anyone in the world!" we said.

Yes, they all nodded their heads again.

"This is a very important radio station," we said.

"Yes, Patron."

"It is too big and important for us to call our friends in America."

"Yes, that may be true," they said. Sixty puffed chests paraded back to the hotel, calling out along the way to neighbors. "We have been to the radio station, and the white people say it is very important."

How could we have let them down? Their village pride was pumped up. Life was confirmed as they knew it to be.

We stayed in Karabane several days while Robb's foot healed. Most days were winter-gray and chilly. The harmattan dust from the Sahara blotted the sun from November through March. One unusually sunny afternoon, I found a cove in a mangrove swamp to do my exercises. I thought I was alone until a group of school children happened along the path. "White woman what are you doing?"

"I am making exercises so that I will be strong and healthy. Do you make exercises?"

"No, we do not. But we want to be strong and healthy—will you teach us?" I chose a skinny little girl out of the crowd. And within minutes the beach was a circus of kids trying to turn cartwheels, stand on their heads, and do push-ups in the sand. It was the kind of craziness that would make a physical education teacher sing. In a short while, their parents started to gather. At first they watched shyly; then they mimicked the motions themselves. The children were ecstatic. "No, Mother, watch me. The teacher said to do it this way." The private cove filled with people. I tried hard to teach them something about warming up and form so they wouldn't hurt themselves, but their enthusiasm was uncontrollable. Only when I promised to teach another class did they let me quit.

When I returned to the beach where I had left Robb soaking his foot in the salt water, he was giving swimming lessons to another thirty people. "No, no, lift your arm over your shoulder, cup your hand this way." We exchanged laughter over an island gone wild.

From that day forward we were known as The Teachers. "Teacher, we want to learn English, we want to know. . . ." The title would precede our arrival in every village. It was also a turning point. We would teach, but in return people taught us, fervently and with passion. "So you will know what to teach about us," they said.

Mousa had to go to the mainland, and he arranged a *pirogue* for all of us at a discount price. He also offered us a ride to Ziguinchor in his car. Along the way we passed several young boys in blood-stained, tattered white dresses. Another group was outfitted in feathered headdresses and bells. They tried to stop the car by feathering out across the highway but Mousa just blasted through them. They scattered unharmed.

"What was that?"

"Do not pay any attention," Mousa said. "It is nothing, they ask for *cadeaux*. These are the young boys who have been circumcised and now they return to their villages as men."

January and February marked the start of the dry season in West Africa and, with it, the "coming out" parties for new initiates, most of whom were young boys and girls. I was curious, but Mousa would not say any more on the subject. I was to learn later that it was taboo to witness, or even speak of, the secret rites.

- 12 -
Guinea-Bissau

Bissau is a small country of flatlands and meandering estuaries. The population is only 800,000, which includes the fifty-three Bijagos islands. Either the harsh Portuguese rule or Bissau's subsequent excursion into Marxism produced a system unlike those of former French and British colonies. The French, we were learning, integrated Africa better than the English and, for good or bad, continued to economically prop up their ex-colonies. The British left a legacy of education and bland food. In little Bissau, the Portuguese colonials had taken everything and given them nothing but a language; the Russians gave them military aid and dogma. It was a hybrid of cultures, languages, tribes, political histories, and economic resources.

Up-country roads and the broad streets of Bissau city had not been ravaged by neglect or by machinery. Very few vehicles were available. And in the Portuguese colonial quarter of Bissau—

usually the first section of a city left to decay from disuse—the
buildings were neatly maintained and lived in. Scarcity of goods,
food, transportation, and money meant that each and every resource had to be utilized. Everything was difficult to find in Bissau except beauty and hospitality. From as far away as The
Gambia, investors spoke of Bissau as the potential tourist giant of
West Africa. "The drawback to development is a lack of infrastructure. Tourists will have to be flown in along with food from
Dakar, and then shuttled to the resorts—after they're built."

Resorts would not save Bissau's economic future. Precious few
dollars would ever touch the hands of the population. Local pundits were perplexed by the problem. "The International Monetary
Fund is ruining us," was a common lament. "We thought by join-
ing things would improve, but now we have higher inflation while
the minimum wage is held at thirty thousand pesos a month.
Watch, things will get worse. There will be more crime and more
begging."

Socialism had not worked either.

"The Russians are still here but we want them out. They have
done nothing for our country except give us military aid," said an
unemployed school teacher educated in Moscow on scholarship.
"Capitalism is the path to our economic survival, but it will be
very difficult. We must first learn to work together as one."

He had taken us to his "house," a small, windowless room, to
show us the impoverished conditions in which the majority of Bissau's people lived. Outside, pigs rutted in the deep mud of the
path that wound around garbage heaps, sewers, and compounds.
Unable to afford a candle, he struck matches to illuminate a meager collection of ratty books, his greatest pride.

"I hope for something more for myself and for my people."

Loka, another educated Guinean, was employed as a secretary.
By most standards, she lived well but modestly with her son and
mother. She identified the development problem on a more fundamental level.

"Africans don't like to work—this is our biggest problem." she
said. "Our men are very lazy. We don't think to the future. If we
have rice today then we eat it all today. People are abandoning
their fields and moving to the city, so that even our rice must be

imported. Some days we don't eat. How can we solve our country's problems with this attitude?"

This was one of the few countries where a semi-public dialogue of its past, present, and future was couched in terms of national identity. Bissau's unique history and isolation forged some sort of unity among the twenty-three major tribes, including the Balante, Fulani, Manjanco, Mandinka, and Mesticos. Problems were distributed equally, and they had little choice but to face them.

Not until we tapped into the almost clandestine network of resource allocation—for everything from food to transport—did we enjoy Guinea-Bissau. The first few days were difficult and perhaps colored by a rude introduction to the country. Between Ziguinchor and Bissau lay 275 kilometers of rough travel. As usual, the camaraderie among passengers multiplied with the obstacles. By the end of the day, we had again formed what I now thought of as "a temporary community" because of our mutual dependence. Movement, any movement, was so fraught with problems that no one in their right mind would subject themselves to such travail unless they had to. If not for the friendships forged during those trials, we would have feared travel altogether. It wasn't just the breakdowns that made it unpleasant, it was the police.

Outside Bissau city, we encountered one of the worst police checks of our trip. It was bad for us because it was a white peoples', *biombos*, inspection station. Robb and I, the only *biombos*, were taken to a bed in a dark dorm room. By candlelight, ten cops ripped every seam out of our clothes, turned every pocket out, and leafed through each piece of paper in our packs. They wanted our medicines but I told them, "No. They are dangerous, they will kill you. They are for a rare *biombo* disease that Africans cannot catch because you are too strong." (Africans definitely believe they are immune to the diseases that plague foreigners. They don't get diarrhea, they say, although they complain of it as much as the tourists. They don't get malaria, polio, etc., they just get bad juju.) The inspection made us nervous. I think it was the bed, darkness, and panting men that upset us. The situation was rank with malice. I would have fainted if it hadn't been for our fellow passengers who tried to intercede at great personal risk. When the door closed on them, they opened the shuttered window. When that was locked, they shuffled their feet. When they were ordered to stop making noises, to go away, the taxi driver started blowing his horn. I will be forever grateful to our temporary community for our rescue.

From the car park in Bissau city, Mercado Bandim, two passengers escorted us in search of a cheap hotel. They were embarrassed for the way we had been treated by the police and wanted to make amends. We eventually found the Ta-Mar Hotel. It was a "budget" hotel, only $18 in hard currency for a sordid room with one broken, sagging bed, and communal bath/shower rooms with feces on the walls and an empty water barrel. We paid with smuggled CFA. We hadn't eaten all day. That night we feasted on clear soup with a floating chicken claw and a sandwich of fried intestines. We went to bed with outrageous headaches.

The next day was no less trying. The National Bank did not accept travelers checks—only hard currency could be converted to pesos. We had CFA 150 but, with paying for hotels and probably visas, it would not last long.

Two British women squabbled with the bank manager to no avail. They only had travelers checks and owed $50 hard currency for a night at the Grande Hotel. Robb said he recognized them from one of the taxis the day before, so he approached them with an offer to team up over the problem. The two blonde-haired, freckled women turned their backs to his overture and teetered up Avenue Cabral on stiletto-heeled shoes as if we were street hustlers trying to pick their pockets. I snickered each time their heels stuck in the cracked pavement. Robb told me that I was acting "little and mean." I told him to shut up.

All four of us ended up at the embassy of Guinea-Conakry at the same time. Truckloads of singing, chanting men were parked in front. "Go away," said a man at the door, "we are closed because President Conte is visiting from Conakry, and, as you can see, we have festivities. Come tomorrow at eight o'clock." He slammed the door on our faces.

Debbie and Jane wobbled in front of us, and Robb again suggested forming an alliance. Debbie, the tallest of the duo, spun on her heels and snapped, "What do you want?!"

"We have the same problems," Robb said. "With four of us working together we'll solve them faster. Let's find a place to talk."

Debbie and Jane had flown into The Gambia from London only two weeks earlier. They were fresh meat for the road to Kenya in east Africa. From there they planned to go to the Far East and open a clothing store in Singapore. They had contracts to update guidebooks for women travelers, and would probably write a book of their own. They wanted the "African Experience" and not the *biombo's* version. Robb and I were *biombos*. They said all of this with a defensive air of superiority.

Undaunted, Robb laid out the immediate problems of converting money, obtaining onward visas, and finding food and a place to stay that didn't charge hard currency. "I propose we break into two teams and divide the tasks. That way we can cover more territory quicker. We'll meet again in a few hours and compare notes." He was right. If nothing else, we were united by hunger and the lack of local currency.

We split up with our assigned tasks and gathered a wealth of information that none of us could have amassed alone. From there we made decisions. None of them were really happy ones. The Guinea-Bissau system was unyielding unless we gave up some of our ethics. For self-protection, we had to lie and misrepresent.

We were literally forced to the black market. Even our embassies referred us to the street corner. They too exchanged money there after couriers to Senegal first converted their paychecks into CFA.

Debbie and Jane had to sneak out of the Grande Hotel because they couldn't pay the hard currency bill. They were determined not to stoop as low as the Ta-Mar. But, after inspecting and interviewing every place in town, they took the room next to ours.

The consular officer of the Guinea-Conakry embassy was a royal pain in the ass. He was as evil as his juju brother in Ziguinchor. I wished them both life imprisonment. For four days we went to the embassy seeking a visa and, over those four days, we were stalled, lied to, manipulated, inveigled against, and ejected. We thought we'd hit a lucky streak the day we met President Conte. "What do you think of my country?" he boomed grandiosely as if Guinea-Bissau was his.

"We don't know about your country," we said. "We are trying to get visas, but we are not having any luck."

"What is the problem?" President Conte asked, bearing down on my face and rolling eyeballs to the hovering ones of his staff.

"Mr. President, sir, we don't know what the problem is. Three days now they tell us to go away because they are too busy."

"Give these people visas!" he commanded. Heads bobbed. Then the royal face of President Conte furrowed with smiles, like a grandfather chuckling over the naive antics of young upstarts. "See," he said, "it is easy. Tomorrow you will see my wonderful country. I have ordered it."

Once Conte's back bent into the waiting limousine, the evil consul scowled, "Come back tomorrow."

Tomorrow there was no visa but there was the wounded ego of the consul. Like an injured elephant, he trumpeted and thrashed all over us. Even our embassies were ineffectual against his vindictive rage. It was a Friday: four days wasted with abuse. The consul had ordered us back on Monday to "fill out the paper work."

Debbie, Jane, Robb, and I forlornly picnicked on a green lawn.

"I don't know about you," said Robb, "but I am not sitting around this city all weekend. We can't do anything until Monday, so let's go somewhere."

"Yeah, far away," said Debbie.

"Yeah, like Kenya," enjoined Jane. "Do you think we can fly there this weekend?"

"Nope," said Robb. "While we were checking on transport out of here we asked about flights. The Bissau airline is down for repairs because they didn't pay their insurance. And nothing else has flown into or out of here for two weeks. Not even the U.S. embassy knows when another plane will depart. I say we go to Bubaque."

"And I say that we just stay here in Bissau and be miserable," said Debbie.

Robb glowered like a disappointed father, "You will go to Bubaque and enjoy it," he said. "You will do it for the book." We whined but Robb won. "Do it for the book," became a rally cry.

It was a Friday afternoon and too late for the weekly ferry to the island. We wandered from boat to boat docked at the harbor, hollering, "Are you going to Bubaque?" No. No one was going to Bubaque.

Robb insisted we try the shipping office of Agencia Guine Mar.

It was packed with seafaring men, the kind of men that command big ships through the treacherous straits of the world. The loudest of all was a robust Greek captain.

"I want my rice unloaded tonight!" he hollered. His meaty fist pounded the countertop, which was highly polished from previous fists. "My ship has stood at your dock for thirty-five days waiting for your crane to move the rice. If you don't take it within the next twenty-four hours I'll take the whole fucking load up to Dakar and give it to the Senegalese. Free. Just to get out of paying your dockage fee. Do you know what this is costing?" At one point during his tirade he turned to us and winked. "Year after year it's the same old thing. They starve, we bring them rice, and then they can't afford to unload it from the ships. I have to yell like hell for several weeks and send a mechanic to fix whatever is broken. But I love it," he said unbuttoning his shirt to his hairy navel and pounding his solar plexus. "I love these people." Like a Greek about to step out into a dance, he flung his arms wide. "God, I love them. Don't tell them I said so or I'll never get rid of the rice. Where are you going? Need a ride to Dakar?" said the Greek.

"We are looking for a boat to Bubaque."

All heads swerved to look at one man, whose curly, slightly greasy hair tumbled over his polyester collar.

"Well," said the Greek, "You came to the right place. That man will take you."

"That man" searched the rafters for cobwebs while trying to disappear into his baggy pants.

"Will you take us to Bubaque?" I said to his ear.

"Yes," he said to the wall. "Be at the docks by five in the morning and ask for the Catholic Mission." His voice was gentle, soothing, and resigned.

At 5 A.M. we found the boat—a canoe! It looked so unseaworthy that we were sure it would sink faster than our waning confidence. The curly-haired man in the polyester shirt directed the loading. He was the priest from Bubaque, Father Luigi. Besides us, the boat held villagers and eight Italian tithers, benefactors of the mission.

The canoe pulled into the bay with a young boy bailing seawater faster than the engine pistons churned. Immediately, a storm whipped the sea into frothing furrows that gradually became deep troughs. The Italians turned green.

The helmsman threw up his arms and abandoned the tiller announcing, "I am lost." Great. I couldn't think of a better place to be lost than forty miles at sea. The sun was covered by the harmattan haze; visibility was maybe twenty feet. Father Luigi had a compass, but triangulation had been impossible.

Father Luigi grabbed the tiller. His mood was blacker than the day. He cursed and thirty throats moaned lifetimes of penance. Boom! Suddenly, the hull struck bottom, and the prow thrusted toward the sky.

Moans gave way to screams of terror. "It's a whale!" someone cried. Time stood still, and rosary beads clicked faster than a turnstile at a racetrack.

We had run aground on an embryonic island. The canoe was pushed free.

Grim eyes searched the sea for a more propitious sign. An hour later, a buoy was spotted. We all heaved a collective sigh of relief. The boat nosed into the green archipelago where the water was calm, and the sun almost penetrated the clouds. Our jangled nerves relaxed. Father Luigi smiled and launched not a sermon, but a travelogue. Many of the islands were uninhabited, he said. They were used as farms or as burial places by more remote islanders who had no interest in the outside world. His suggestion that we visit them received no enthusiasm.

Other than the one expensive hotel on Bubaque, there was little in the way of accommodations. We tread well-worn village paths for several hours in search of a room or a "legal" place to camp. Our inquiries were met with "no space tonight." For a while, a lanky, sloe-eyed young man had followed us at a distance. When we stopped under a tree to rest, he approached hesitantly with the offer of a room. Debbie said that sounded like a "brilliant idea" and asked the young man, Mohammed Dee, to take us. He led us down a dirt path past compounds guarded by fierce Balinese-like masks to a thatched hut in an outlying village.

Mohammed Dee spoke a while with "Father" who owned the house. Father nodded several times then ushered us to the doorway. Mohammed Dee said that Father asked no money and, anyway, that was our business. His good deed done, he skipped back to town.

With growing horror we watched Father, a sickly stick figure wrapped in a blue blanket, move his few belongings to the house next door. The room was his own! He assured us he would stay with his wife.

Then unfolded an amazing scene. Neighbors arrived with furniture from their own homes! We were brought bed frames, mattresses, new sheets, mats for the floor, stools, a wood box for our clothes, a gourd, a door lock, candles, and a box of wood matches. Each family—parents wrapped in blankets, shy girls in short grass skirts, grandparents bent over sticks—hovered to witness our appreciation. Clearly, our house was theirs. For as long as we stayed there, we were communal property.

The only drawback was the absence of facilities. This in itself wasn't a problem. The spectators were. Paths crisscrossed the open compound so that a private stub of grass was difficult to find. Bucket baths always attracted a crowd who squatted alongside and chatted. I guess they didn't want us to feel lonely.

One afternoon we encountered on the path a group of women coaching a laborious childbirth. They were oblivious to our intrusion but we hurried on, embarrassed. Two days later, the woman danced through the streets surrounded by women who sang and clapped. The men beat drums. The birth had been successful.

Several families in town cooked. Meals had to be ordered in the morning before the market opened. It was potluck. Nevertheless, their business thrived on take-out wrapped in banana leaves. We usually "ate in" at rickety, candle-lit tables with raspy, overhead speakers pouring loud music into our ears. The owners were always proud of their sound systems.

The best beach on Bubaque, Punta Anino (the only beach free of a sting ray infestation at the time), was on the other side of the island—a 15-kilometer walk past roadside stands of palm wine, home-brewed beer, and coconuts. Birds flew by our shoulders, and a bush rat or green mamba snake was as apt to dart across our path as a fierce-looking man in a grass loincloth toting a freshly cut branch of red palm nuts, used to derive cooking oil.

For once, no one was around to spy on our antics. The freedom was as healing to our souls as the sun and salt water were to our skin. We stayed to watch the harmattan haze shroud the sun. The walk back would be cooler by night. We were preparing to leave when three distant lumps drew near and transformed themselves into three Italians. They were with Father Luigi, who was fishing around the point. They tittered effusively with the joys of Buba-que; a sentiment that we could share. They invited us to join them for the ride back—a less sentimental but more practical joy that we also shared.

Some days the weather was fierce. Not even the fishing boats stirred from shore. We used this phenomena as an excuse to stay on Bubaque a few days longer and to throw a beach party.

Debbie and Jane wove plates from green palm fronds. We bought tomatoes, onions, bread, tangerines, and plantains. Robb trimmed sticks into skewers, collected firewood, and cleared a cove of the viporous green mamba.

The green mamba is a small snake with one of the most deadly venoms in the world. It is hard to detect because it blends into tree branches about the height of the average human face. It is also one of the few snakes that attack without provocation. Zappo! Its poisonous talons sink into the vulnerable area of the face. Sup-posedly victims die within minutes. I literally twitched with fear for Robb as he shook long palm fronds into the overhanging trees. Two struck at the branch then slithered away. Since Robb sur-vived, we were grateful for his macho noblesse.

Unfortunately, the fishing boats did not go out that day; not even a fish fin was available for our skewers. It was a poultry day, and they were all claimed early in the morning. Forlornly, we gazed at the bright fire and the empty banana leaf plates in the sand. That night we discovered new recipes. Canned sardines roasted over an open flame with toasted tangerines were abso-lutely delicious.

The Pope would arrive in Bissau two days later. In spite of the adverse weather, Father Luigi and his Italian benefactors had to be there for the ceremonies. They offered us a ride back in the mission canoe. When the gale didn't clear by late afternoon, we set out anyway. The canoe was ladened with flowers and passen-gers in their best ceremonial clothes. Lastly, reverently tucked among us for protection was a carved, miniature canoe complete with figurines. The Pope would bless it and thereby bless all the fishing fleet.

How hard could it be to miss the continental mainland of Africa? Easier than it seems. The gale tossed the little stick boat like a Ping-Pong ball. Once again, Father Luigi had to take the helm. Ten hours later, at midnight, we made landfall in Bissau.

We were headed with all our gear to the Ta-Mar when a persistent hustler took up our footsteps. Once he saw where we were headed, he claimed to be the owner's son. The desk clerk was not on duty—probably asleep somewhere. What ensued was a loud, physical tug-of-war. The hustler demanded money for taking us to the Ta-Mar, then demanded twenty dollars extra for each room. Robb threatened to call the police if he didn't leave. The hustler said he would call the cops himself because it was his hotel. Robb snatched room keys from the unattended desk and started up the stairs with all our luggage. The hustler tugged at the luggage, ranting that his father would arrest us. Stoically, Robb ascended, yelling with each step, "I am calling the police right now."

At that moment a door flung open, its knob forever denting the wall behind it. A sumo wrestler in jockey shorts burst forth. "What the hell is going on?"

Robb talked, the kid yammered, and the wrestler bellowed, "I am the manager, and he is not my son! I kill him for his lies!" The pretender was kicked down the stairs.

The next morning the Guinea-Conakry consular official unofficially denied our visas. "You were ordered to reappear last Monday, and you did not come. Go away, don't ever come back here!"

We appealed to our respective embassies. The British High Commissioner, who owned the hard money store, threatened to cut off the ambassador's charge account. The American ambassador took a different tack. "This fellow has given us trouble since we caught him forging documents for his buddies." It figured. "It is high time I straighten this out." He ordered his limousine and flags.

This time, our reception at the Guinea-Conakry embassy was cordial and diplomatic. The Conakry ambassador opened his well-stocked private bar and ordered the accused man to serve us. Mr. Evil groveled.

"Make your charge against this man," invited the ambassador.

Really, it was tempting to skewer him like we had the canned sardines. We didn't. It was enough to depart under the American flag with visas to Guinea-Conakry stamped in our passports.

Meanwhile, Debbie and Jane met two Frenchmen who either vouched for them, or paid the bribe to Mr. Evil for their visas. They would travel with the French, in a private vehicle, to Conakry. The Frenchmen also offered to put them up for the night at the Sheraton.

"What if they come on to us?" asked Debbie and Jane, wringing their hands over the dilemma of a hot shower, food, a free ride, and possibly the hidden agenda of the Frenchmen.

"Sit in the back seat together and snuggle with each other," advised Robb, "Occasionally kiss and they'll think you're gay."

"When will we see you again?" asked Debbie.

"If not in Conakry, then in Ghana," said Robb. "Go to Busua Beach, we'll be there in three months."

"Brilliant!" exclaimed Debbie. "We plan to be in Kenya then."

"Meet us in Ghana," repeated Robb. "Do it for the book!"

- 13 -
Guinea-Conakry

Juicy oranges, green on the outside, were the main source of fluids during the two-day trip to Conakry. It was the type of travel best fortified with fatalism and resignation. New bruises tenderized our buttocks. The cars spent as much time roadside for repairs as they did in motion—seven flat tires, a dead reverse gear, and all the vital vehicle fluids drained from multiple leaks. The drivers seemed optimistically determined to cross the one thousand kilometers on one liter of gas. They scratched their heads in wonderment when the tanks ran dry.

Only in one six-hour stretch did we make any time. The driver did not stop at any of the numerous police barricades. He sped past the screaming, gun-waving, whistle-blowing officials. At each barricade, all ten passengers would crouch on the floor in a giggling heap, just in case the police started shooting. The driver's lunacy, or anarchy, both invigorated and frightened us.

The road from the border wound through the Fouta Djallon mountains, the wellspring of the 2,600-mile-long Niger River. Reputedly, it was breathtakingly scenic. Unfortunately, the harmattan obscured the valley vistas and rendered an overcast drabness to the brittle dry grass and scrub.

We got out in Dalaba, a small mountain town famous for its scenery and for the nearby homes of President Lansana Conte and Miriam Makeba, an exiled South African singer who was given refuge in this country. Although road-weary, the pulse of travel beat steadily in our hearts. We didn't pay attention to the concern of our taxi friends when they asked, "Who do you know in Dalaba? Where do you stay?" Such questions usually presaged a lack of accommodations. We assumed that in Dalaba we would find a cheap, grand old hotel. Not until the taxi left did we learn that we had assumed too much.

For a brief while we were the center of every would-be social worker in Dalaba. Our presence caused a stir of excitement. "What to do with the white people?" They would decide the matter among themselves.

Kerosene lamps twinkled from the vendors' stalls along the dusky main street of town. A toothless woman sidled up to Robb and playfully linked her arm in his, then tugged him as if he were hers. "Take him," I said, "I will pay you to take him," and held out a few guinea francs. She laughed raucously and repeated my English words aloud several times for all the other vendors. "These are my daughters," she said, introducing two women selling peanuts, candles, and canned sardines. The old woman grabbed her breast and pointed to her daughters to underscore her meaning.[1]

Mist-shrouded Dalaba wore a friendly charm. When it was learned that we were not with the French Foreign Legion, proud parents invited us to inspect their children's copy books and report cards, to share greasy "ragout" (a vegetable and meat stew), or a big bottle of beer.

Finally, a UN jeep was rounded up and we were driven to the Region Administrative Dalaba quonset huts. "It is closed but the caretaker is my cousin," explained a man from town.

Cobwebbed rooms were filled with cracked and torn, overstuffed furniture. Stapled on the walls were crinkled, full-page advertisements for food, cologne, fashions, and cars that had been ripped from French magazines twenty years earlier. The site felt haunted. Long-departed voices of French colonizers ranted against the ungrateful audacity of Sekou Toure, the uncompromising Guinean who led the colony to independence from the French. "Quick, pack, De Gaulle said we must leave!" Another ghostly voice urged, "Not a minute to lose. Take the phones, take the generator...*depeche*!" The one-time French resort was, in its ramshackle abandonment, a haunted mausoleum.

We ran away—to life, to town, where the kerosene lamps flickered all night like encircling arms of security. Where the blown-out bass speaker at the disco summoned lovers into its dark, discrete nooks. "Come to me," the beat pounded, "do it now," it suggested. The dance floor heaved with swaying bodies like snakes hypnotically compelled by a mystical flute.

In Dalaba, our list of "Things People Carry on Their Heads" lengthened. Heretofore, the list included water, firewood, and piles of cloth. Now we added an umbrella, a pair of shoes, three sacks of rice crowned with an old fedora, and a hand-driven Singer sewing machine.

Dalaba to Conakry took a full day by bush taxi. During the ride, it was easy to resist the temptation to explore. In Labe, Pita, and a few smaller towns, our white faces elicited undisguised hostility. People spat through the car window. And it wasn't meant as a benediction. Our companions shuffled us into the center of the car to shield us from "the rude Susu," or "the uncultured Malinke." Most likely, it was an excuse to stick us on the unpadded hump in the back seat, a place to be avoided.

To both sides of us mothers breast-fed their babies. Suckling infants traveled with their mothers until they were at least two years old, some three. Extended breast-feeding was a form of birth control, the women said. It was also a pacifier: never did we hear a child cry. After the first two years of total security, the child suddenly lost his special status and joined the other children of the compound.

Missing was verbal and visual stimulation as we define it in the West. Very few mothers played with their children, and colorful toys certainly were not available. Only in a few tribes did we see males actively participate in child care. Parents complained that children were becoming brattier and more uncontrollable. They couldn't blame it on television, so what was it? I had studied child rearing since entering the sub-Saharan countries. I had looked for the effects of child rearing practices on adult behavior. What, for instance, made adults so passive toward authority, or toward the future?

Conakry, the capital, spilled beyond the natural boundaries of the peninsula. Uncertain of where we were going, we rode the taxi to the end of the ride, until every passenger but us had been dropped off. Our minds swarmed with images of people, taxi stands, cement buildings, and squatters' huts patched out of paper, plastic, and scrapped sign boards. Every inch of space looked occupied, and Conakry looked impenetrable.

Usually after such a "tour" we had some feel for the lay of the land, but we were lost. We hired a local taxi to shuttle us in search of a cheap hotel. Again, every hotel was either full or closed from disrepair. The driver and his assistant, a sort of Cheech and Chong duo, took the edge off the hunt for a bed with a good-natured narrative of the city.

"Landmarks, you need landmarks because we have Conakry One, Two, and Three, and only a few buses or taxis that cross from One to Three, or Two to One," they told us. "Stupid, but that's how they operate. Now here is the president's palace and the big waste of money—the OAU mini-palaces. Remember it, because this is where Conakry 1 and 2 divide. Stay away from the government-run hotel, L'Independance, they are thieves."

When they suggested The Nimba we did not argue. The ride cost CFA 2,000. Slightly high, but considering the two-hour tour and the countless inquiries for rooms, it was not bad. Unfortunately, we didn't have it. The French owners of The Nimba, Hines and Marcel, paid the bill.

We were broke on a Sunday. No CFA, no Guinea francs. The Nimba men kept a taxi on standby, so they sent us in it to Wall Street: the infamous black market block. Our driver threw up the engine hood to make it look like we were stopped due to a mechanical breakdown. I am sure it didn't fool the police. The moneychangers weren't fooled. They flocked to the taxi with calculators to display offers the same or lower than the official rate—617 Guinea francs. Considering bank commissions were as high as 25 percent, Wall Street was often an acceptable deal.

The Nimba was a nice house, nestled among African planked houses on a dirt road. Something was sad about it though. We were the only guests. The few African nymphets that hung out in front gave it the appearance of a whorehouse. Red-nosed French expatriates slurred over the bar with nothing else to do, having given up on life.

"I want to go home but I would lose everything here. And if I did, what could I do? I have no skills. I have stayed here too long now to fit anywhere else." In bits and pieces they confessed to shattered dreams. Like Graham Greene's characters in *A Burnt-out Case*, they had sunk into alcoholic stupors and self-hatred. Immobilized by fear.

They spoke real French, however, and not the pidgin French we learned in taxi brousse—pragmatic words hung on present tense verbs. We had expected to learn French—it was the one big expectation of the trip, and our one big disappointment that we didn't. Ironically, the African guests translated many of our conversations with the French expats.

Some cities wear well, and we were partial to the small, sleepy ones like Banjul or even Niamey, where you could walk end to end in one afternoon. While Conakry had received rave reviews for music, nightclubs, restaurants, and security, it topped our list of most-hated cities in the world.

Walks were unpleasant, and always an impossible distance laid between points. The streets were congested with traffic, dirt, gas fumes, and too many people. We hiked across Conakry several times during the day, but by night we cruised the quarter where The Nimba was. The streets were lined with small shops, eating benches, market produce—banana, pineapple, mango, and vegetables. Cubbyhole bars blared oppressively loud music for their yellow-eyed clientele wobbling on crude benches. Tiny sundry stores stayed open as long as anyone wanted to buy detergent, and kids with Molotov cocktails—bootlegged gas sold in bottles and plugged with a twist of cloth—darted among the all-night traffic waving siphon hoses. The vendors, the guardians of the street, patrolled and enforced behavioral ethics, at least within their view. They watched out for our path, so I always felt safe among them.

Every mouth repeated bleak stories of violence: gangs, break-ins, robberies, and murders. Crime and warnings were never spoken without reference to the economy. Economic frustration boiled like a cauldron ready to spill over. A Guinean woman said, "President Brigadier General Lansana Conte is more progressive than Toure. He's opened the market, and it is now possible to find food . . . if you have a job and have money. Some nights my children cry from hunger. It is difficult to listen to them when you have nothing to offer. We must lock our doors and windows at night against thieves. If it is hot and we sleep outside, then we must keep the fire all night." Many compounds glittered with the sleeping fires. Long ago they were burned to discourage lions and hyenas, now they are used to discourage the urban beast of prey. At night, people walked in groups, "It's unsafe to walk alone," they said.

Part of the problem was blamed on the influx of immigrants from Mali, Senegal, and Sierra Leone. "They come here to work to get rich. We are a rich country. You see our agriculture, we have great reserves of bauxite, iron, copper, magnesium, uranium, gold, and diamonds. But something happens to the minerals. They disappear from our country without any payment. People move from their farms into the city, and now we are too many people without enough work or money. We are desperate."

Increasingly, fathers sold their daughters into prostitution at the age of ten for 500 to 2000 Guinea francs. Daughters could earn maybe five times in a day what their fathers could in a year. It was lamentable, "but what can we do?"

The white travelers claimed they were unprotected targets of crime. In an unusually long discourse, Bernard, an expat from France of twenty years, expressed the expatriate opinion.

"In 1952, President Sekou Toure said all white people are bad and that the Guinea people should steal from them. It has since become an unofficial policy. A white man buys a house, but then a Guinean presents papers that say he is the new owner. Voila! The white has lost everything. Paper is for sale here, all kinds of paper, from deeds to passports, but it means nothing if you're white. This mentality won't change for maybe another forty or fifty years. There is no heart here. You can try and try, and what you find is blank."

This was the first place we felt generalized, anonymous hostility to whites—an unwanted minority. Guinea-Conakry was the first nation to reject membership in De Gaulle's Franco-African community. The pride of successfully rejecting the white man lived on in everyone's memory. Coexisting was a nebulous animosity for De Gaulle's punitive retaliation; he had ordered everything French removed from the country. The infrastructure was never rebuilt and was in shambles. Conte, in hopes of stabilizing the currency and stimulating the economy, was moving the Guinea franc into line with the French franc. Many Guineans saw it as a sell-out, a restoration of white domination; it irked their pride and renewed their anger.

Conakry was deadly serious and very unhappy. Violent crime was extremely unusual in West Africa and unheard of in rural regions. As soon as our visas to Sierra Leone came through, we would flee the city and turn our smiling faces to the road south.[2]

One concern gnawed at the future: a rumor of a civil war in Liberia, and it grew into a reality. Only at the American embassy was it denied. "Nothing is happening in Liberia that we know of," they had said. On the streets, it was common knowledge, although the details were fuzzy. "Don't go there," person after person warned. "Liberia is very dangerous. They are killing each other and anyone else. Just last week an American woman had her throat slit by the military. You are American? Well, don't go, I tell you."

At Alliance France we dug up an article in *Le Soliel* newspaper. Opposition rebels to President Master Sergeant Samuel Doe, led by Charles Taylor and allegedly trained by Libyans in Burkina Faso, crossed the border from Ivory Coast into Liberia on December 24 and massacred a village. Two hundred civilians were slaughtered, ten thousand refugees had fled to Guinea, and another twenty thousand to Ivory Coast. Liberian borders were reported closed.

Well, Sierra Leone stood between us. We would have time to investigate the developments and decide what to do. Curiosity compelled us to find a way into Liberia, or "Little America," as it was called.

Another article in *Le Soliel* made us cringe. Of all U.S. aid to Africa, 60 percent is military support for strategic goals. What the

hell goals were we supporting? Are we arming repressive dictatorships and equipping generals with new Mercedes while the poor
populations starve?

   If Africa had been an apolitical journey for us, that would soon
change. Disillusionment and desire were cropping up in heated
events all over the continent. Soon, no one would be apolitical.

– 14 –

Sierra Leone

We were advised to cross into Sierra Leone at Pamelape early, before the border guards were drunk and contentious. Although we left Conakry at 5:30 A.M., and arrived ninety minutes later, they reeled and reeked of palm wine. "Money talks," the guards slurred with glassy, unfocused eyes. Later, when throbbing headaches replaced their drunkeness, they would remember we did not pay.[1]

It was here I met my first woman cop. Without looking at my pack, she said, "Give me all your fine lotions and expensive perfumes." I laughed madly, thinking it was the funniest thing anyone in Africa had ever asked for.

"Take it," I said as I flung open my pack. "Take it all!" She saw the heap of dirt-stained clothes, turned on her heel, and left me chuckling like a deranged lunatic.

Our first impression of Sierra Leone was that it was a country with a thriving black market. Our taxi was stopped five times in fifteen minutes by police searching for foreign currency. My hatred for police checks escalated and threatened to engulf my affection for Africa. The passengers joked at having beaten the police. Because Robb and I were "rich whites," the police focused their attention on us and didn't search the Africans, whose bricks of money were hidden in the door panels.

Something in me snapped. I think it was my adaptability. I did not see the cracked tarmac road, nor the jungle thick with flowering bromeliads. I did not hear the jokes that were integral to rebuilding dignity after each demeaning police check. I did not even feel happiness to be in an English-speaking country again. I saw and heard only my own anger.

Police barriers meant we did not arrive in Freetown, the coastal capital of Sierra Leone, until dark. By night, central Freetown looked bombed, decrepit, and devoid of any charm. Again, our list of cheap lodgings was useless: some places we couldn't find, and others were closed.

Stepping around drunkards sleeping in burned-out doorways among broken glass, we found the Hotel Lamar. The manager said he had one room left on the sixth floor. It was a bit expensive, because it had air conditioning and a private bath. Both sounded great but neither worked, nor did the door lock, nor was there electricity to run the elevator.

Robb and the manager shouted at each other until the price of the room was adjusted down for each deficient amenity. The manager would not budge, however, on the need to pay up front, and we hadn't a single leone. One of the ironies of Africa was that every service had to be paid in advance, but getting change back took hours, and even days, to receive.[2] In the end, we gave the manager a passport for collateral.

We were starving. I was grumpy. So was Robb. It was time to splurge at a restaurant that accepted credit cards—an indulgence we had promised ourselves if our spirits got down. It was time, perhaps, but not the place. We found several restaurants, but only one accepted credit cards—The Paramount Hotel. (Fish dinners with salad and warm beer came to a total of $7.90, including tip.)

Life looked a little better over a full belly, yet I harbored rancor for the events of the past weeks. Self-indulgent despair sought sympathetic company, and Robb was the only other person in the dining room.

"I've lost my adaptability," I said as introduction. "I've had it with West Africa. Tomorrow I want to check on flights to Kenya. There is nothing here but difficulty, and I cannot, do not, want to do it anymore."

"What are you talking about?" Robb said. He was caught off guard.

"I am talking about leaving. . .quitting. I am talking about being sick and tired of police checks, of lies, of living in fear of being caught with our smuggled emergency stash, and of dealing on black markets with strangers. I am talking about four little countries in the last month alone, and searching for food in each little town. My mind is crazy with switching languages from English to French, then to Portuguese, back to French, and now to English again. And most of the people we meet don't even speak those. Oh, no, we've had to learn twenty different African languages on top of it. I am tired, angry, and want to quit."

"Don't you think I'm tired too?" said Robb. "I'm the one who handles all the money transactions. You don't."

"Well, I'm the one who has to talk to everyone. You won't."

"You don't see me quitting."

"Look, we agreed before we started this trip that if it stops being fun, we'd move on. We agreed, didn't we? This is not fun."

"I knew you couldn't do it," he said smugly. "I knew I should have come by myself."

"You are a self-righteous bastard," I said.

"And you are a wimp! You haven't even made it six months and you want to run home to mommy!"

I guess I got what I wanted. The argument justified my self-pity. "Don't yell at me," I whispered, "I don't need to be yelled at again today. Alright?"

"I am not yelling," he said.

"Yes, you are. Can we leave here now? I mean, continue this argument some place else? Private. Like bed? I'm tired."

"Pami, we're both tired. I love you, and I don't want to continue this argument anywhere. The past days have been tough but can't you remember the fun things, like the sardine barbecue on Bubaque? Cocktails with the ambassadors while that creep fawned for forgiveness? You're forgetting our friends, the people on the trucks who looked out for us, the babies we've held, and the smiles we've shared. Remember that old woman on the truck that broke down so often between Casamance and Bissau? No one understood a word she said, but her expressions made everyone laugh so hard that the car problems were hilarious."

"Gee, I'd forgotten her. She was great." I chuckled.

"Okay. Think about her. Think about the others. Think about Debbie and Jane, Golo and Walter. Can we be friends?"

"I'll try. I'm sorry." We walked hand-in-hand through unlit, empty streets to our sweltering, sixth-floor alley room. We splashed water from a bucket, then cuddled in the one hot broken bed before I moved to the floor where it was cooler.

"There's one thing I can't figure out about Africa," said Robb from the blackness. "I can't figure out why there are so many babies. It's so miserably hot I don't want to touch you. My question is, how does anyone do it?"

"Beats me. Maybe they store it up for the rainy season. The first cool night that comes along we'll make love until the sun rises."

"Hmmm, that would be good for a change."

By morning the crises were over—the crisis of arriving in an unfamiliar city by night, disoriented, and penniless; and the crisis in our relationship. Freetown rose with the sun as a new challenge.

Freetown is snuggled among soft sweeping hills on a plateau of fingers extending into the Atlantic. Stilt-like houses with peeling white paint lent the place a lazy, island atmosphere, reminiscent of its first colonizers—freed slaves from the Caribbean. Life sprang from the deteriorating wood like termites from a dead tree stump. Freetown had changed little since Graham Greene described it over thirty years ago in *The Heart of the Matter*, except it was, perhaps, less ambitious, and the City Hotel, where Greene had lived, was now ramshackle with creaky, sad floors.

The bank dispensed stacks of money bricks when we converted the mandatory sixty dollars. Often the bank didn't have money because people hoarded the few bills in circulation. A recent devaluation of the leone, from 60 to 120 for a dollar, made them more scarce. The Lebanese community paid for a printing of ten-leone notes, but the most widely circulated denomination was the two-leone note. Sixty of those totaled one dollar, which, if traded on the black market, yielded 150 pieces of paper, or one brick. the money was carried in plastic sacks.

The people at the national tourism office, a shack full of dusty immigration forms, sent us to the Peace Corps people, who operated the two wildlife parks—Outamba-Kilimi and Kiwai. We wanted to go to the Peace Corps office anyway to locate our friend Mike, a volunteer, whom we had met on the Niger riverboat and later in Dakar. It turned out that Mike lived in Makeni, about half-way to Outamba-Kilimi National Park. The Peace Corps director was going to Makeni the next morning, so he offered us a ride. We agreed to meet him at six the next morning.

We then went to the American Embassy for information on Liberia. The embassy was so unfriendly and inefficient that, for the first time, we were embarrassed for our country. The file on U.S. sports was updated more rigorously than travel advisories. The consular office produced a sterile, cautionary statement about possible disruption of travel in Liberia but that was it. For more information, we went to the British library, where we pieced together more of the story. Charles Taylor led the Gios against the all-Krahn military force of Liberia's President Samuel Doe. The fighting was called tribal warfare, genocide, although we couldn't figure out who was massacring whom, nor the location of Nimba County—the seat of the fighting.

When we left the library, the day was drawing to an end along with our list of things to do. It was a good time to contact the family of an ex-student of mine. Before we left Florida, Sequeen had asked me to visit her parents. I had asked her where they lived in Freetown, and she had replied, "All you have to do is ask. Someone will tell you." She had said it as if Freetown is a small village and not a city of 400,000! Now the task gave us an excuse to widen our explorations. Luckily, her surname was well-known. A "Selonese" librarian put us on the right track, but, unlucky for us, there were several branches of the family, and we found them all.

I think we frightened her mother. "No problem, Sequeen is fine," we hastened to soothe her. Within minutes we balanced drinks and the family photograph album while listening to tales of the family history. Her gray-haired mother was retired from the UN and animated with plans to open a restaurant in her front yard. Her father was a judge. Like an urban paramount chief, he ruled when community arbitration failed.

Here, finally, in the bosom of a family, the inescapable aliena-tion of travel melted. Tension and emotional rigor mortis dissi-pated. The frustration and weariness of too many experiences too quickly were pacified by the security of a family. It had been a good day. Freetown, indeed, set us free. Africa was once again a land of magic, a land of the possible. This was the Africa we were beginning to love.

We stayed in Makeni a week while waiting to connect with a ride into Outamba-Kilimi National Park near the Guinea border. A small- to medium-sized town, Makeni offered all the diversions of a soap opera: Sex, violence, intrigue, love, loneliness, cannibal-ism, secret societies, bush moguls, and a cast of thousands. It was a hub of volunteer aid agencies from around the world: Canadian, German, the British VSO (the equivalent to the U.S. Peace Corps), UN workers, religious missions, etc. Townees and trans-planted aid workers were cozy friends and not-so-secret lovers.

One reason for Makeni's integration was Pa Carbaugh. He served almost-chilled beer on his popular-but-tiny veranda, while Ousman grilled meat sandwiches good enough to dream about. This corner bar was the catalyst for interaction in northeast Sierra Leone. It was an oral newsstand, a place to swap contacts or to leave messages.

Friday evening at Pa's attracted all the international aid work-ers. Beer and shoptalk flowed in equal parts. They all professed various states of disenchantment and devout commitment. Yet, the PCVs (Peace Corp Volunteers) were unanimously voted as the worst of the lot. The Peace Corps has many problems in Africa: lack of central support and indiscriminate recruitment of people with no skills or training have led to a poor image.

Larry, a seventy-three-year-old PCV economist from Califor-nia, said, "I want to make it one year before I quit. I don't need this bullshit, I am retired, and I have a pension. They don't screen us at all. I passed their physical, and I have only partial lung ca-pacity, a weak heart, and am subject to fainting. I am at a blind school that is a five-mile walk to the nearest road or town. I'll leave before I'll die here."

Larry sweated profusely under the torpid sun. His breath came out in short, shallow gasps. "They sent a group of old, obese women out here. Out into the bush! Alone! Can you imagine? Some of them had sold their homes, but they didn't make it beyond a few weeks. If they let them stay in the cities they would have been okay."

Most of the PCVs were young, just out of school, and had never before worked unsupervised. A political science major taught fish husbandry to fishing men, and a young male nurse with a bachelor's degree worked in water quality. He shrugged weakly, "I suppose it's related to health care."

Members of other organizations expressed more contentment with their work. They tended to be professionals working in their fields of expertise. Mary, a VSO nurse, worked with emotionally handicapped children. David, another VSO, was a mechanic who cruised the country in search of broken vehicles. "Everyone is glad to see me," he grinned. And Abdul, the Selonese CARE director with a master's degree in business, reorganized cooperatives. "We've cut out the market middleman. It was difficult to teach them the economics, but now that they've found the difference in their pockets, we're making plans to export products ourselves."

They all agreed on one thing—most aid projects fail because they are short-term. "Change, even the slightest change, takes years, maybe decades." Mary the nurse added, "I am no fool, I know no one follows through on treatment, so eventually it fails."

Melinda, a PCV in her mid-forties, taught home economics. She was reviving a women's tie-dying (called gara) cooperative that was started by a former PCV.

"When her hitch was up and she wasn't replaced, the co-op treasurer ran away with the money. They wanted me to hold it this time. They always want the white person to hold the money, or the baby, or the bundle, because they don't trust each other. They can't help it. The pressure to share, to give, is so strong that sometimes the person holding the money runs away with it. Possessions are communal. If Uncle Johnny or Cousin Mimi has a problem like a debt or a funeral feast, and Mary has money, she is obligated to give it. Here today and gone tomorrow.

"Anyway, I won't do it. I won't keep the money for them. The Selonese must find a way to temper greed and engender trust of each other. Until they do, no enterprise will work for long. So I've written a new constitution that provides for these factors. I'll present it today at our first meeting. Why don't you come along? It should be really interesting."

Robb and I were guests at the Peace Corps rest house[3], a modest cement house like the others of Makeni. A painting party was in progress, and I really didn't want to paint anyway. I accepted Melinda's invitation and followed her down the path to the meeting place—the home of a Selonese woman.

Roads were for cars; paths were for people. Paths were quicker and more direct, yet I never felt totally at ease walking through the middle of family compounds, as we did on route to the gara meeting. Melinda and I ducked under laundry lines and past tired women pounding casaba greens into a pulpy sauce while their men slept off the palm wine. We passed one group of men castrating a howling dog with a sharpened scrap of metal. Hair was braided, and pot-bellied kids with protruding navels chased scrawny chickens for the dinner pot. Adages were painted on many walls. The one that stood out for me was, "I don't trust my friends not even you."

The meeting was held in Nafsa's compound. It started an hour late, because "everyone is watching to see who comes." Neighbors nonchalantly spied from under nearby trees. Suddenly, twenty women quietly materialized. The benches of the compound sagged under their weight. Silent anticipation vibrated the air.

One man strode defiantly into the compound with two shrinking women in tow. After a heated exchange with Nafsa, the resident organizer, he scowled and left, shouting something that sounded like a threatening order.

Melinda interpreted for me. "Both women are his wives, but he says only one can be a member. He gave Nafsa the 500-leone membership dues for her. The other wife cannot be a member, nor is she to be paid any profits from the cooperative. He says she is only a helper, but if she does not work hard, he will beat her. Nafsa says that if the second wife works, she, too, will be paid. The man says that Nafsa has no right to interfere." Still the meeting did not begin. I did not know what was holding things up until several men came bearing freshly tapped, bubbly *poyo*—palm wine.[4] Smiles spread as fast as the *poyo* was distributed. The constitution was read and accepted with one amendment: "No special favors for friends."

More *poyo* was passed around. "This is god's natural gift to all men," said one of the women with a salute. Sleeves were rolled up and work began. Large cauldrons of boiling water squatted over fires. Dye was added to the water and stirred until thick, then the cloth was tied with cords to make the patterns, thrown in, stirred, dried, or thrown into another vat, squeezed, and hung out to dry. There was plenty of work and plenty of *poyo* for everyone.

The job of stirring emerged as the one with the most status, because the worker could rightfully issue orders. Each woman took a turn at stirring and calling for "more cold water" to be poured into her gloves. The one non-member of the group was the most cheerful and hardest working of all. A clandestine vote admitted her into full membership rights. A pact of secrecy was sworn.

More *poyo* was delivered. The heat of the day, the fires under the cauldrons, and the hard labor created an insatiable thirst. Eyes glistened; laughter and trust replaced the initial formality and apprehension. I was sent to get my camera. "When we sell our gara in the market, we will use your pictures to show how we make it. Yes, yes." For that job, I was honored with the first piece of gara out of the vats.

One woman leaned to me and said, "Next year past I live in Chicago with my husband. He goes to Roosevelt University for his master's degree."

I was astonished. Maybe I thought I was a female Burton Spekes translating for the first time the secret ceremonies of the Temne tribe, and here was this woman from Chicago. I asked her if she liked the United States.

"I don't know," she said. "My husband is bad. He do not let me enjoy myself. All de day for four years I stay in de house. I watch television, and I learn about Florida."

"What do you know about Florida?" I asked.

She brightened into a big smile and sang in contralto our most famous and infamous promotional lyric, "Come to de Florida sunshine free, fresh squeezed oranges fo you 'n 'me." She grinned again on the final note.

"That was wonderful," I said. She squeezed my hand in appreciation. "You know Florida well."

"Yes," she said, her smile abruptly sagging into a frown. "I tell my bad man to leave. Now I work here and make money. One day, I will go back to America and enjoy myself."

Another conversation was about Charlie, whom everyone but me seemed to know.

"Charlie lost 80,000 leones in a diamond scam. He gived the money in Freetown and never see it again," someone said.

"That Charlie knows nothing. You tell him if he wants diamonds to come see me. I get very good diamonds." These women, it seemed, were real wheelers and dealers.

The secretly enfranchised helper came to hold my hand. "Do you know Bundaba?" I thought she was talking about a town, and I asked her where it was. "Shh, shh," she hushed, "they are a secret society. They are sooo fearsome. I run away. You should run too. You see them, you turn your head. I tell you, they are fearsome. Ooh-wee. Bad." Inexplicably, a shiver crept up my spine.

Secret societies were active now that the bush grass crackled with the dryness of the season. Like the feathered boys we saw in Guinea-Bissau, in Sierra Leone we saw lone beggars with white, painted faces, or in blood-stained coarse gowns; and cadres of women dancing down dirt paths, tapping on buckets and tin cans, clapping frenzied rhythms to announce their coming out—their circumcision, the graduation into womanhood. Some nights, the drums and chanting were so loud it drowned out the bark of village dogs or the otherwise loud, late-night music that emanated from almost every window.

It was illegal, bad juju, to even witness the ceremony. In parts of Sierra Leone, a fine of twenty-five leones could be levied if you were caught looking. Even worse was possible retaliation by the secret society. We tried to abide by local laws, but it was impossible.

In one morning we encountered two different *poro*, male societies, parading down the street. One man hobbled slowly with a sabre impaled through his chest and a dagger through his leg calf. Red, blood-stained bandages wrapped his middle like a cummerbund, yet they didn't seem to bind the instruments in place. He wore a red, museum-vintage, British-style, admiral's cap trimmed with gold braid. A circle of men followed while clapping coconuts and chanting.

Another group was painted white: circles around their eyes, dotted, patterned bands on their chest and legs. They slashed the air with wooden daggers and fanned it with palm-frond switches. Another band of chanters and coconut percussionists followed. Little boys ran and hid, adults turned their backs, and we stared not too discreetly.

To talk about the secret ceremonies was bad juju, so people talked about them in roundabout ways. Customs were in flux. Traditionally, boys or girls retreated to the bush for three years of training for adulthood. Recently, that period had been shortened to three or six months. The culmination of this was a circumcision ceremony for girls as well as boys. Usually, boys were between the ages of fifteen and seventeen and girls were between the ages of twelve and fourteen. Now, with increasing financial pressures and more children surviving, all siblings of the same gender were sent to the *bundo* house in the bush at a group discount when the eldest child reached maturity. While other people wondered if alterations in tradition weren't responsible for their childrens' ill behaviors, we wondered at female circumcision.

No one would speak directly about it. However, it was a public issue, as evidenced by the Malian movie *Finzan* and a Nigerian law prohibiting female circumcision. Originally introduced by the Muslim traders, circumcision was adopted by non-Muslim people as a way to keep women chaste. With the clitoris removed, sexual arousal was impossible. Ironically, women have become the perpetrators and enforcers of this practice. It was estimated that in Sierra Leone alone, 90 percent of women had survived some form of clitorectomy.[5] I found myself staring at women, gawking at their amazing beauty and graceful, seductive movements, and wondering at the many joyless sex acts needed to produce so many children. Africa was one of the wellsprings for the mother goddess, and she was, perhaps, the most revered deity. How could she allow this bondage?

We also heard rampant and alarming gossip concerning cannibalism. Somebody was eating the children. A rash of children were showing up scalped, or with fingers and/or toes bitten off or eyeballs missing. Some children had disappeared completely, purportedly because their hearts were taken. Many people blamed it on Liberians sneaking across the border to take the coveted body parts to renew the juju strength of their leaders. The Selonese denied cannibalism as a part of their rituals, although three men were arrested in Kabala. Parents kept watchful eyes on their children, and some locked the youngsters in the house during these sprees, just as they did during rainy season, when the roar of the rain masks the noises of intruders.

Juju sometimes required the sacrifice of an animal, but only occasionally did it require human parts. The juju doctor, a *moniken* or *moriman*, often combined animism, Christianity, and Islam to create his charms. The *seba*, a gris-gris that looks like a leather envelope pouch, contained selected words from the Koran, "the direct power of God," to favorably direct aspirations, e.g., to get a passport, to be a boss or do in a boss, to be number one wife instead of number three, for fertility or illness, or to lift a spell invoked against you. The treatment was expensive. When it failed, the person would return for another treatment. Women sometimes traded sex for the juju potions.

Makeni was a fascinating town because of its friendly openness. It was a comfortable place, yet we grew restless to explore more of this vibrant country. Outamba-Kilimi National Park laid slightly further north and east along the Guinea border. When no other transport materialized, we hitched a ride on a gravel truck, stacked high with stones and passengers, destined for Kamakwie—the last town before the park.

Progress was excruciatingly slow. The heavy truck lurched through potholes deep enough to sit in. Rolling hills gave way to neophyte mountains; bush land grew dense with tropical jungle. Many new, mud brick houses dotted the roadside.

Moses, one of the passengers, explained, "The people are moving in from the hills to form communities for social reasons, but also to escape the dangers. The big dangers are big animals, but the worst is fire."

Omar, another passenger, shrugged in disagreement. "They are fools that they don't build fire breaks," he said. They build with mud and grass so if it burns, they can move to a new place. It is economical, but, when the fires come, they lose not only their fields but their villages."

The truck creaked past smoldering skeletons of corn, tobacco, and cassava. "The fires start from nowhere" some riders said.

"Maybe the hunter, maybe lightning," claimed others. Some fires were intentional, although those, everyone agreed, never got out of control. "See this burnt field? That is where the village is preparing a new tobacco garden. After the tobacco is harvested, then we plant rice, maize, cassava, and groundnuts. The next year, we make a new field. It is very efficient."

The truck dropped off and picked up passengers along the six-hour route. Always the conversation was of agriculture. Oranges and cigarettes were bought along the way and passed among the passengers. One spry man with bright eyes boarded and waved to a singing group of women left behind. His presence turned the ride into a sort of parade with people running from their homes to wave to him.

"You know many people," I said.

"It is their business to know who I am," he replied, "I am the paramount chief. I have many cattle."

I was not quite sure what to say, so I said nothing. He turned a big brown kola nut in his hand several times, then bit a crack into it. He extended it to us for the first piece. Usually, the chief gets the first piece of the bitter fruit. All eyes were on us. We could not refuse. I took the bite and chewed it slowly, Robb took his piece, then the chief took his bite and passed it around. Life was good.

We arrived in Kamakwie at dusk, too late to travel further. The passengers decided we should be taken to the house of Mr. Glenn or Mr. Al, two Peace Corps teachers in the village. Al gave us a fishing pole and sketched a map to and around Outamba-Kilimi.

"I worked there for a year. I loved it," he said. "Try to see the elephants if you can. We've had problems with poachers, so the elephants are hiding from people—can't blame them. You will probably have to walk the 26 kilometers in and out of the park, but it's a nice walk."

Early the next morning, Robb and I hiked out. We were hailed from verandas that fronted the eight-mile walk to a river and the ferry. "Pushay! Hello. Ow de body? De body fine, tankee. We go see you past Outamba-Kilimi." Of all the African greetings, this Krios greeting was perhaps the most endearing.

The ferry was a floating wood platform transported across the Little Scarcies River by tugging on a liana. The river severed any relations with the twentieth century. On the other side of the river, traditional compounds—round huts with high peaked grass roofs—nestled in clearings cut from the jungle. Occasionally, a file of people emerged from the jungle. Their giggles and chatter stopped abruptly. Surprised to see us, they would stand and stare. A few of the men might dangle a small animal collected from a trap; topless women clutched babies and roots or fruit. Then the screech of a green monkey from the treetops would break the spell, and they would walk on.

We reached the camp by mid-afternoon. Not too surprisingly, no one was there but two Selonese park rangers. It was a nice set-up with tents pitched on cement slabs, twin cots, porches with tables and chairs. If we could find food, we would stay.

A tree-shaded river flowed past the site. Within minutes, we had waded in, clothes and all, and within a few minutes more, the black flies had zeroed in on our flesh. Their voracious bites leave puncture wounds and globs of blood; sometimes, they also leave river blindness—an incurable disease. Even long clothing and repellent would not dissuade them. They've been known to chase an entire village inland. In the quiet eddies lurked other possible dangers, such as bilharzia or schistosomiasis, painful diseases caused by microscopic river flukes.

Trails had not been bushed for some time. Tangled brush prevented exploration by foot, and machetes would frighten the very animals we wanted to see. We would wait until the day cooled, just before dusk, wrap ourselves in many layers of clothes, and explore by canoe. The animals that hid from sunlight came to the river at dusk: crocodiles, duckier, wart hogs, bongos, civets, and chattering colobus monkeys dancing through leafless baobab trees. The hippos ambled from their pond and crashed ungracefully through the jungle to their grassy feeding grounds. The full moon rose like a big eye in the sky while the smaller, red glow of animals' eyes watched the movement of our canoe upriver. A symphony of night sounds serenaded us. The best sound of all was that of the Nile perch scooting across the water. The river was thick with their twenty-pound bodies, so thick that, in places, I imagined walking across their finned backs. We'd drop the fishing line and, within minutes, feel the runaway tug of a strike. They were strong fighters that broke the rod and reel, so we resorted to a drop line.

Our food stores were depleted because we stupidly hadn't allowed for the travel days. Food was not readily available, but with two or three of these monster fish, we fed ourselves. We also traded some fish for coveted grains of rocky rice and hot peppers.

Slowly, we recovered strength and a sense of peacefulness. Along with it came a sense of belonging, of being at home. Home—the one across the ocean—now seemed like a remote concept, like something we once saw in a magazine that had nothing to do with our lives here.

The hike out of the park felt longer, maybe because we knew how long it would be. Our packs, now emptied of food, felt twice as heavy, the sun twice as hot, our thirst twice as great.

The pontoon ferry had sunk, and only one partially submerged canoe serviced the river. Something or somebody had wrecked the ferry during the few days we were up country. That small change in the world made us feel like we'd been absent for a long time. Not until we made moves to commandeer the semi-submerged canoe by ourselves did a man offer to haul on the rope for us. As it was, we had to balance the packs on our heads and bail like crazy to escape losing canoe and all mid-river.

People sang out from the shade of trees or their verandas, "Oranges fo de dey" or "*Poyo!*" It made more sense to join them than it did to trudge the road under the midday sun. We stopped frequently and visited with the tipsy, sometimes rowdy parties. "We go see you," our drinking buddies hollered to our departing backs. Around the bend in the road would be a new group.

"Have you ever seen a mean drunk here in Africa?" asked Robb between *poyo* breaks. "If we were any place else in the world, Asia, Latin America, or the United States, and I saw a group of drunks, I would avoid them like a plague. Inevitably someone would get mean. I haven't seen that here yet. They just get drunk."

We did not reach Kamakwie until evening. Al and Glenn had left for Freetown, but four-year-old Albert, Al's eager errand-runner, roused the houseboy to unlock the doors for us. It was too late for the market. We found sardines and spaghetti, however, and I stirred up a dinner that only a hungry hiker could love.

Our candle-lit dinner was interrupted by a big ruckus in the streets. Strident clanging of pots, thumping of drums, and frightful shouting and chanting quickened to a loud, frenzied tempo.

Abu, the houseboy, threw open the door. His eyes were wild and his lithe body tight. He panted with urgency, "You better come quick, quick, I think something is happening!" His actions and words told us it was an emergency. We ran into the street where the noise was deafening. It was too dark to see anything.

"What is it Abu?"

"I am not sure. The people say the cat will eat the moon, so they must scare it away. I think you call it an eclipse?"

Sure enough, something was gobbling up the full moon. We were all barely saved from a catastrophic total eclipse by the persistent and effective pot banging. By and large, Africans were afraid of the dark, and, that night, I assimilated their fear. I knew the mechanics of an eclipse, but such knowledge was irrelevant in the darkness of a more powerful phenomenon. I was relieved that we weren't alone on the river. It would have been too scary. I rubbed my protective gris-gris. A noisy celebration of thanks persisted through the night.

Back in Makeni, we made a beeline for Ousman's sandwich stand and Pa Carbaugh's semi-chilled beers. There we met Paul, a missionary, who offered us a ride into Freetown. He drove a brand-new 1990 Nissan jeep with air conditioning, velour seats, lots of dials, and a cassette stereo that blasted Peter, Paul, & Mary. We went. It was more fun than ice cream topped with fresh whipped cream, more fun, even, than a shower.

Paul was a swashbuckling crusader for the good life. His chatter was liberally laced with cursing. During the trip, he made frequent stops at watering spots to swill a beer or two. What he didn't stop for were police checks.

"They see this nice new car and they see me, a white man driving it, and they think I am powerful," he said. "They've seen me for ten years, and they know I give them money." He made it sound like voluntary tithing. "You have to feel sorry for them. Police aren't paid well. The harder times get, the more blockades you'll see.

"I am an African now," he rambled. "It's stupid to work unless you have to. It's not a matter of can I do it, can I work, rather the question is: is work necessary? I have to send in reports on how many conversions I've made. It's unrealistic to quantify conversions. The first five years I didn't make one, now I've got seven. The lack of pressure here is wonderful!

"We've got a big house, a generator, refrigerator, freezer, VCR, and television, the mission imports our food, my son will go to the university with mission aid, they pay for a family vacation each year, buy me nice cars, and I have unlimited gasoline because the church makes a big cash deposit with the government. We also deposit with them, so visiting church members aren't searched, and a helicopter picks them up from the airport, then drops them at one of the nicest hotels on the beach. Ha, I love it here! I love the people! Occasionally I think about moving back to the States, but I could never live this well there." So much for the hardship life of missionaries.

Big news rocked Freetown. Mike Tyson got KO'd in Tokyo, and the film of the fight was on the way! Second in importance: Nelson Mandela was released from prison. The streets of Freetown were clogged with revelers, parades, and school marching bands. The other news was the "SCIPAgate" scandal. SCIPA, an Israeli-owned diamond mining operation, was the largest diamond exporter in Sierra Leone. The company was known to be rolling in money, yet their end-of-year revenue reports showed not a single leone of income for the previous year. It might have gone unacknowledged, but the newspapers caught the story and soaked their banners with the scandal. Implicated in collusion were high government officials and banks. Officialdom professed to be shocked.

Actually, any person on the street could tell you what was going on—diamond smuggling was leeching the country into bankruptcy.

"Diamond exports in 1967 totaled $175 million. By 1987, twice as many were mined, yet export revenues had fallen to $50 million," Paul said.

One Selonese, a wallowing fat man who gave us a ride in his new Mercedes, said, "Sierra Leone once had the seventh highest per capita income in Africa, and now we are broke. We don't have electricity and can't afford to import gasoline. We are what the World Bank calls a fifth world, one in economic retrograde. This should not be, because our diamond production has not dropped."

From others we heard that diamond smuggling out of Sierra Leone funded every illegal war in the world. "Go to Lumley Beach where they all hang out. You'll find the KGB, the CIA, the Mossad, Hezbollah, the PLO (who have an embassy in Freetown), everyone is here!" Another Selonese said, "The biggest businesses here are wealth and poverty. You either tap into it or your children go hungry."

This time in Freetown we got a room at the YWCA. They were, perhaps, the most coveted rooms in the entire country, and there was a long waiting list for them. The rooms were cheap, clean, and cheery. The building received intermittent electricity, and the hearty kitchen served Star beer as long as an eyelash fluttered. Luck was with us, we thought. Luck fled our first night.

A dog yelped from dusk to sunrise. This dog was so obnoxious that a horn blaring at 3:00 A.M. was soothing in comparison. We stuffed underwear in our ears and filled our pockets with rocks. "Die you bastard," swore Robb with each stone he tossed into the alley. Then one night the dog was quiet. All that could be heard were radios, an all-night evangelical crusade, squalling children, a lovers' quarrel, shuffling feet, and the constant pounding of cassava. It was too quiet. "Where is he?" Robb asked, perched at the window sill with a stone in his hand.

"Maybe he's dead. Maybe someone else killed him."

"I feel terrible," said Robb, "maybe we should have wished that he went hoarse, lost his voice or something. Death was perhaps too extreme." Even dead, worry for the dog kept us awake.

Not since Algeria had hitchhiking been so good. Rides came as regularly as the sun. Afternoons were for the beach and mornings for work.

We continued to pursue information on Liberia. At the Liberian embassy, a mumbler denied any problems in that country. The American embassy was appallingly mum. Despite vociferous demands to see a consular officer, no one would talk with us about "Little America." Nothing much was coming out of that war-torn country except unconfirmed tales of horror, such as the rumor of indiscriminate decapitations. Even the merchants who normally shuttled between countries with trade and news stopped going there. The scuttlebutt was that the borders were closed. Street news was usually reliable, and, with nothing more to contradict it, we decided to fly to Monrovia rather than risk the un-known overland route. Air Guinea allowed us to pay in leones, which, after the black market, brought the airfare within the cost of bush taxis for the same distance.

The beaches of Sierra Leone were gloriously clean and expansive. We soaked in the crystalline blue water for a long time, rubbing dirt from our pores and soothing the itchy lumps of black fly bites. Lumley Beach was by far the most touristed of the country, with big semi-empty hotels not too far from the breakwater. By day, expatriates and Selonese basked in the sun and surf, fruit vendors roamed, ready to split a watermelon, pineapple, or mango in pieces. By evening, it was the happening scene for spies on expense accounts who crowded the cane-thatched bars. The accents were different, the bricks of money plunked down for gossip and drink were indifferent. They sported a distinctive air about them. It wasn't the cold swagger of a mercenary soldier, nor the jumpy eavesdropping of the political reconnoiter, theirs was more like sleaze.

"I cry for my lovely country," said one Selonese woman. "We deserve better."

We agreed completely.

- 15 -
Liberia

I hoped that Liberia, our thirteenth country, would be lucky for us. It wasn't so lucky for the people who lived there. The evening of December 24, 1989, Charles Taylor crossed the border from Cote d'Ivoire with a small band of Gio rebels and attacked a predominantly Mandingo village in Nimba County. Swift retaliation came from Doe's soldiers, all of whom were Krahn tribesmen. Beyond that, the story was confused with accusations and counter-accusations of tribal genocide, vengeance, and coup plots.

Because of the uncertainty of the situation, the Peace Corps in Freetown referred us to the Peace Corps in Monrovia, the capital of Liberia. The director guided us into his office, shut the door, and whispered with a wagging finger, "Don't talk to the police. Don't talk to anyone about politics. Don't take pictures, especially do not take pictures of the Masonic Temple. A visiting volunteer was jailed for doing that, and it took the entire United States government to free him. I don't know if we could pull it off again. Try to stay at the Lutheran or Methodist guest houses, they are the only safe places. Take a taxi, don't walk," he said giving us fare. He was very nervous.

Liberia was established in 1822 by freed slaves from the United States, whose descendants came to be known as Americos. They dominated the government until 1980, when an indigenous master sergeant staged a coup. Many Americos fled when Samuel Doe inaugurated his presidency with a televised execution of thirteen former ministers. During the decade that followed, human rights abuses escalated. Nevertheless, the United States gave Doe's government more than $442 million in economic and military aid— the highest amount of aid paid to any African nation during the same period. Technically, the United States did not colonize Liberia; however, to Africans and Europeans, Liberia is "Little America."

After much persistence, we were assigned a room in the Methodist mission on the beach. The peaceful garden and beach location were offset by numerous posted warnings: Swimming Prohibited—Dangerous Undertow. The Methodist mission was between the Baptist and Lutheran missions. Behind the mission, the Israeli Embassy stood fortified and heavily guarded. Like much of Liberia, beneath the facade of order and harmony flowed dangerous waters.

There were few taxis and no buses the afternoon we went in quest of Little America. Traffic lights blinked red, orange and green while traffic police wore uniform blue like New York's finest. Kentucky-style fried chicken stands competed with restaurants serving meatloaf and mashed potatoes or potato salad, dill pickles, and cajun blackened fish. Canned dog food sold in the few grocery stores. The national flag—the red, white, and blue "Lone Star"—flew over government buildings. AT&T phone booths with direct dial to the United States sprouted on Monrovia's street corners.

There was one bookstore in Monrovia. "I am going out of business," said the owner. "A government minister bought the printing presses, then raised the price for copy books. The kids can't afford paper, and I can't afford to import books any longer. I am charged a huge import duty, then charged for the warehouse until

I pay an additional fee for paperwork, and I have to pay a bribe to do that. Then I pay for the store, and daily bribes to the police, who always find some objection to my license. My customers see that the price printed on the jacket cover is less than what I charge. What can I do? I am the last bookstore in Liberia, and next month I lock my doors."

The grocery stores were owned by Lebanese who traded Liberian dollars at three times the official rate. They said they needed the currency to import; in truth, many were converting for a bailout.

Everyone, even residents, had to go "downtown" to central immigration within forty-eight hours of arrival in the country for permission to stay.[1] Something about the place gave us the willies. We paid our fee and falsified our addresses on the registration form.

People were terrorized by "rogues," roving street gangs, and the military. Except in the markets and around the university, no one lingered. They seemed to scurry about as if to hide. Anyone walking openly was likely a bad guy. We too scampered along the paths between houses to skirt the streets and the weed-choked lawn of the infamous Masonic Temple.

President Doctor Doe (both were honorary titles he bestowed on himself) had closed the temple as a symbolic strike against Americo imperialism. In its emptiness and neglect, the temple became a monument to the freedoms that no longer existed.

The American embassy would not, or could not, offer travel advice. "We don't know much, said the consul official. "As far as we know, everywhere is safe. If you want travel information, go see the people at CLO."

The staff of the Community Liaison Office was very friendly and helpful (they sent us to the U.S. commissary to change for dollars). But maybe they were too helpful. They gave us pamphlets for tours to Sapo National Park and encouraged us to visit PCVs around the country, including those in Nimba County.

It didn't take long to learn that something was rotten in Liberia. How anyone could ignore it was incomprehensible. Insecurity and fear suffocated Monrovia like an ominous cloud. We had the distinct feeling that one unlucky step and we—or anyone else—were goners. Pitfalls, like the undertow, tugged beneath the surface. A

1984 decree made it a felony to disseminate rumors, lies, and disinformation, so warnings were whispered, not posted.

Residential neighborhoods were locked tight. There were more guarded, walled residences and "bad dogs" than in Dakar. Wackenhut Private Security Guards seemed to employ a bigger army than the armed forces of Liberia.

Civil liberties were unofficially suspended. Corruption was as out of control as inflation. With the "incursion" under way, military checkpoints proliferated, and the standard bribe escalated from five dollars up to fifty dollars. Everyone told stories of detention and imprisonment for failure to pay the bribes.

One missionary said, "It costs so much money that you have to grab money yourself. . .as quickly as you can. I would lie or steal for money, it is survival."

Andy, the one other traveler we met, was harassed by rogues on Broad Street. He complained to a nearby policeman who had watched the incident. Andy was summarily arrested, detained for the night, and his passport held until he paid a twenty dollar fine.

Although newspapers labored under censorship, letters to the editor revealed a citizenry terrorized by the military—rogues in uniform "who harass, rob, and intimidate peaceful citizens." *The News*, *The Mirror*, and *Daily Observer* somehow published reports of six prisoners starved to death because the prison officials had pocketed the prisoner's food allowance. Another article, "He Called Me a Heartman," carried the denials of Gary Allison, the defense minister, and his wife, who were accused of eating a soldier's heart to solidify a juju-based coup attempt. (Juju was also blamed for a baboon who disrupted a soccer match.)

The Liberians, rich and poor, were under political and economic siege from their own government. A pathetic shantytown squatted on a portion of the Monrovian beach. The inhabitants survived in a wretchedness worse than in Haiti. The beach was so littered with human excrement that not even the tidal undertow could wash it all away. We stood with missionary doctors on the perimeter of the inhuman ghetto not daring to enter. Coughs, not the harmattan coughs of sand clogged-lungs but the rattling coughs of death, shook the cardboard walls of the make-shift shelters.

Despite heavy censorship and severe injunctions against gossip,

gossip flourished: Israel, the largest arms supplier to Liberia, was completing construction of a new Ministry of Defense. (A gift to Gary Allison, the "Heartman.") Wackenhut was a mercenary army, spies on the U.S. payroll. ELWA, a religious mission from America, maintained a gigantic field of antennae and was said to be a CIA listening post. And, of course, the largest Voice of America transmitting station in Africa was a propaganda tool for the Doe regime. Firestone, which operated the largest rubber plantation in the world in Liberia, was planning massive layoffs. With 50 percent unemployment, that was not happy news.

Another rumor concerned two United States colonels who were spotted in Nimba County acting as advisors to Doe's troops. They had directed a massacre of Gios and Mandinkas. A counter-rumor claimed they were there to investigate human rights abuses and, as a result, a Liberian general was removed from power. No one believed the human rights story.

Linda, a Methodist mission doctor, and her husband Dave (a computer analyst in Minnesota but a low-tech problem-solver in Liberia) were assigned to a hospital in Ganta, Nimba County. The worst of the fighting took place in Nimba, just 167 miles east and slightly north of Monrovia. Linda and Dave told us their story.

"We heard that two U.S. military advisors were asking questions of the villagers, who are afraid to speak. They never came to talk to us—we would have told them how the military shot people sitting on their front porches; how the military closed down the roads and rivers, and how they took over the hospital and airstrip so no one can get in or out. We cannot make hospital rounds after the six o'clock curfew unless escorted by the armed forces, and then, they call us only if it is one of theirs who we must treat for free. They slaughter the people, rape the women, and loot the towns. It is very dangerous. It is a massacre, and if a massacre can get worse, it will. We fear for all the people of Liberia."

Another story circulated of 150 children, all under the age of ten, who were left behind in Nimba during the panic and chaos of flight or were orphaned by the cross fire. The military transported them to Monrovia. Reputedly, President Doe said, "When they grow up they will want revenge. Bury them now!" Some people said they were shot and tossed into a mass grave while others said they were simply buried alive.

Everyone called what was happening genocide of Mano, Gio, and Mandinka tribes by Doe's Krahn tribe.

"Things are getting worse every day, no one knows how many people have been killed," people whispered. "It won't stop in Nimba either, it will reach Monrovia." Reportedly, the number of refugees in neighboring Guinea and Cote d'Ivoire (Ivory Coast) was uncountable.

"If you want to know the truth, you must go to the refugees. People are escaping through the bush. Monrovia is cut off, surrounded by the military."

America was indicted by the public, our role was inextricable from the massacres. It struck us that Monrovia would not be a safe place for Americans if the war escalated. "Ha, don't worry about the Americans," said one Monrovian, "they never come out of their compound on the hill. We don't see them, and they don't see us. But if I were you, I'd leave right away. You don't have protection, and the people up-country hate Americans."

His words imbued us with apprehension. We had not encountered an iota of animosity; indeed, the Liberians encircled us with their grief, fear, and what in better days might have been conviviality.

Monrovia, however, was a cauldron of politics and speculation. We wanted to know more about the people but the war made any excursions into the interior impossible. One road, among the hub of roads radiating from Monrovia, was supposedly open: the road to Robertsport on the coast.

Three checkpoints blockaded Monrovia from Robertsport. At each one, everyone in the "money truck" was ordered to baggage search and internal immigration. Once, a soldier with a machine-gun shouldered Robb.

"Are you Peace Corps?" he growled.

"No, we are tourists," said Robb.

The soldier's eyes flicked slowly, his jaw slacked like a man trying to remember something. Slowly he put out his hand, "Welcome to Liberia!" He smiled warmly. Underneath all the brutality glimmered human civility.

Robertsport snuggled between lush green hills and the blue ocean. It was truly a splendid place. Prior to the 1980 coup, it was an Americo community and a resort. Now, abandoned houses, a mixture of Caribbean and southern US plantation architecture, were empty reminders of the hope for peace and prosperity. For now, Robertsport was little more than a fishing village. There was a vitality to the quiet streets, the colorful little market with sundry items and dried fish, and neighbors hailing one another. Hillsides, on which coconuts, mangos, papaya, breadfruit, and bananas grew, fringed pristine beaches. Not a footstep marred the sand. Under clumps of palm trees, entire families repaired nets, launched dugouts, and sorted the catch.

At the one hotel, the Wakalor, we were the only guests. Five dollars treated us to two queen-sized beds and a spacious private bath overlooking the ocean. The county had stripped the kitchen the month before as payment for taxes, so only one meal was available, cooked over a beach fire and served in the lovely-but-empty dining room.

Usually, we shuffled into town to one of the three chop shops for fermented foufou, sauce, and dried fish, or to sit on the wooden porch of the dry goods store and share a warm Club beer. One day, an old man, wizened, brillo-headed, with chocolate skin and sharp eyes came up to us. He gave us each an orange, we exchanged greetings, and he invited us to his compound.

"I stay there next number two pole," he said. "You must stay to my compound? I am Old Man Chief Willy. I am chief of this region and all this." He pointed to several streets of houses. "This house here is the talk-palaver hut; it is long time business, like me," he chuckled. "Before first, I show you where I sleep. You must come."

He led the way up rock stairs into a round hut with a tin roof. It was as neat as a pin, with two beds draped in mosquito netting, one cassette radio, and a trunk. He sprawled on one bed and indicated the other for us while a wife served coffee. He wanted to know about us and, in turn, told us he had come to Robertsport from Ghana in 1917, and that he owned much of the land, including the hotel. "Awa no geh one money from dem," he said.

"Before I go sleep, I make presentation to your woma'," he said to Robb. "Because she wear *lapa* you give us pride to see. You are welcome here." From his trunk he removed an uncut double *lapa* with a fish pattern and laid it on my lap.

"I want you wear *lapa* in America and tell all the people that

Old Man Chief Willy is here." It was an extravagant gift, a humbling honor, as we had nothing to present him with in return, except our promise to deliver his message. "You fini leave me now but you come back. We talk-palaver. Stay to my compound. Wear *lapa*. If you come I may be sleeping so come back again. If I sleep the sleep of my fathers you must...." Chief Willy raised his hands to the sky, threw back his head, and smiled.

As often as we could, we joined the manager of the Wakalor hotel to listen to BBC news broadcasts. (The Voice of America did not mention Liberia.) The manager, Austin, had spent much of his life banging around the world, and he was a news addict. The announcement of Violeta Chamorro's victory over Daniel Ortega in the elections in Nicaragua caused his face to erupt in grins.

"This is very important news for all Africa, especially West Africa," his finger gestured downward to indicate Liberia without saying the word. "This election, coupled with Mr. Gorbachev and the Berlin Wall, will cause great change on this continent." He nodded sagely.

One day three new Peace Corps volunteers were relocated to Robertsport. News of their arrival spread because they came from Nimba County. We, like many others, sought them out to hear their stories. They were not present when "the incursion" began and had not been allowed to return to their villages. They heard the villages no longer existed. Their spirits vacillated between mourning, anger, and hurt. They were fragile. They blamed much of it on the United States.

"Before the Peace Corps sent me here, I believed the United States was irreproachably right," one volunteer said. "And now, now, I've learned that it is all a lie. I've been betrayed by my country, the people of Liberia have been betrayed, my village massacred because of these lies. Even the Peace Corps is a lie."

The woman sobbed and the small band of volunteers closed around her for support.

"They sent me to a village where the previous female volunteer was raped. Did they tell me? No. Did they give me a chance to protect myself? No. All they care about is their image. I thought we were non-political, but I guess there is no such thing."

Unfortunately, the Robertsport haven erupted with gossip of an impending military invasion. Supposedly, guns were being run along the coast and into Robertsport for an attack on Monrovia. The townspeople were scared. Memories of the 1980 coup d'etat haunted cooking fires, the market, and replaced the usual fishing stories.

"We will not wait this time for the military to come. We move our children into the hills and hide. Everyone will be suspect."

"The soldiers went door-to-door in 1980, smashing them open with their rifle butts. Many of us slept with our children, but they pulled us into the streets. The military stayed a long time, took our food, closed the roads so we could not pass and the beaches so we could not fish. Many people died."

The cook at the Wakalor worked there then. "I remember many guests were in the dining room. They kicked down the doors and came with guns and shouted many things. They took the jewelry from the guests and shot some who tried to jump over the balcony. The soldiers went behind the bar, drank all the whiskey, and smashed glasses. One military grabbed me by the collar and put his rifle to my throat. I just went limp in his arms. Then he hit me, said O.K., and walked away. I never forget that."

When we boarded the money truck back to Monrovia, I raised my arms to the sky, threw back my head, and smiled wide enough to swallow the sun. I did it for all the lovely people of Robertsport who, if we should return, might be sleeping the sleep of Old Man Chief Willy's fathers.

The border between Cote d'Ivoire and Liberia was rumored to be closed, and the border with Guinea, semi-closed. We'd have to take a flight to Cote d'Ivoire. The sooner we left, the better.

I was reminded of Sartre's *No Exit* when we tried to leave Liberia. It was as if Doe had ordered, "No survivors." Exit permission from the police in Monrovia was to be obtained exactly forty-eight hours in advance. It was a hassle. Person after person claimed an irregularity with our documents.

Nausea accompanied us to Spriggs-Payne Airfield. We both felt like our lives, our freedom, had only minutes left on the clock. Immigration was hell. So was our health examination, which was usually a cursory glance at our international health certificates. In both offices, interrogations, false indictments, and arbitrary seizures of paperwork resulted in last-minute refusals to allow many passengers to exit Liberia. The atmosphere was as intimidating as waiting for torture.

Robb was pulled from Immigration and shoved into a room by the Chief of Security. The move was unannounced and roughly executed. I waited outside the door and prayed to any and every god or goddess with the slightest jurisdiction over travelers. Occasional yelling, but not Robb's voice, shook the frosted glass on the closed door. Oh, please, let us out of here! Twenty minutes later, what seemed an eternity, Robb emerged pale and shaking.

"He told me I wasn't going to be allowed to board the plane and took my passport."

"What did he want?"

"Hell if I know! Probably money. But I wouldn't give him any, eventually he gave me my passport and told me to go."

Then began the "legal" extortion. Airport tax was twenty American dollars for each person. Customs inspectors appropriated luggage until additional fees were paid—one for the inspection and another for returning the luggage. Baggage handlers harassed us for money to guard the luggage. We sat on ours and refused to pay until a circle of police closed in and we dug up a few Liberian coins from our pockets.

Finally, we were stamped out of the country, safe from the terror of Liberia and free to go to Abidjan, Cote d'Ivoire. But, the plane flew over without landing and without explanation. The next scheduled flight was a week away. Boom! The bomb in my gut exploded.

We went ballistic. This could not happen! The Air Guinea manager suggested two alternatives: get readmitted to Liberia and wait a week, or catch the northbound flight to Guinea-Conakry. "We don't have visas for Guinea-Conakry!" we screeched to his indifferent shrugs.

The head of immigration was a woman, Lt. Colonel Seekey. I saluted her and congratulated her for her high rank. She rose with massive height from her desk and embraced me to her bosom.

"Thank you, thank you," she said. We were off to a good start. I told her our plight. She assured me she would take care of everything for us.

"Thank you, Lt. Colonel, I will tell my husband that you are a strong woman. You give me pride for all women."

She beamed and gave me her card. "Thank you, sister," she said, "We are friends, I will help you." It was a touching moment. Because of the sincerity, I trusted her. Unfortunately, we did not trust the men standing behind her.

Traps. The problem was recognizing the traps. Air Guinea pledged responsibility for us. "I will be on the same plane," the manager said, "I will talk to immigration and there will be no problem." No matter what happened in Conakry, to delay in Liberia was not prudent.

Upon disembarking in Conakry, we were promptly arrested. The passengers, all Africans who did not need visas, protested in our defense as the police dragged us away. The Air Guinea personnel slithered another direction in silence.

The chief of police threatened deportation, "Fine, we did not want to come here anyway. Deport us." Our only valid visa was for Cote d'Ivoire—we could be deported nowhere but to our destination.

"You will remain in this office as prisoners until the next plane to Cote d'Ivoire, three days from now." We accepted our sentence with fatalism. It was preferable to Liberia or jail.

We made ourselves comfortable as prisoners. We sprawled across the floor in the small office and napped. By six o'clock, the chief was rabid.

"What! Are you still here? In my office?" he bellowed.

"Sir, you ordered us to stay. We are under arrest, remember?"

Our guards confirmed the chief's orders. Doors slammed, people were called in and out, more shouting was heard from behind closed doors.

At seven o'clock, we were escorted by a detective to a nearby restaurant. As we walked out the airport door, we bumped into Cheech and Chong, the taxi team from our first visit to Conakry. They ecstatically threw hugs and handshakes.

"Mon amies, you are back! So nice to see you again," they said. The detective pushed them away. "What is going on?" they asked in unison.

"We are under arrest. This man is our guard," we explained.

"Non, no, these are good people. They are friends. Let them go and we will take the responsibility."

I didn't know we had made such an impression on them. The detective warmed up a little and said he was under orders.

"Then, my friend, tell us how we can help. We will wait here, or we can give a message to someone...?"

Sometime later, Air Guinea admitted to minor responsibility. Our passports would be held until the flight to Abidjan, but otherwise we were free to go with Cheech and Chong to The Nimba. Home at last.

The staff at The Nimba doted on us like nursemaids. Without passports or Guinea francs they once again arranged for us to visit Wall Street. They worried we'd never see our passports again, at least not without paying a big bribe. Finally, to calm them, we went to the American Embassy to alert the airport expediter.[2] Once again we roamed the streets of Conakry Two, greeted by old friends and treated to extra dips of okra sauce with our foufou.

The embassy expediter never showed up at the airport. The detective who took us to dinner while we were under arrest did, and he handed us our passports. He interceded when Air Guinea insisted that we did not have reservations, and again when they tried to levy a 9,000 Guinea francs departure tax. He walked us to the plane, shifted from foot to foot uncomfortably, and shook our hands.

"You should not leave Guinea so quickly," he said. "You do not like us?"

We reminded him that we were ordered to leave.

"I am sorry for this," he said. "We are friends. You see, many people live here, but once you meet a Guinean, you have a friend, and friends of his friends are yours too. You are welcome here."

He pointed to the observation deck where Cheech and Chong, Hines from the Nimba, and "a friend of a friend" all waved to us. The detective stood on the runway, the force of the twin jets blowing his hair and jacket, until our plane was a speck in the air.

"This is a strange continent," I said to Robb as we were served breakfast, "from massacres, to near arrest, to real arrest, to release to our friends, to this magnificent meal. Just when events seem irretrievably desperate, something comes along to change it all."

He answered with a mouthful of link sausage, omelette and

jam, "Hmmm.... When in Africa expect the unexpected. It's juju."

"Good juju."

- 16 -
Cote d'Ivoire

Abidjan shimmered with as much conspicuous wealth as any first-class city in the world, but its long-standing reputation as the most expensive city on the continent was tarnished by the poverty of its underbelly. Abidjan was cheap if only because there was a great diversity of goods and services. Also, the economy was faltering and luxury prices were floating down. Some people blamed the fall from affluence on President Houphouet-Boigny's cathedral (the world's largest) in Yamassoukra. "He build it with our money so now he tries to make things look good." For whatever reasons, Abidjan in 1990 was not the budget drain we had feared.

A distinct aura of class and privilege reigned in the downtown plateau and in wealthy suburbs. As the saying goes, "Everything is available for a price." In Abidjan, it was certainly true. Everything—from electronic equipment, clothes, books, and food, to an ice-skating rink and bowling alleys at the Hotel Ivoire, and a slick system of water taxis comparable to those on the Seine—was for sale, and all echoed Abidjan's previous prosperity.

We stayed in Adjame, a low-rent residential area, at the dreary Hotel Liberte while waiting for visas to Ghana.[1] Although Yamassoukra, in the interior, was the capital of the French-speaking nation, all embassies were located in Abidjan. Our continual need for visas necessitated that we spend time shuffling paperwork and waiting for our passports to be returned from embassies. Abidjan was a nice place to wait in, though. It was a bigger city than we liked. However, a well-engineered public transport system made all four peninsulas and the many quarters of the city accessible.

Days and nights were unrelentingly hot. One of the best places to cool off was at the pool at the Hotel Ivoire. Admission to the pool was inexpensive and, by afternoon, it was filled with splashing kids. Mornings were peaceful however. It was a great place to pen postcards and write in my journal, and to lie in the sun and enjoy our hard-won freedom.

A cute, perky American woman approached one day and invited me for a haircut. She said I looked as if I had been traveling a long time. One amenity of cheap rooms is the lack of mirrors: you never have to confront your own face. Her eyes, however, confronted my delusions of neatness and unmasked my lies. I accepted her offer.

Her house, in the wealthy suburb of Cocody, was elaborately secured, as befitted her husband, the head of the American embassy Marine guards. The couple demonstrated the house's alarm system and guided us through a mini-warehouse of food imported from home. Before the last snip of hair fell to the floor, we had endured an hour of Africa-bashing. To them, everything and everyone was a potential threat.

Robb and I walked from there as quickly as we could. The haircut felt nice, much nicer than the disquietude we felt among our compatriots. Almost sadly, we realized how alienated we had become from Western culture. We were bored by the useless "things" they so proudly displayed, appalled by a lifestyle bound by the constraints of fear. That, which from the outside looked desirable, was on the inside stupid and silly. It was no longer a familiar culture.

On the other side of town, in Adjame and Treichville, the streets pulsated with enterprise by day, and by night they were alive with laughter and friendship. Food vendors—the *maquis*—filled the streets with kettles and grills, and displayed irresistible spices and ingredients: fish, bats, meat brochettes, chicken, and *attieke*, a grated manioc. Bowls of scented water for hand washing were brought to the streetside benches, someone else brought the food, and, inevitably, someone at a nearby table sent a beer with a welcoming salute.

An enormous Adjame market began at the *gare*, the bus station, and sprawled for miles. It was an urban jungle of multicolored plastic buckets, radios, hair straighteners and skin lighteners, cloth, electronics, cassette tapes, meat, fish, and vegetables. Sequestered in one obscure stall was the juju doctor.

He examined the scalp of a little girl for symptoms, then wrapped together a tuft of raw cotton and pinches of stuff from various bags. I asked him about my prickly heat rash. He tugged at some pieces of bark, and he prescribed an elaborate procedure for applying it. I would require two follow-up treatments, he said. At $20 per visit, I decided to stay with medicated baby powder. Instead, I asked him for a new gris-gris, "One for strength and courage." He picked through a box of tattered animal pelts and horns, dried bird claws, crocodile heads, and snake skin then selected a tuft of lion's mane. That gris-gris had an odd effect on me. I started thinking that I was invisible.

Then, suddenly, strikes disrupted the city. Doctors refused to treat patients, shops closed, the university students rioted, and many voices called for the resignation of President Boigny who, at eighty-four, was "too old, had ruled too long, and should make way for democracy." Boigny addressed the nation via radio and pronounced edicts forbidding strikes. Riot police, with special headgear, rubber hoses, machine guns, and tear gas canisters, were deployed throughout the city. It wasn't frightening like in Liberia. In fact, it carried a charge of excitement, of change.

At the *maquis*, issues were expounded, opinions and statements bantered. More than one person followed us into the street to privately express what he could not express in public. Late one night, after conversation and beer with a group of dancers from the national ballet and students from the university, one of the students followed us home. His name was Ali, he wore a white Muslim robe, and he stooped to whisper in our ears what he didn't want others to hear.

"I was there for the first student riot," he said. "It was over the economics of the university and overcrowding and not about democracy like people say. Two hundred students sit in a classroom, and then we must share our rooms with ten, fifteen others. It is difficult to study. The teachers are not free to teach—nor students free to ask questions. Much is forbidden here. The government makes it look nice, but it is not true. You have to be here to know. We cannot speak about it. It is dangerous.

"People are taking advantage of the student strike and say it is for other reasons. Some say we want a multi-party system. How can we have many parties? We are many tribes. One person must take care of all his family and his relatives. He must take all he can get with no care for anyone else. If we want multi-parties, we must first act together.

"I want to be a teacher, I've always looked up to teachers, and they get a room from the government. I don't know if I'll finish the university with all these problems, so if not, I want to be in the army because you get respect. Although there is always someone above to whom you must show respect, everyone else is below you and they must give you respect. I think that would be nice."

That night I tossed in my sweaty bed and pondered the mechanics of democracy in a tribal society. I gave up, it was too hot to think—which, in itself, didn't portend much future for participatory government in Africa. Under the fan in our room, sleep was attainable but not sustainable. The neighbors moved their mattresses or cardboard sheets into the cooler streets, where voices murmured all night like a slumber party.

Then one afternoon it rained! The relief was only temporary, though, and the rain was dirtied by more than five months of composted ashes, dust, and sweat of the dry season. It was also a harbinger of the rainy season, when torrential monsoons would render the mud roads impassable and release hungry, malaria-carrying mosquitos. Our sights were now on the Congo/Zaire River in central Africa. We hoped to reach it before the rainy season set in. The shower spurred us to move up-country to the Man region of Cote d'Ivoire in search of Liberian refugees.

The Man region is in the west and borders Liberia. It is mountainous in an otherwise flat country, so it is known for natural beauty. It is also known for the artistry of its crafts—especially masks. To us, it would be where we'd find the Liberian refugees.

The bus ride to Man from Abidjan was luxurious. The bus was air-conditioned, and videotaped movies made the distance pass swiftly, as did a high-ranking military officer riding in the front who waved us through all the police barricades.

Man the town wasn't much. Superficially touristy, it looked like the kind of place that caters to the occasional brief visits of tour buses. Kids begged *cadeux*, souvenir shops ringed the real market, and many of the *maquis* were fake-tourist restaurants. A cadre of French elitists lived in patronizing grace. It took us a full day to dig beneath the veneer and find the real maquis serving delicacies such as giant *agouti*, or bush rat. "Choose the meat nearest the bone it is the best," a passerby coached. The best local bars were the open-air ones in and around the market. For the price of one tall beer, you could sit for hours, sipping with new friends and watching the glorious parade of life.

Side trips to surrounding hillside villages were necessary. Tisni/Siabli was supposedly a mystical site. A ruin of rock walls on a hill was guarded by kids and old women who, like the beggars in European cathedrals, demanded *cadeaux* to approach the sanctuary.

I pondered the relationship of religion to money as we strolled through the tiny market. We stopped to watch a leather worker spin a thong for my new gris-gris. With one end of the leather strips tied to his big toe, he braided, twisted, and spat on the thong. He rocked and sang over it, his burnished, leather-like fingers caressing it into a life of its own. After an hour, he tied it around my neck. "This will live longer than any of us," he said.

La Dente mountain, also known as the Guardian Angel, snagged the sky at 881 meters. Its rugged, snaggle-toothed shape jutted above the village of Glongouin, whose population made a living from tackling and hog-tying tourists. "Special price madame, I guide you to the top for only CFA 5,000. Some people pay 13,000."

We pushed through the kids with an indomitable spirit of independence. How difficult could the climb be? After all, we'd traveled this far without a guide. We made a few false starts up jungle trails, across fields, and over rocky terrain, and found ourselves no closer to La Dente.

"How do we arrive at the top?" we asked people hacking brush from their yam fields.

"Ooohee!" they said. "Return to the village and pass around the mountain."

We pressed on several more hours until, in total defeat, we accepted the a man's offer to guide us for CFA 1,500. He was a very athletic fellow. He ran up the rock cliffs, ducked under low hanging branches with green mamba snakes curled to strike, bounded over ravines, and shimmied over huge smooth boulders. He was like a mountain goat trying to shake himself free of a nuisance. We might admit we were lost, but we were not about to admit we couldn't keep up. We kept up, but my heart and lungs threatened to explode.

The view of the canopied valleys from the top was grand, but not as grand as the congratulations of our guide.

"A team of French climbers came here to make a documentary, and I was their lead guide. We used ropes for same climb."

Robb and I were puffing like steam engines, but we didn't want him to know, so we made busy slicing pineapples we carried in the backpack. The sticky juice bathed our faces in sensuous delight and trickled down our elbows. From below wafted the voices of women singing in the fields. It was like being perched on the spire of a cathedral. The sun caressed us to sleep.

The next day we caught a rickety bus to the town of Danane on the border, where the refugees were rumored to be. The ride was nasty. The police were viperous. They assessed the value of each item the passengers carried and took the best cloth, the newest pots and pans. Owners moaned and upped their bribes from CFA 3,000 to CFA 5,000. One man crawled on his knees, the ultimate supplication. Robb stood by his side, trying to spread an aura of white man's influence, but the police were impervious.

The men massed in solidarity with the women, who piled all the babies on my lap. Forty passengers confronted the police with demands that their goods be returned. Everything was lost. One of the supplicants urged the truck driver to leave him; he would stay with his belongings.

Oh, did things get ugly when the driver left! A sacred rule of the road was violated: never, never abandon a passenger. "You did not protect us! We give you the bribe, and you too greedy, you keep it for your own," the passengers railed.

Later, the roof straps came undone, spilling and breaking the remaining merchandise. Tears replaced anger, and mourning replaced agony. By the time we reached Danane, we were a sad group.

One man followed us from the bus into the dirt street of Danane. He identified himself as Abit, a Liberian refugee from Nimba.

"I heard you speak American," he said, "but I said nothing to you on the bus because of the trouble with the police. I want to explain that the police took those things for the refugees in the camps who have nothing." (United Way take note.)

A real refugee! We invited Abit to walk with us and tell his story. He had been a teacher of mathematics in the town of Bahn in Nimba County.

"First the rebels came but they did nothing. After, the armed forces came and said that we helped the rebels, that we gave them shelter and food." He shrugged to imply it was irrelevant. "The military first shot all the chiefs, from the paramount chief to the clan chiefs. Then they started shooting everyone—bam! bam! Those that weren't killed ran into the bush. In the end, the only people alive in Bahn were the military and Mandinka.

"My family, my wife, my parents, we go to the bush and hide for two weeks without food or water. We were very hungry and weak. We had to leave my parents behind—they could not finish the trip.

"At first, the Ivoirian army made it very difficult for us to cross the border. All Ivoire helps now, as you see. We have a special camp at Zouan, but we are too many and the people too sick. We have nothing and no work. We will return to our homes when we have assurance of safety and help with resettlement. It will be very difficult."

Abit left us to catch a truck going to a refugee camp further north. "I am inspecting the health conditions for the UN," he said.

We found other refugees in Danane by greeting in English anyone who wore a correctly spelled American T-shirt. (Only in Liberia did they get the real thing, e.g., Chicago Cubs instead of

"Chikago Socs".) Soon a large crowd was gathered around us, and several animated and vocal Liberians were telling their stories. The elder men of town listened and nodded their heads intently, as if it were an important ceremony.

"On January 2, the rebels entered Compli village and kill every Mandinka and Krahn man. They cut off their heads or shoot them with gun. Half my family I lose. I am Mandinka but I speak Gia good like my own. The rebels speak Gia, I hear them. After the second time the rebels come, they pour gasoline around the doors and side of the house and they light it. When we run out they shoot us. My family and I stay in the house and it burns. We run around the rooms but when the roof come down four die—all burned up. The military come to help. Everyone is dead or gone."

We heard story after story of ruthless death and equally miraculous survival. People told of being separated from their families and hiding in the bush for weeks without food or water. They told of illness and poverty.

"I have no money to buy the medicine I need," one refugee said. "One man bought me six tablets for the water that made me sick."

"The United Nations must come and help us go back to our villages. It is not safe. There must be guarantees. We were Mandinka, Krahn, and Gios, and we lived together in peace. But now it will be a long time before I give this other man work, or work for him. I can only speak for myself and how I am now.

"I hear rumors, stories. People say that the Ivoirian military is preparing to invade and help the rebels. I don't know. I don't read. I only hear."

We felt humbled, maybe even irreverent, listening to them. I think the Liberians felt differently: for them, telling us of their suffering was a catharsis. It was a ceremony.

We tried to sort it out, to make sense of it. To take sides. There were none. Just as the realities of Africa were different from person to person, so were the realities of war. Liberia had gone berserk, with neighbor turning on neighbor, friend on friend, tribe slaying tribe. It did not fit neat political models of good guys and bad guys, of principles and causes. I think pundits who tried to describe the events this way were way off the mark. In the words of Ali, the student in Abidjan, "You have to be here to know. We cannot speak of it."

– 17 –

White Men Don't Have JuJu

On the map, Ghana is a green country. Remarkably, it *is* green! The coastal road was enveloped by lush leafy trees, hills, impenetrable bamboo forests, and palm and rubber plantations. Strip-logging didn't look to be as big in Ghana as in Cote d'Ivoire, where highways buckled under trucks laden with bleeding tree trunks. Many of those felled jungle giants measured six feet or greater in diameter.

We left Cote d'Ivoire with an immense feeling of "good timing." The morning headlines cited President Boigny as saying, "The government will enforce order!"—by whatever means, utilizing all its paramilitary forces. Between Abidjan and the border were no less than fifteen police checks, sometimes only one mile apart. The driver twice collected duty on luggage to replenish the bribe "kitty."

Whatever joy we felt in reaching the Ghanaian border dissipated when we went through customs and immigration. The border crossing was unusual in that searches were literally brutal. Women were strip searched behind semi-drawn curtains, and men were ordered to drop trousers where they stood. The chief wielded a big cane that rarely rested. His job description seemed to require frequent thrashings of the pilgrims. Somehow we managed to avoid all that. Meekness maybe, downcast eyes? Robb admitted to having bought cedis, Ghanaian currency, on the bridge between the two countries. Our lives scrolled before my eyes. Surprisingly, the officials only scowled. No special taxes, tips, or bribes were extracted from us. The lion mane gris-gris made me invisible after all.

Once inside Ghana, the harassment stopped (although I flinched with fear every time I saw a cop). The refreshing greenness of the countryside, the ease of speaking English again, and the anticipation of reaching Busua Beach filled us with a sense of well-being.

Busua was a long-term goal. When we separated from Walter and Golo in Niamey, it was with the promise to meet in Busua. The same pact was made with Debbie and Jane. Neither a date nor specific meeting place had been set. We did not have far to look, however, because there was only one place to stay in Busua. It was named in the tradition of a Club Med: Busua Pleasure Beach, several rows of pumpkin-yellow bungalows on the ocean's edge. There the similarity to Club Med ended. For $3.50 (1,100 cedis) a night, we got a bungalow with a cement porch, umbrella, and oily water barrel. The surrounding palms had lost their crowns to a blight. The blue ocean heaved white, curled tubes at the beach like milkshake froth. The waves were ripe for surfing, body surfing, or windsurfing—all the surfings.

Many foreigners ended their journey across the Sahara on the shores of Ghana. And Busua was a popular "weekend getaway" for families from the capital, Accra. We searched the thick registry for the names of our friends. Walter and Golo's names had been inscribed three months earlier. We had missed them, but not Debbie and Jane.

The town seemed unscathed by the influx of tourists. It was only a T-shaped dirt road with a basic market of wimpy vegetables, canned sardines, and candles. Actually, a comfortable symbiotic relationship flourished between the town and the tourists: the providers and the consumers. Soon after the fishermen beached with their catch, the vendors began the 6:30 A.M. parade through the bungalows. Fish, lobster, and fruit orders were taken and delivered to your cook, or your bungalow, by 9:00 A.M. Many folk in town opened their kitchens, actually their cooking fires, and peddled their services. It was cheap and fun, as long as you didn't sleep late and miss the morning rounds. After nine o'clock, nothing would be available except sardines.

It rained several nights in a row—heavy, tropical downpours. The bungalows flooded. Mosquitos swarmed in clouds, but the rain did nothing to alleviate the severe water shortage. The deep well was almost dry. The grandmothers, who were employed to transport water from the well to each bungalow, took longer each day to deliver less and less water. On laundry days, I hauled my own. It was muddy and thick with plankton and coated our clothes and skin with what looked like green sequins. Drinking and cooking water was brought in by an ice truck. When the truck broke down, thirst became desperate. There was nothing but beer to drink for five days. It was a tough time at Busua Pleasure Beach.

Ghana admits travelers for only forty-eight hours, during which time travelers must report to immigration for permission to stay longer. The nearest immigration office and the nearest bank were in Takoradi-Sekunda—a several-hour ride to the east. We left early in the morning and returned so late we had to walk the last eight miles in moonless night.

Debbie and Jane were sitting on our porch when we dragged in. They were in high spirits, but were physically worn down. "Because of you we tarried," they said, "we knew you were traveling slower than us." They stayed in Busua three days before pushing east toward Kenya. It was three days of lobster feasts and discussions of roads already traveled and ones to come. In a way, their roads had been tougher than ours: they came through the Guinea highlands by truck, crossed borders that had never seen a white person, were dined by the military, almost raped by an evangelical minister, racially and sexually harassed by Ghanaian men, and were now recovering from cholera. "We're doing it for the book, but from here we'll move faster. Honestly, we've had enough."

Robb and I dawdled nearly three weeks in Busua. We enjoyed the luxury of rest by promising ourselves to move faster in the future.

There was plenty to explore around Busua. Seventeenth-century forts dotted the Ghana coast. They were remnants of the Dutch, Portuguese, Danes, and British who exploited Africa for slaves, gold, and ivory. In recent years, the forts had become popular "hostels." While we were there, however, they were closed to campers for renovation.

One famous fort was in nearby Dixcove to the west. However, without travelers visiting the fort, the town had fallen into economic hard times. People crowded around us with the hope that we signified the return of the recently departed tourists. To the east of Busua stood another Dutch fort. Perhaps because no road led to the village, it was little known, and we were ignored when we explored it. It crouched on a hill overlooking cane-walled compounds and a lovely tropical cove. The romance of the site quickly dissipated, however, when we stepped foot on the beach. It was strewn with raw sewage. The villagers had squatted on the beach for so many centuries that their feces had piled up.

One village woman wanted to hold my hand. She told me her name was Ama. I told her that, in Spanish, that means love. She and her friends picked it up as "life." Before I knew it, I was encircled by maybe fourteen women and pushed down a muddy path to a cane shack. "Say her name again," cried the original witnesses. The faces were expectant. Okay, so maybe their translation of love is life. Isn't it the same? I put my hand to my head and said, rather theatrically, "This woman's name is Life."

"Ooowhee!" Murmurs passed around the gathering. "This woman is Life." They probably thought I had some sort of white man's magic, because they all begged to learn the meanings of their names. One time was enough, I couldn't do it again. So I told them, "I am tired now and must rest."

Soon after that, one big event probably earned us a page in local history. It all began when Robb left the day pack on the beach while he rode a few waves. He saw a thin, half-naked man dart from the jungle, grab the pack, and disappear into the jungle again.

"I was lucky," Robb told me later, "at that moment I caught a

was surprised, because he threw the pack out to me. I was barefoot and couldn't follow him too far, so I went to look at the place
where I thought he'd thrown the pack from. There, under a log, I
found everything but my reading glasses and about a dollar in cedis. I also found this!" He held up a pair of patched cut-off shorts
and a cutlass. "They're his. I haven't exactly decided what to do
with them yet. Any ideas?"

We both agreed that the scales of justice should be balanced. A
certain leniency toward crime against white people was condoned,
almost fostered. We had witnessed the imbalance with growing
anger, because the permissive double standard seemed to say that
white men didn't have souls. As we turned the cutlass over in our
hands, an idea slowly evolved.

That afternoon we took the cutlass to town and displayed the
grooved cross-hatchings on the handle.

"Do you know this man?" we asked. No, no one knew him.
Why did we ask? Reluctantly at first, and then with growing frustration, we explained, "This man tried to steal from us, and we
are looking for him."

Beginning at dawn the next morning, every man, woman, and
child strode past our bungalow. Each swung a cutlass by his side
as a public disclaimer of guilt. We didn't know who among them
was missing—but they knew.

We waited patiently. Mid-morning a man came to our bungalow and offered to buy the cutlass for a price just below the cost
of a new one. Again we asked, "Do you know this man who steals
from us?" No, he did not. "Then why do you want to buy his cutlass?" Because it was old, he said, and because it was of no use to
us. "I have use for this cutlass," countered Robb, slicing a coconut
in two. The man left quickly, but another came in his wake who
offered to pay even more money.

The thief, we suspected, would not be able to work without his
cutlass. The cutlass was the do-everything, miracle tool. It was
more useful than fire—it killed and cleaned the fish, cut the palm
fruit for oil and the coconut for the rice, it harvested the fields,
bushed the trails, killed the snakes, and built the houses. On the
plantations of Ghana, it earned a cash livelihood. So we could understand why he wanted it back, but why he was willing to pay

more for it than its street value could only mean that it symbolized something very important.

Community arbitration was usually swift and sometimes brutal. We were accustomed to using it to appeal disputes and to right wrongs, but here in Busua, the double standard corrupted the system. If we were to confront the thief, we would have to smoke him out of hiding ourselves. That's when we foolishly escalated our strategy.

With great seriousness and pompous ceremony, we entered the jungle and made a big to-do of gathering weeds and cutting roots. We did not interrupt our nonsense chant to return the familiar greetings. We did not go into town, but ate quickly at the restaurant. We then locked ourselves in our bungalow.

The very next morning, on our porch, we erected a lower torso mannequin dressed in the patched, cut-off shorts. It was stuffed with weeds and sprinkled with baby powder. We rocked in our chairs, waiting.

The first man to come by asked, "What are you doing with weeds stuffed in those pants and all covered with baby powder?"

We were aghast at his question and floundered for an explanation. The truth was, we didn't know what we were doing with it. It had been an act of inspired impulse. With our entire reputation, our credibility in the sling, I blurted, "It's juju."

"Oooh?" he said, leveling a scathing eyeball. "Everyone knows that white men don't have juju."

We were in trouble. The bluff hadn't worked—white men didn't have juju. "Oh, yeah?" I stalled for another inspiration, "You are foolish. We have very powerful juju!"

He laughed, snickered, chortled, and giggled. "How do you know juju, if white men don't have it?"

I dug into my memory. Juju was voodoo, it was magic, it was, at least, the power of psychic belief. We must believe it ourselves in order to make him believe.

"If we tell you what we do, then it is not juju. If you knew juju, then you would not ask me, you know that I cannot tell you the secrets. We do not do juju on you, we do it on the thief. He will know, ask him."

Loud guffaws of disbelief lingered in the air after his departure. We thought ourselves sunk dead in the water, so we added blood-red Betadine and feathers to the mannequin. Late that day, another person came to us.

"How do white men have juju?" he asked.

Ready with an answer, I said, "We may look white to you, but we are not, your eyes lie to you. We come from the land where your people were taken as slaves. For all these years they practice the juju. Our parents come from this blood, they know these secrets, and they teach me all my life."

Aha. That one got him. The story had credibility. If ever there was an African princess, born of the masses, it was the woman whose skin was as light as a white person. She was given the choice seat in the mammy wagon, men carried her bundles, and the military bowed and scraped to her. Latin blood and genes beat through my body, although side effects from Paludrine and cholorquine had bleached me to whiteness next to this man's black skin. Nevertheless, I had successfully introduced an admissible doubt.

"What do you do to this man? How do you make this?" To uncast the spell, the original spell had to be known.

"Why do you ask, do you know this thief?" we asked. No, he didn't. "It is not your business then, the man will know."

He left. Robb and I grinned. The white man's juju was working! Lingering doubts as to its effectiveness gradually disappeared as each new person came to ask us about our juju.

"This man suffers, when will you stop the suffer?"

"Do you know this man?" we asked.

"No, I only know that he suffers."

Sooner or later, we feared, someone would take out a juju on us, and we didn't want to be standing there when it happened. We had not rooted out the thief, and we were running out of ideas, and out of a desire for revenge. So, without telling anyone good-bye, we caught the first morning mammy wagon out of Busua. Before we left, we stuck a carrot through the pant zipper and chopped off the end of it. It was overplay. The act made us feel low, mean, and dirty. Perhaps we should have taken the pants back to the log and done it there for the man to find privately, as Robb suggested. And I might have agreed. We might have left the man with many happy years of sexual potency ahead of him...if it hadn't been for that one statement: "Everyone knows white men don't have juju."

Several days later, way down the road, a policeman asked us about our cutlass. "Why do white men need a cutlass?" It was a gift from a friend we told him. He slowly turned it over in his hands, examined the worn blade, the sweat-polished handle with the cross-hatchings, and handed it back to Robb. "This is not a good gift," he pronounced, "your friend was not a good friend, or he would have given you a new cutlass."

– 18 –
The Gold Coast

Robb and I argued in Accra, the capital of Ghana, where we stayed several days while waiting for visas.[1] I guess it was the "travelers' six-month itch," delayed by two months. We really didn't understand it, although home was one recurrent and unresolved theme. I left Robb for one luxuriously private night and slithered back when I realized that he had all the money and the passports. We didn't talk about it again. Between us it was obliquely referred to as "The time...." Africa, many months of uninterrupted companionship, and no news from home were partially to blame.

The countries of the Gold Coast—Ghana, Togo, Benin, and Nigeria—flowed easily from one to the other. People flowed easily too. The indigenous Ewes of Togo were swamped by the blue-robed, northern Tuareg salesmen who snapped the lids of their souvenir wood boxes like crocodile jaws. The Nigerian Hausa spewed English over merchant counters in French-speaking Togo and Benin. We took our time exploring regions of each country, yet days passed without names or dates. Few events distinguished themselves from the almost monotonous familiarity of West Africa.

Thunder and lightning slashed the velvet night. Torrential rains, like a nightly custodian, bathed the streets in preparation for the next humid day, when the brilliant white sun would blind us like the lamp of a torturer. Under this light, Lome, the capital of Togo, looked as if it had popped out of an artist's canvas. Lome was truly one of the most beautiful cities in the world. Justifiably, it is the "Pearl of West Africa." Coconut palms wave along wide sandy beaches, where fishing nets are hauled to chanting songs. Much of the coastal architecture transforms the buildings and their grounds into sweeping sculptures. The presidential palace and large, antiquated hotels smugly face the water: the Benin, the Gulfe, L'Paix, the Sarawaka, and our own modest L'Abris.

Produce was vibrantly colorful: fat orange carrots, leafy green lettuce, yellow onions, red tomatoes, purple eggplant, yellow corn, rotund cabbage, avocados, endive, bananas, apples, spiky pineapples, and spices. The market women arranged displays of their produce in baskets, with flowers to complement the colors.

Food was excellent and cheap. Walking through town was a stimulating olfactory experience, and a variety of music emanating from patios and street parties lent it another dimension still.

Rain nudged us east to skinny little Benin. Like Togo, it is only 120 kilometers wide along the coastal highway. Cotonou, the major city (although Porto Novo, a few kilometers to the east, is actually the capital), was less extravagant than Lome, but the people were hopeful of change. Benin's long record of coups following its independence and its subsequent embracement of Marxism had ravaged the country of four million people. But a new, recently approved constitution was making people joyous.

"In another six months we will have all new paperwork saying the Republic of Benin. There will be no more problems with visas. This is a free country. You can go anywhere or say anything freely. We are getting Democracy!"

Visas to Benin were a problem. They were issued only at the border and were for only forty-eight hours. To travel the country west to east took an hour, but to go up-country took much longer. We were preparing to do just that when I was stricken by fever and a debilitating headache. I went to bed with a flu-like ache in my neck and shoulders, and I did not move again until we left for Nigeria. Robb scouted Abomey, once the home of a king who kept a personal guard of six thousand amazon women, and Ganvie, a lakeside fishing village built on stilts.

Most travelers zip across southern Nigeria and Lagos in particular, as if the devil were chasing them. Lagos suffers a reputation for the worst crime on the continent. But, we needed to stop in Lagos for onward visas and to fulfill a promise to meet with the family of another ex-student.

The *taxi ordinaire* from Benin to Lagos was the wildest ride in all of Africa. And that is saying a lot. None of the passengers were the nationalities they claimed, and none but us had identification papers. One woman bore elaborate facial scars, a suckling child, and several kilos of palm nuts that caused a multitude of problems. We called her Urdu. She spoke a Nigerian tribal language semi-shared by the driver. Probably because of her vulnerability, she was a susceptible target for police harassment.

A slouch-shouldered gentleman with a beach-ball belly told us he was from Benin, to the authorities he claimed he was Nigerian, while in reality, he was from Cameroon and spoke no English nor any local tribal language. He was very quiet. Of course, he carried no papers.

"The Nigerians will arrest the Cameroons just to take all their money," said a woman who was Togolese but claimed to be Nigerian. She was a true heroine—beautiful, as a heroine should be, demure as an orchid, and unintimidated by anything or anyone. She was never asked for her papers so we never knew her true nationality, or if she even carried papers. She told us she had once traveled to Brooklyn on a "business trip." How does Lagos compare to New York City? we asked during a lull. "Hah!" she snorted, "Lagos is nothing like New York, it is more like New Jersey." She was right.

The driver was the hero counterpart to the heroine. He almost lost his car, his permit, his passengers, the luggage, his dignity, and perhaps his freedom several times that day. He fought for us in the tradition of any hero. He stuttered slightly and by the time we reached Lagos, the stutter twisted his tongue in bondage.

The problems began at the Nigeria border. Urdu didn't return to the car. We waited and waited until Heroine ordered the car to wait by the highway while she searched for Urdu. Heroine returned sucking an ice cream and towing Urdu, who had been arrested. We were off. No, our car was suddenly surrounded by police! A great tug-of-war ensued, with the driver at one end of the sack of palm nuts and the police at the other. Urdu wept prostrate at their boots. Heroine hissed the police aside for a confab.

"Let's go," she said, sauntering casually to the car.

"What happened?" we asked.

"The police wanted ten naire from Urdu, who has nothing," she said. "Let's go."

There were fourteen police checks and each with a similar hassle. If they weren't confiscating the cargo, then they were confiscating Urdu or the other man without papers. In the middle of another tug-of-war, a policeman formally bowed to Robb and me.

"I am sorry for these problems, if these people had proper passports . . ." he said.

Heroine went rabid. She flung open the car door and wagged a finger in his face shouting, "We shouldn't have these problems at all! We shouldn't need passports in our own country!"

When ordered to "come down," she would reply, "No, we don't come down. We stay here. We have no problem." Sometimes it worked but mostly it didn't. The hero and heroine paid a lot in bribes that day. Robb and I bought banana ice cream sticks for everyone. The police tried to interfere with even this. It was well-known that white people should not eat anything made with untreated water.

In Lagos, Urdu and her child left with the heroine as their protectress. The Cameroon man stayed with us as our protector. The stuttering driver was so incapable of speech or further movement that he didn't even lift his hand to accept our tips.

Lagos looked like New Jersey and New York City rolled into one teeming mass without end. Once again we had to position ourselves within commuting distance of the embassies, which were located in the high-rent district of Victoria Island. After much searching, we found a small guest house over a restaurant on a res-

idential street in nearby Ikoyi. The Beneshade Restaurant and
Guest House catered to working Nigerians in an area of international restaurants that catered to a glitzy clientele.

Much of Lagos is a juxtaposition of rich and poor. A maritime
port and industrial complexes exists alongside a crumbling public
infrastructure. Modern, reflective glass buildings house phones
that do not work. Once an oil exporting nation, Nigeria has become an oil importer. Where amenities once came quickly and
easily, there are now long lines for the basics. Inexplicably, new
construction sprouted at a time when banks would not lend. Lagos is a giant organism of change and movement.

Kobos, the nearly obsolete coins that operate public phones,
were only available from candy vendors. We bought pounds of
stale chewing gum in order to place a call to Mr. Niji, the father of
my ex-student in Florida. The telephones ate the kobos, but not
even street urchins would eat the candy. Finally, we asked at banks
if we could use their phones. It took a full day to place one local
call!

At a popular restaurant near our house, the owner singled us
out from the crowd.

"Are you with Exxon? he asked. "An embassy? No, you are different, you wait with patience. . . .who are you?"

Patience is an African trait, one we had learned in over 12,000
miles of travel to his doorstep. We told him our story.

"Never in my life have I met such a people," he exclaimed.
"This travel is everyone's dream. You will be my guests in my restaurant any time you come here. Welcome to Lagos."

He was true to his word. And his graciousness, along with that
of many other people, warmed us to Lagos.

Mr. Niji unexpectedly came to our guest house. A uniformed
driver entered the restaurant first and announced that his boss,
the man in a sleek new Mercedes, was seeking us. The busy restaurant patrons gawked with curiosity at Mr. Niji's powerful presence. He commanded attention more by his aura than by his
words. But his words were spoken like a man who had never been
refused. So, when he invited us to dinner several days later, and to
accompany him to "the most important site in all Nigeria," we did
not tell him we were planning to leave. We accepted, along with an
invitation to use his office phones to call home.

That night my fever returned. An ache in the back of my head paralyzed my neck. Feverish gods of hallucination swooped to comfort me. "Come with us you are safe," they cooed, like the sirens who led sailors to their deaths. I tried to hide the trembling of my hands and legs when Mr. Niji's driver picked us up on Saturday.

After a large family dinner at home, Mr. and Mrs. Niji took us to the most historic city of Nigeria—Badagry. The west Nigerian coastal town was so obscure we couldn't find it on the map. Only dirt roads led to the tiny coastal town.

"This is it," proclaimed Mr. and Mrs. Niji, proudly.

"It's nice," we commented lamely. The four of us stood in someone's compound. "What is it?" we wondered. No sign marked it. And we were left to wonder until Mr. Niji paid $10 for each of us.

A lithe man dressed in sweat-stained clothes mounted an imaginary podium and bellowed as if he addressed a lecture hall of many hundreds: "This was the compound of a great chief, and I am his great grandson. The story I tell you is as my ancestors tell us. This was a slave cell," he pointed to a cement reconstruction of a round house. "After the slaves were captured in the interior, they were brought here to wait for the ships. We go inside now." It was a smallish, low-ceilinged room draped with a few chains, yokes, and manacles. "In this room, two hundred people or more stayed without food or drink until the slavers took them away. Many died here, men, women, and children. These were the instruments of torture . . ."

Either something was wrong with this scenario or I was still hallucinating. I held up my hand like a child in elementary school.

"This is the compound of a Great Chief?" I asked.

"Yes."

"This is where the slaves were brought, held, tortured, and died while waiting for the slave ships?"

"Yes."

"Can you tell me what made this chief so important?"

Sniff. "He was the chief of all this coast."

"Yet, the slaves were brought here, to his compound where many died and the living were sold?'

"Yes."

"Did he try to stop the slave trade?"

"No, why should he? He was the king."

"You show us instruments of torture, and you tell us this chief was great. How was he greater than the slave traders who came here?" Momentary confusion while the question was translated several times.

"The chief, my great grandfather, did not care for these slaves. They meant nothing to him. They were from the interior, a different race, a different tribe. It meant nothing to him if they died or were sold. He was great because his people, the people of his village, did not go."

The Niji's exchanged looks with the grandson as if the explanation was totally satisfactory. Robb and I exchanged looks of puzzlement. I searched the spiked neck collars and leg irons, and our five black and white faces for the missing clue. Suddenly, I felt angry at Mr. Niji for bringing us here. What was the purpose? Was he making fun of us? Or did he truly believe this had been a great chief?

I must admit it had a profound effect on us. There, on that hallowed ground, we renounced for all time any guilt for anyone's misdeeds but our own. We swore to never lie to ourselves or anyone else about racism or slavery. I wanted to kick, punch, and tear the heart from the whole system of lies. The lies that absolved the African from his slave guilt, yet allowed him to ignore the continuing brutality against his own people, such as enslaving women in torturous labor. The lie that declared "Africans are brothers," when tribes slew each other, or members of one tribe referred to another as "too black and ugly." The lies that ignored the conquest of Africa by Arabs, the first foreigners to exploit the system of slavery.

White men knelt and burned candles at an altar of forgiveness for their role in slavery. Ridden by guilt, they heaped aid money, "gifts" that inadvertently stymied domestic production, and military aid that bought new cars for the chiefs and helped them maintain their abusive regimes. Aid was as much of a lie as the myth that white men alone were responsible for slavery.

Surely, there was more to Nigeria's history than slavery and colonialism? The Africans must have been great inventors. Large empires had thrived on her land, which meant widespread social, political, and economic organization. Africa has been called the birthplace of human evolution; yet, no one, not even the Africans, spoke of Africa's own history. Why was the most historic site in Nigeria a slave pen?

We were guests. We said nothing of our personal battle with "white men's guilt." Tactful inquiries into the Niji's presentation of Nigeria's history led us nowhere.

The Niji's next stop took us further down the road to the first Christian mission house in Nigeria. Unfortunately, or ironically, it was established the same year the slave ships arrived. The Niji's were "high" Christians, so we were not surprised that the mission was also high on their list of important historical sites in Nigeria. They also showed us the university and housing abandoned by the British. "They thought we would eat them if they stayed for dinner." A wave of the hand got us through the same police checkpoints that had given us such grief on the way into Lagos. Sharply spoken criticisms of the government were tempered by illustrations of success. In the brief time we spent with the Nijis, we knew them to be intelligent but understated. We struggled hard to understand them in order to resolve the dichotomies and paradigms Mr. Niji presented.

The next morning, just as we were leaving the guest house, I collapsed under my backpack. "I can't make it," I said. Like a sadist's vice, fever and pain gripped every muscle and joint in my body. Diarrhea emptied my body of organs, and, when I coughed, my head felt like a roller derby rink. I was beyond miserable, beyond caring, and nearly beyond life. Based on the symptomatic pattern of fever and pain, our guess was that I had cerebral malaria. Robb dug out our medicines and pumped me full of quinine, doxicyline, and salted water with sugar for rehydration.[2] For three days I fought against, and mated with, fevered ancestor spirits.

I could not tilt nor turn my head for several weeks. But once the fever and pain dissipated, I was eager to get on the road again. We left in the rain for Calabar in eastern Nigeria.

Calabar was an ugly city. Still, it was where we got visas on to Cameroon. We decided to take the sea route to Cameroon rather than the overland route. A fluid, water surface would be more gentle than potholes.

It sounded straightforward. A ferry ran from Calabar to Oran, and, from Oran, boats crossed the Sea of Guinea to Limbe, Cameroon. What we didn't anticipate was it being so bizarre.

We were hiking to the Calabar ferry when a man spun up on a motor scooter and blocked our way. He flashed a plastic identification card that said Secret Security Service.

"I want to talk to you," he said, "I want to see your passports."

The week before, the SSS kidnapped two Nigerian human rights workers. One was murdered and the other escaped to tell the story. The newspapers went wild with reporting the details of these and other missing people. We wanted no part of it.

"We can't talk now," we said. "We must hurry to leave town."

He said he understood and would meet us at the ferry. We thought we'd never see him again. It was a fool's dream. He was waiting at the ferry.

He worried us. The old warning buzzer rang. When we couldn't evade him and he got ill-tempered, we grew bold.

"If you must question us then we demand official witnesses," we said. Together we marched into the maritime office. Again, he showed his identification card to six men. "We want more proof. Anyone can buy a plastic identification card. It means nothing to us. Do you know this man?" We asked the witnesses. Four of the six "witnesses" showed police identification. Not a good sign.[3]

The dock master then said, "When the SSS say they want to talk to you, you must answer."

I doubt if our interrogation followed standard procedures, however. The SSS man said Nigeria was having bad economic problems, and they were trying to build up tourism. "Many people don't understand who tourists are, and they may not treat you kindly." We assured him that all Nigerians had been very kind and the "country is lovely." They seemed to want us to confess to taking photos. Photography was not illegal in Nigeria, so we didn't understand this line of questioning, but their eyes glinted in pursuit of something. Finally, we admitted to having taken a photo of a family in Lagos to give to their daughter, my student in America. We were released with warnings of thieves and thugs in Oran.

Oran was an armpit, like an old sailor's port of call that never progressed beyond whorehouses and knife-stabbing bars. Mean-looking people glared at us as if they would like to crush our skulls. A group of women signaled me to sit on a step with them. "This is a bad place," they whispered. "Thieves follow you on the street, you must be very careful." Robb swatted flies with the cutlass. "You sit here with us and our husband will find a safe room." After a while, the husband panted back with directions to a guest house further down the street.

One young man followed us so closely that, if we stopped or suddenly changed directions, he walked up our heels. Menacing, pendulum motions of the cutlass did not get rid of him. We heard a scream, and a man across the street waved his arms at us.

"Go away from this boy! He is bad!" he shouted.

We explained that he would not leave us alone.

"Come with me," said the man tugging our sleeves. Thirty people or more encircled us protectively. "We try to make our town good for people, and then these bad boys make everything worse. Where do you go?"

They told us to wait while a delegation went to the Nosara Guest House that we mentioned. Meanwhile, the crowd swelled to a mob and blocked all traffic in the street. The bad boy might have been lynched on the spot if the hotel delegation hadn't returned with a favorable report. The mob confabbed, and finally it was decided. The boy, who was called Ephram, adamantly denied the charges against him, but he would take us to the Nosara. Great! Just who we wanted for company: Ephram, the delinquent.

Three new SSS men flashed plastic identification cards at the entrance to the Nosara. They loudly interrogated us before they turned their vehemence on Ephram. We almost felt sorry for him as he cringed under their wrath, but when the sentence was pronounced, my sympathies switched to us. "This boy must stay with you until you leave. He is responsible." Ephram, Robb, and I rolled our eyes at each other. We were mutual prisoners.

"The one good thing about this," said Robb after we stepped over Ephram's sleeping body to bed, "Ephram will not try anything." When the SSS and immigration again interrogated us the next morning, Ephram stood by our sides, and he waved good-bye as we departed Oran with thanksgiving into the Sea of Guinea.

It was a flying boat. That is, a fiberglass hull with twin outboard engines and eight other passengers. As soon as we moved out of sight of the dock, four boats descended on ours: The Nigerian Naval Police.

"It is illegal for you to be on this boat," they said, waving machine guns. "You are under arrest."

We showed them our passports stamped with permission to be on the boat. Then they demanded Nigerian money, naira, as a fine to be released from arrest.

"We don't have naira. It is illegal to export naira," we said. The boat man urged us to give the money so they would release the boat. "It is true, we don't have naira," we said showing empty pockets and an empty wallet.

The waterway scam was that the police first collected from each individual passenger, then they fined the boat ten to fifty naira more for each head, which the boatman was also to collect from the passengers. Since we didn't have any naira, the other passengers were forced to pay our portion.

Six more times we were pirated by the Nigerian Naval Police, and each encounter was increasingly ruthless. On the boat, we were open marks and totally helpless against their lawlessness. "Shut up," the police yelled, "or you must pay me one hundred naira. Now you owe me fifty more because you won't shut up." No one had uttered a word. The demand for money was punctuated with slaps, which escalated to senseless beatings with brass knuckles and garrotes.

When the naira ran out, they appropriated the cargo under charges of stolen property or "smuggling." The only other woman on the boat, Jeannette, who transported clothing for resale in Cameroon, tried to protect herself with invoices. She was slapped, then half her clothes taken as a fine for lying. One man kneeled in the boat and cried, "I beg you," he choked with tears, "I have nothing left to give you." They beat him unconscious.

They turned their machine guns on us and teased the triggers. "Give us all your money or we kill you."

In the confusion of their shouting, Robb leaned to me and whispered, "Want to bet their guns are too rusty to fire?" I nodded.

The policeman held a pistol to Robb's head and again ordered him to give naira that we didn't have. Robb took a slow, calculated breath, crossed his arms, and leaned back against the gunwale.

"No." he said, emphatic, clear, and without negotiation. I wondered if we would hear the shots before we felt them.

I don't know what happened then, but suddenly the naval police got into their boats and left. A few minutes later, one boat circled around and came back. Jeannette started crying, the boat man cried, others moaned. "They're coming to kill us all!" Our knees were jelly. Without a word the police tossed into our boat everything they had stolen! We were too stupefied to react. The boat man was the first to move. He started the engines and nosed the flying boat out of Nigerian waters.[4]

Hosannas were sung to the sky. We washed the blood from the head of the man who had been beaten, hugged each other, and the engines died. We were adrift, but safe from the pirates and free to talk. As usual, no one mentioned the last mysterious occurrence. Maybe they understood it in a way we did not. At any rate, dignity would have to be rebuilt first.

Jeannette tried to explain the problem to us. "The Nigerians are all greedy. They don't care for nobody or anything but money. They want what we in Cameroon have, our CFA and our freedom. You see, we are free people, we can go anywhere and say anything and the Nigerians think if they take what is ours, it will make them rich and free, too."

"You do not have beatings in Cameroon?"

"Not so much because we are free people. Some people do beat on others, yes. They are the people in the north and west who were treated in this manner themselves."

When the boat man started the engines, one of the engines only puttered to life—it would fly no more. The boat followed the coastline, past cypress swamps and small thatched fishing villages, past green mountains and verdant rain forests. In late afternoon, the waters filled with meandering sailing boats of all kinds— yawls, ketches, and sloops with ingenious quilted sails of plastic and cloth scraps. A few sails defied the laws of physics—they were completely blown out!

We originally had not planned to travel into Central Africa. We had neither a map nor a book to guide us. Instead, we would rely on faded memories of political borders, and hearsay.

West Africa was our original focus of interest. It had lured us, not for its physical beauty or wildlife, but for its people, for its rapidly disappearing cultures and arts. Yes, we'd found the carvers, the weavers, the iron makers, the farmers, the market mammies, the boat builders, the fishermen, the illiterate, the college graduates, the paths through the bush, the secret societies, the voodoo doctors, the musicians, the dancers, and tribe after tribe, language after language. More importantly, we found people and not vocations; people and not textbook references, picture postcards, or geographic documentaries. We found kindness and generosity, hundreds of teachers who taught us to listen—to listen for the shaking leaf that announced a visit, the silent giggle hidden in a smile.

What we found too was violence and inhumanity. And, even within ourselves, we found a docile acceptance of it. We raged against oppressive systems that dehumanized people into slaves and devalued women, who were the strength of Africa. We wanted to gather our new friends into our arms and give them salvation from their own demise. But we couldn't.

We found a view of the white, westernized world simplified by movies, magazines, and boastful tales. No one worked in America. There, material possessions and money hatched on trees. Everyone was rich, and education was free. Even we seemed to illustrate that illusion. The only people who didn't want to go to America, or Europe, were those who had been there.

The foreigner's view of Africans was as simplified. Africans were all lazy. They were thieves and liars, dependent and childlike, boring and stupid. Foreign aid assuaged white guilt, paid for a rich lifestyle, pacified the folks at home, and perpetrated the mutual myths. The white people in Africa kept to themselves, no more dependent on the toil of the African than the African was on the white man's paperwork.

The African did not accept blame or self-accountability, but he accepted juju plots against him. On a grander scale, he blamed the white man for injustices, for slavery, neo-colonialism, and racial exploitation. Mistrust and racism were facts of African life.

Africa was a web of deception and realities. Which was which was the question.

PART IV

Central Africa

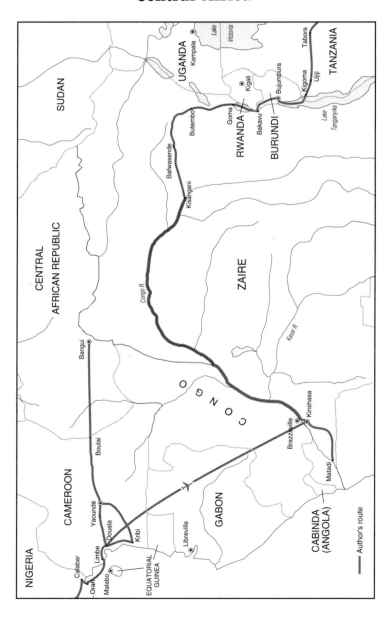

— 19 —

Cameroon and Central African Republic

Our relief at reaching the shores of Cameroon was so great nothing could daunt our smiles. The Nigerian SSS men, the Naval Police, Oran, and ten hours on the "flying boat" were behind us. Cameroon was the gateway to central Africa and, symbolically, a new beginning for us (we hoped). The ride from the port to the town of Limbe confirmed these hopes. Absent were the familiar police barricades. Instead, we passed small but impeccably neat and tranquil villages. Green arms of trees, a color rarely seen in western Africa, waved their welcome. The hulk of Mt. Cameroon could be felt, though not seen, behind a veil of sunset clouds. English was the official language in the southwest corner of Cameroon, while in the rest of the country French officially "dominated."

The driver took us to the Victoria Guest House, a cute gingerbread building in Limbe. Satisfied, Robb paid with CFA from our

West Africa emergency stash. Unfortunately, the CFA was unacceptable. Although Cameroon was a CFA country, their bills were slightly different in coloring. The Guest House paid the driver for us. No problem, we could pay them back when we got money. However, the banks were closed for Easter—a four-, maybe five-day holiday had just begun. No problem. The guest house would extend us credit. No problem, we thought, we would find the money changer and be on our way.

We prowled pleasant Limbe with sing-song steps. "There must be a money changer, there is always a money changer...." Our mission took us into and out of shops, restaurants, and the large hotels until our feet dragged with despair. No one knew a money changer. The Victoria again reassured us that we could stay, eat, and drink on credit there. In African terms, that meant we were taken care of. What more could we want?

The terms were gracious and very kind. Victoria's was comfortable and the kitchen good, but we wanted independence. We went back to the big hotels that attract people with big money and power. There we whored for a solution. We were lavished with attention, drinks, and food. We were introduced to everyone important in town or strolling through town. Offers of credit were extended, but no one wanted to part with cash over the long festive weekend. We were embarrassed by our plight.

Back at Victoria's we gave it one last try. "We must change money, we cannot walk like beggars," we said. "The shame is too great."

Without a word the owner opened the till and handed us CFA 20,000. Almost $75!

"You are right," she said, "you must keep your respect. Take this money and pay me when the bank opens."

We nearly fell over. She would not change, but she would lend so that we could have respect. We spent very little of that loan, and, for the most part, we gave our business to the guest house. For the five days in Limbe, we were free to walk with respect, to buy an ice cream or big beer to share with friends, to attend the soccer match of the year, and to ride the bumper cars and ferris wheel with kids on our laps.

Some regions just flow with a rhythm of goodness, and south-western Cameroon is one. The radiating circle of Limbe was bountiful in so many ways that, for us, it was a region of magic.

Banks reopened on Tuesday. We changed travelers checks, re-paid the hotel's kind loan, and were on our way to Douala.

Douala, Cameroon, was a bust in all ways. It was only the titular capital; all important functions were carried on in Yaounde, 275 kilometers away to the north and west. Off and on, we spent six days in Douala. We got to know its streets, the neighborhood restaurants where "consumption" tax wasn't charged, and all-night clubs that pulsated with more music than dancers. It was the most expensive, frustrating city of our trip.

The religious missions, touted as cheap, were either full or closed to the public. Luckily, we found a hotel much cheaper than the missions. There were many European-style restaurants with European-style prices we could not afford. No one knew where anything was, even if it was a block away. Pickpockets were so prevalent that Robb carried a brick. We never felt comfortable there and never shook the gloomy sadness that penetrated Douala.

The scuttlebutt was that the CFA was collapsing in Cameroon. Their export products had risen in price above what the international market would tolerate, and domestic consumption had also dropped for the same reason. They had priced themselves out of their own market. Other gossip told of demonstrations spreading across the country from the west. It was a cry for democratization and independence from French control. Traditionalists argued that France would never let go nor allow the CFA to bankrupt. Nevertheless, financial insecurity pervaded all transactions. We received ninety fewer CFA to the dollar than six months earlier. While newspapers reported the dollar gaining, in Cameroon it was wilting. Inconsistent and undervalued exchange rates coupled with inflation raised the price of a beer CFA 100 in one week, and the price of the five-hour bus ride to Yaounde went up CFA 500. The issues of economics brooded more ominously than political issues.

Off the coast of Gabon in the south, French warships stood ready to evacuate her citizens from the riots and demonstrations that severed and threatened the country. Nigeria to the west was in an equal mess with the plummeting naira, a coup attempt, and disappeared persons. Central African Republic (C.A.R.) to the east of Cameroon was reputed to have succumbed to lawlessness and violent robberies, a response to economic frustrations. The *International Herald Tribune* called for cessation of all foreign aid to Mobutu's regime in Zaire. This quiet corner of the world, one that we knew so little about, was on a headlong suicide crash course with its leaders.

Since the announcement that the Berlin Wall was coming down, pockets of rebellion erupted almost daily throughout west and central Africa. It was the "They did, why can't we?" syndrome. It was the first political awakening in Africa since independence. Previously unchallenged despots clashed with their people in Niger, Mali, Senegal, The Gambia, Liberia, Cote d'Ivoire, Benin, and Nigeria. We heard rumors of other civil protests in Burkina Faso, Ghana, and Togo. We scraped through the unrest just as we scraped through the dry season, but now, with rain on our backs and discontent in the wind, the chances for drama multiplied.

The city of Yaounde was a full day's ride from Douala. The climate, atmosphere, and prices were more agreeable in Yaounde than in Douala. And, as the financial capital of Cameroon and seat of all the foreign embassies,[1] it was also more vibrant. Much of the city had a newness about it, as if a huge infusion of capital and people had come at one time—then stopped. We stayed at a weird Presbyterian mission that was patronized by French travelers. Some had crossed the Sahara in their jeeps and still wore the tough, macho swagger of "adventuremen." We gave them wide berth.

The city was crisscrossed with paths that shortened the distances between banks and embassies. They wound through affluent neighborhoods guarded by the same Wackenhut security guards as in Liberia. Their muscles and presence failed to instill me with a sense of security. The paths also took us past "chop shops," benches burnished from years of butt polishing. They were cool, dark refuges from the sun.

We were having a cola in one chop shop, nodding sagely with all the other sages, when the chief of police burst in. Nothing less would do than he buy us a beer. We thanked him and stood up to leave.

"You don't drink with black men?" he snarled. "You are too good to drink our beer?" His hand brushed his pistol, his guards crouched.

The nodding old folks sat up straight and telegraphed trouble to us. We knew he was trouble without the quickening heartbeats that filled the room like thumping drums.

"Yes, we drink beer. Yes, we drink with black men, as you can see. We leave because we are late for an appointment with the American ambassador."

"You white people are all the same," he roared. "You know nothing. You insult us with your stupidity. If I offer you a beer, you must take it."

He was right, of course. We must accept his offer. To do otherwise would have been a grave insult. Yet, he was wrong. We attempted to leave because he was trouble. As it was, we took the beer and hobnobbed on the edge of disaster. He had a retinue of prostitutes with him, and he ordered them to make us happy.

"Teach them the African way," he said over and over. Everyone wanted to run away, but the doorway was blocked by his guards.

Only after we groveled and agreed that we were stupid and knew nothing about Africans did he relax. He signaled a woman to his bellied lap as he talked. "You are different, I see that," he said, "but I think you come here to know the real Africa, and you don't know it." He flagrantly massaged the woman's breasts and thrust a hand between her legs. She smiled and moaned with fake pleasure. The elders averted their eyes in embarrassment.

"Tonight you will come with me," he said, enveloping Robb in a vice grip around the neck. "And you," he pointed at me, "you will go with the women. Tonight we will teach you what it means to be African." His lips slathered salaciously, his eyes glossed with an undisguised memory of a triple-x-rated pornographic film.

We promised to meet him for a night of licentious abandon, African style, after our dinner with the American Ambassador.

"It is done," he said, slapping his beefy knees. "You will know lovely Africa like you never imagined."

"Thank you," we chorused. The room once again started breathing. Heads nodded sagely. The elders abhorred his vision of Africa, of course, and we made a swift exit—not only from the chop shop but from Cameroon to the Central African Republic

(C.A.R.), the country next door. We had our visas and felt it wise to leave Yaounde after breaking our date with the chief of police.

We didn't stay long in C.A.R., either. The overlanders who funneled through there were, in their own way, as obnoxious as the chief of police. The military and the thieves were unpleasantly indiscriminate and grew fat and surly on the tourist dollars.

The most direct overland route from the Sahara to Kenya, and therefore the most popular route, crossed the C.A.R. to the capital, Bangui, near the Zairean border. From Bangui, the route dropped almost directly south to Lisala, Zaire. If the travelers were lucky or had enough time and patience to wait, they could pick up the riverboat for the remaining three days on the Zaire River to Kisangani.

Three hours in Bangui was enough time to decide that the popular route was not for us—it was too crowded to be enjoyable. The company of the overlanders would be unavoidable, and, as we had learned in Cote d'Ivoire, we were no longer comfortable in the white culture. The more we thought about the Zaire River, the more we wanted to travel its full navigable length, which meant going to Kinshasa in western Zaire.

Airplane flights out of Bangui to Kinshasa were expensive and infrequent, but from Cameroon they were rumored to be much cheaper. We decided to return to Cameroon and fly from there to Kinshasa, the Zaire capital near the headwaters of the river.

Another factor in our decision to reverse our steps was Denis. He was a Swiss malcontent who had traveled with us from Yaounde to Bangui. Denis was intermittently likable and nasty as hell. The vacillation in his personality made me suspect a mental illness, but Robb diagnosed it as malaria. Robb argued it was our moral responsibility to help him.

"You could be him," Robb said, "think about it . . . you just got over malaria. Suppose you had been alone . . . you'd be dead now."

The only hospital we could find had no medicine. The patients bought medication themselves at the pharmacy, which didn't have them anyway. The patient's family was expected to provide the linens and the cooking pot, and to stay in the same dormitory as the patient, too. We didn't have the time, expertise, or affiliation to go that far. And, anyway, we suspected Denis did not take the pills we gave him from our own stash.

When Denis was sane, he talked of returning home, or of flying to Kenya to get medical treatment. He insisted on returning to Cameroon where airfare was cheaper, and we followed.

Then we did something we had never done and were hesitant to do after our near deportation from Guinea-Conakry: we reentered Cameroon with the same visa. It worked. Our passports were such a mess of ink and autographs that immigration gave up on sorting it out. Back in Yaounde, Denis parted company with us. He snuck away one night. We presumed he went on to Nigeria. Denis needed intensive care and treatment too sophisticated for us to tend to. He was better off moving on than staying still.

Our flight was not scheduled for several days. The preacher at the Yaounde Presbyterian Mission offered us a house in Kribi, on the southern coast, to wait in. It would be our last look at the ocean, and we took him up on it. We also were hoping we would be able to avoid the chief of police.

Not much happened in Kribi, ever. A new road was going in, however, and that would change the place forever. It would make things easier for the loggers, who were already stripping the landscape as fast as they could cut and haul, and hotels would be built along the sand beaches.

We met a Dutch couple in town. For two years they lived among the Pygmies. "They used to be hunters, and they still are by tradition, but the forest is shrinking so rapidly there is nothing for them to hunt. We teach animal husbandry, but how do you teach hungry hunters not to kill chickens? Hunting is all they know, and all they want to know, even if it means their extinction. Did you know that in Cameroon it is legal to kill a Pygmy? People hunt them for sport! The forest is their only protection, and, when it is gone, they too will disappear. What I can't understand is why people will preserve animals in wildlife parks, but nobody, nobody cares for the preservation of his own species."

Snoozy, indifferent Kribi, it seemed, was on the same cataclysmic course with progress as the Pygmies.

– 20 –
Zaire

Protocol was unfurled to welcome our arrival in Kinshasa, Zaire. Immigration placed us under quasi-arrest because we did not have an onward flight from Zaire. I suspect it was because we were the only passengers not met by a facilitator, a "fixer" retained by governments, missions, and businesses to protect their own. Police guards marched us from room to room. We followed with fatalistic resignation. Zaire was infamous as a corrupt military state. In anticipation of problems, we had stapled into our passports a letter from the American embassy in Cameroon requesting permission for our entry and safe passage through Zaire.[1] It was a flimsy ploy, but without a facilitator, it was our only chance. Perhaps because of the letter, or perhaps because of something that President Mobutu said in a long-winded speech broadcast over the airport loudspeakers, the officials released us, with apologies, after two hours.

The bus we took in search of a place to stay broke down in hot traffic snarls. Most passengers got of the bus. If we had known where to go, we would have jumped bus too. Kinshasa and its environs sprawled relentlessly through indistinguishable neighborhoods. The capital of Zaire, with more than two-and-a-half million people, Kinshasa would be one city in Africa we'd never get to know well. We had a hand-drawn map to get us to the vicinity of the boats and embassies. Black Xs marked the approximate location of missions and cheap hotels. Typically, they were all full or closed. We found the Hotel Guesthouse. It was popular among Zairean families and so, we hoped, an unlikely place for surprise visits from the military.

The national security forces were known to rob people of everything down to their socks in broad daylight, and to pay surprise, midnight visits to foreigners. The pretense was to check visas and currency declaration forms; the reality was to plunder their belongings.

Paranoia motivated us to devise elaborate precautions. We removed the sacred letters from the American embassy from the passports. If challenged to produce identification, we would show the letter, rather than risk having our passports seized by the police—a popular technique to extort large bribes for their return. We hid the passports in our passport cases or locked them in the hotel safe, and stuffed everything else of importance above the ceiling panels in our rooms. The letters were accepted when we said that our passports were at "an embassy."

The first order of business was to book onto the Zaire River boat. It was a procedure more complex and tangled than any we had encountered on the continent. A boat would leave three days later. It was sold out. Another would leave in two more weeks. We pleaded in the office of the big boss, Paul, and networked all the employees of ONATRA, the riverboat company, in search of the exception—the cabin that just opened.

Paul was not rude, just short of time. He pushed us off on Claude, the young supervisor of ticket sales. Claude patiently explained in broken English and in French, "Reservations go on sale five days before the boat departs, then two days after you must buy your ticket. Cabins sell early, and no one ever gives them up. The first to get cabins are high government people, the police and military, then family, and then friends of friends...." Claude studied our silent dejection. "You must learn Lingala."

His message was clear. If we wanted to go on the next boat, we would have to become family, or a friend of a friend. And to do that, we would have to prove worthiness.

Robb looked at me, "Well, Pami, you're the one fluent in languages, get to work." No one spoke English and few people would speak French. Lingala was the most widely spoken of the two hundred languages in Zaire. We would need it in order to become someone's friend. Someone like...Claude.

"Don't worry," Claude assured, "Lingala is easier than the European languages, you will know it quickly."

Claude began the lessons on the spot. "Let's start with the greetings and move on to verb tenses, plural negatives, gender noun agreement...." He was a thirty-year-old university student with a facility for grammar, and he was an apt teacher. As an object lesson, Claude took us on a tour of the riverboat, the *masua,* at dock. Second class was on the barges. The cabins were steel, windowless cages without ventilation or electricity, and barely wide enough for four bunks. A stench of rotten animal feces permeated the cabins from adjoining pens. First-class deluxe was an air-conditioned suite with brocade curtains, settee, and private bath. Regular first class, was basic with two beds, windows, electricity, and a walk-through, rusty bathroom adjoining another cabin.

"We want this one," we told Claude. We did not need luxury, but we also did not want an abysmal cave for two weeks.

Each day Claude refined the Lingala we gleaned from the streets and markets. *"Mbote. Sango nini? Sangote,"* launched lesson after lesson, until the three of us grinned with mutual pleasure. "You are family," announced Claude. His benediction released us to escape Kinshasa.

Escape was a good word. The political climate in Kinshasa was charged with unrest. Mobutu's speech was acclaimed by political analysts as forever changing the political climate in Africa, but it was whispered by the people that it would change nothing. Mobutu said he would allow opposition parties to his own Popular Movement for the Revolution; he would install an interim government until a special democratic election could be held. The constitution would be rewritten and the military placed under civilian control. He also said he would remain head of state, above all parties, above criticism from the legislature. Only one decree made any concrete change: men could wear neckties.

Since seizing power in 1965, President-for-Life Mobutu Sese Seko, the all-powerful warrior, had imposed a policy of authenticity. The name of the country was changed from Congo to Zaire. Likewise, the Congo River was dubbed the Zaire River, Leopoldville was changed to Kinshasa and Stanleyville was changed to Kisangani. People's names were also changed to African ones, and all titles of respect dropped except "citizen." Men were required to wear the high-necked jacket so favored by Mobutu that they were called Mobutu jackets instead of the more familiar "Mao jacket," and neckties were outlawed.

Secretly, people clung to their Christian names and addressed each other as monsieur and madame, or mama and papa. Within hours of his speech, neckties appeared on the streets—old-fashioned, soup-stained ties hidden for twenty years and ones so new that sewing strings dangled from them. On one street corner a shirtless man ceremoniously draped a big paisley tie around the scrawny neck and bare chest of his son. He deftly tied a fat Windsor knot. It was a technique that must have been taught him by his own father and practiced in secret these many years.

Further on, hundreds of people rushed down a street that led to the boat docks. Jubilant cheers and applause rippled the still air. We stood on tiptoes to see. A wide corridor parted, and down the middle strutted a man, short enough to be a Pygmy, who sported not just a tie, but an entire suit with lapels that flared beyond his shoulders. It was a small, symbolic civil liberty, yet monumental in a country with few liberties or hopes.

Kinshasa was not a happy town. A specter of fear, shortages, and desperation quaked its core. One in twenty people carried hand-held radios. By six o'clock each night, markets were shut up tight, intercity buses stopped running, taxis vaporized, and only a few restaurants remained open. The night was eerie. Boulevards were deserted except for the patrolling security police. We got caught in this disappearing act the first night.

Two policemen waved their guns and demanded cigarettes or money. Only minutes before, people were on the streets, but suddenly they were as empty as if swept by nuclear holocaust. "Keep walking," I said to Robb. The police followed. Doorways were all locked, but we slithered into their darkness, crouched behind garbage bins, and scurried from shadow to shadow. The menacing men in uniform pursued us with drawn bayonets, which they poked into the recesses we had just abandoned. Sometimes they were so close we could have tweaked their pants leg. I was sure they could hear my panicked heart beat. Robb and I split up so if one of us was captured, the other could find help. For an hour they hunted us with deadly intent. I'll never understand people who pay to play war games. When the pursuers' footsteps could be heard tromping off in resignation, we attempted to cross the boulevard.

"Stop. Stop now!" came a shower of voices from under a shadowed lintel. "Stop, or we will shoot!" I don't know what possessed us—fatalism, optimism, or the panic of finding you are a mouse between the paws of a cat—but we did not alter our pace. My back went rigid in expectation of bullets ripping my spine apart. Nothing came but their hollered threats and demands for money or cigarettes. It was a long way home dodging police, hiding and watching for their coffee break or a turned back. No wonder the streets were empty! Never again did we stay out past the unspoken curfew, except to slither to the shadowy, unmarked bars and restaurants sequestered in private compounds of our neighborhood.

For the next week we traveled south and west—to Matadi on the bank opposite Angola and, finally, to rest in the small towns of Kisantu/Inkisi. Set among hills, the climate was refreshing after the closeness of the cities and the mugginess of the Congo delta. The towns were small and unhurried. Our bruised spirits healed as if soaked in a medicinal spa.

I bought local fabric at the market and took it to a seamstress. Within two days, I had a sharp "Zairean" ensemble: a wraparound skirt, a boat-neck blouse with puffy short sleeves, a scarf that could be tied in myriad ways, from a flower to a bow, and a matching "sling" to carry babies or goods on my back. A crowd gathered at the door of the seamstress when we went to pick it up. There was nothing to do but model it. The women took my hand and led us through town to nods of approval, applause, and invitations to "come sit with us." While men might wear neckties, women remained the guardians of tradition. My new Zairean clothes encompassed us in their guardianship.

Local specialties were prepared as treats. "Come to me tomorrow, I make you squash soup or *mkindso*"—a stew of caterpillars cooked in their own juice. (It wasn't bad; it tasted a little like snails.) Flowers floated in the bowls of washing water. The entire town rallied to teach us more Lingala, and one man appointed himself our French teacher. The only time we got a break from our lessons was when we hid in our room.

With great sadness, we left our friends in Kisantu. We were different people than when we arrived. The people of Kisantu, with open hearts and homes, had taught us much. Lingala, French, etiquette, new foods, and new clothing outfitted us for the rest of Zaire. Sometimes I tried to imagine what they knew about us. I am sure it was everything, as secrets did not exist any more than privacy. I hoped what they learned was good.

We arrived at the *Gare Fluvial* in Kinshasa one hour too late to get a cabin on the next riverboat. Reservations had sold out within the first hour. Claude anxiously ushered us from the head office to his own and handed us our reservations. He had to return to Paul, his boss, and explain a "mistake." We added our voice to Claude's, but in Lingala. Their jaws fell open in surprise, then they beamed with pride. Paul lightly berated Claude for his lie, but it was very light. Claude pronounced us, "ready for the riverboat."

Not exactly. An inventory revealed we were dangerously low on Paludrine, money, and books, and our cholera vaccinations were expired. The boat would not leave for another six days—time we would have to spend in Kinshasa restocking our supplies. It took five arduous days to find what we needed through Kinshasa's underground. Expatriates reluctantly admitted us to their network of resources. "You will have a bigger problem several weeks from now if you don't help us today," we told them. Cholera vaccinations were useless against preventing cholera, yet Zaire, like most of Africa, required semi-annual vaccinations. Likewise, without Paludrine, chances were excellent we would have to be evacuated for medical reasons at embassy expense. The American embassy stamped our health certificates, and the Peace Corps helped us with a supply of Paludrine.

At the American Embassy we talked to a political officer who was ecstatic over Mobutu's turnaround. "We anticipated a full blown rebellion, a civil war on the day he made his speech," the official said. "Mobutu averted it by hours or minutes, now all has changed." Just as idealistically, he reported no problems with travel in Zaire.

But, behind the walls of the expatriate bastions, we felt betrayed by him. Posted everywhere were warnings against Kinshasa at night, against the military, and against travel.

"This is a dangerous country," said one Peace Corps employee. "We cannot afford to let personnel travel even 150 kilometers, or we would spend all our time trying to bail them out. Our presence is barely tolerated."[2] This, in a country where the US alone provides $60 million annually and untold more in military credits and through churches! The very foreigners who sustained Mobutu's power were barely tolerated by him. Foreign aid had made Mobutu one of the richest men in the world. His personal fortune was estimated to be over $6 billion, while the annual per capita income of his people was below $150. Yet his benefactors cowered behind walls rather than offend "the all-powerful warrior." It was more diplomatic to hope that travelers would simply disappear without a trace rather than issue an offensive travel advisory.

An embassy nurse said, "We call it the walled city. Walls, visible and invisible, are everywhere, and you can't get through them. I am sure there are some lovely people and lovely places, but the walls...."

An expat "businessman," who provided critical services to other "businessmen," proposed another theory for the walls. "They (referring to the international community) are getting rich off this scam, and no one wants the other person to know by how much. I watch them send out vouchers for their so-called projects. Vouchers for house, driver, guards, food, per diem, travel, 70 percent over salary, hardship pay, and subsidies. You can live here for $200 a month, don't tell me you need an additional $5,000 to $6,000 to make ends meet. Phhh! Projects! Better to build a road to nowhere. If they wanted to make something with their money, skip all the projects and send these people out for vocational training."

Of all our tasks, the most difficult was to replenish our supply of reading books. In the past, we had walked up to ten miles on bush trails to swap a book. Here in Kinshasa, we searched embassy and mission libraries and hunted down rumors of white travelers.

Our rounds brought us in contact with some of the strangest people since Tamanrasset, Algeria. Worthy of mention, not for their strangeness but for their intrepid fortitude, was an overland group from London who had forged a new route through The Congo. They spent fifty-seven days crossing from north to south and rebuilt eighty-one bridges—some after their truck had plunged into the river below. Seven members remained to jokingly speculate if, and when, they would reach Nairobi.

Across the Congo/Zaire River gleamed Brazzaville, The Congo. It shimmered like a promised land. For some reason, Zaire did not easily permit its people to cross between the two cities. A *laissez-passer* was so difficult and expensive to get that Brazzaville grew in legend. Several times we risked staying out past twilight to sit by the river and watch the distant twinkling of lights. I am sure it was little different from Zaire, but because it was visible yet unattainable, it was magically alluring.

– 21 –

The Zaire River

South of the equator, the rainy season officially ends May 15, when it swings to the north until September. The equator cuts through Zaire and the river snakes twice across the line so the northern half is wet while the south is dry. "Not so much rain comes this year," said one man, "see, the water is low. The river trade will be little."

The boat, the *Colonel Ebeya*, with its six barges, stood tied to the Kinshasa dock. It was ten o'clock in the morning, and the boat was not scheduled to heave-ho until three o'clock that afternoon. We were there early to stake out our cabin. Claude, our protective brother, had to intercede when our reservations for cabin number eight were "lost" under another person's name. All day huge bundles of furniture were ported on the tops of men's heads, and they filled every available inch of space. Ovens and even freezers clogged the gangways. "Room sitters" staked out space for the occupants, who arrived in formal dress and uniforms just before the whistle blew. The elite of Zaire surrounded us.

Our first-class room, like theirs, was stifling. Once out of sight of the dock, friends, relatives, and obligatory entourages, the Zairean passengers took off their formal clothes and changed into leisure wear. Sleeping mats, babies, cooking braziers, and even laundry were dragged out of rooms to fill the decks. Whiskey appeared, and a festive-but-waiting spirit settled over the ship. There was little apparent difference between first class and second.

Gossip said there were more than two thousand people aboard the rafted boats. Certainly there were too many to count. We clambered from barge to barge and deck to deck, no easy feat with steel cables and lianas lashing the barges, and slippery wet decks and railings. No one level matched up with the other. The tricks of balance used to leap and climb came through attentive practice. One, sometimes two, stairways connected the levels of each barge. They were hopelessly barred by vendors, clothing, livestock, and families. The quickest path was to climb the outside railings—a question of nerves and faith more than dexterity. I had great difficulty navigating at first. Although it wasn't serious, one of my legs had stiffened like a board. While in Kinshasa the inevitable happened: I walked into an open sewer.

The boat atmosphere was subdued that first night. It would take two weeks to reach Kisangani in eastern Zaire, so there was plenty of time for activity. Along with the families of the boat workers, we watched sunset from the transom. Dinner was served promptly at seven—rice with mixed vegetables, and a tough piece of meat. Not exactly the fare we enjoyed on the Niger River, but neither was our cabin as deluxe.

By the second day, shipboard life was organized into a beehive of activity. If movement from barge to barge was difficult the first evening, it was now impossible fun. Gossip reported four others from our tribe were on board—two white people in second class, and two in first. The two in first class shared our bathroom so we met them immediately. Desiree and Ien were Dutch medical students conducting malaria research. The two in second class were Stephanie and Josef. Stephanie was a Canadian who was on vacation from her job in Malawi, and Josef was a student from Germany. We spent the first few days exploring the ship, so we did not see much of them.

The Zairean women of first class did not eat with the men in the dining room. When the meal bell clanked, they would enter first and fill their bowls to eat outside on the deck. It was at lunch the second day that the women upbraided me in Lingala for eating with the men; I should sit with them on the deck. I would be shunned and my life made miserable if I didn't do as they said.

I didn't doubt them for one second. On the positive side of their argument was the better choice of food and the more spectacular ambiance of open-air dining. I was easily persuaded.

"What did they say to you?" asked Robb, tugging me aside. I translated as best I could the torrent of words and menacing gestures.

"You will not!" he said. "I don't care who they are or how they threaten, you will eat dinner by my side. And, you will learn to say in Lingala, 'You come eat with me in the dining room.'"

What I really learned to say was, "I am with my husband. I go with him according to his command." It was closer to what I felt the women would understand. I could no more change their belief systems than they could change mine.

Nevertheless, I still felt I was in a headlong clash with these women, until one very strange, horribly embarrassing incident.

On the foredeck and rooftop of one of the barges, a variety of recreational activities were held at sunset. At least four Christian groups gathered to sing and gospelize. About 10 percent of the passengers went to bow to Mecca and chant evening prayers. Others lazed around and toked on Congo weed. Still other groups exercised. There were boxers in full headgear, joggers, gymnastic tumblers, and, most astounding of all, a Tae Kwon Do class!

I was an exercise addict more than a specialist. I tried to find a private hour each day to work out, and when the opportunity presented itself on the trip, I attended both aerobics and karate classes. I was a proud white belt, so I had no claim to expertise, only exercise.

I am not really sure what got into me. I could speculate forever: it was rebellion against the claustrophobia and lack of privacy, or maybe I believed myself invisible with my gris-gris. Without a thought for consequences, I asked to join the Tae Kwon Do class. The instructor's warm welcome was all I needed.

The instructor barked the cadence for a vigorous military-style warm-up. Rusty slivers from the metal roof penetrated my skin and bled during the knuckle push-ups. In my mind, the boat and everyone on it disappeared. Masochistic calisthenics were replaced by forms, singular displays of techniques in mock battle, which was in turn replaced by raw aggression—punch-and-kick drills and sparring.

My partners, all men, towered three feet over me, their mammoth chests ripped their uniform cloth, their fists and feet were the size of sledgehammers. "Advance! Attack!" the instructor bawled, and the mastodons moved forward with full body contact. I trembled; I was scared. It was more like street fighting than a drill. I concentrated on survival and found myself driving my opponents to the edge of the roof over and over again, not by expertise but by sheer fear.

Cheers and applause echoed off the river banks. All two thousand passengers watched from sagging rooftops. A few had even climbed the smokestack for a better view. We did not notice until the captain sent someone down to stop the action. The captain said so many people were on the barge roofs that he could not see to steer, and he feared the roofs would collapse. He was right. The spectators jumped up and down as if they were at a stadium.

Robb told me later that the entire crowd cheered for me. I had not heard a thing. As the adrenalin quelled, I slowly realized I caused the spectacle. I probably violated all laws of propriety. A woman fighting men! It had never been seen except in the movies. I had acted stupidly. I sat in the rusty bathtub filled with muddy river water and tried to figure out a way to expiate my shame.

That night I dressed in the Zairean ensemble and fluffed the head scarf into a nice feminine flower for dinner and dancing in one of the barge bars. Both the dress and the dancing caused another stir. The stuffy nightclub rocked with fast-paced Zairean music. Empty cans were used as drums, tin maracas shook with beans. Maybe a hundred people jammed into the little room, and as many more through the doorways and windows. Everyone danced to a sweaty slather. The women and I swapped dances I had picked up from different regions. They taught me a Zairean dance too obscene to be called a "fertility dance." Ovations, kisses, and hugs culminated each song. Big bottles of Primus beer were kept standing at our seats. They were gifts from well-wishers. The debauchery might never have ended if the bar hadn't been ordered to shut down.

Three scenes in one day was too much. "Tomorrow I think I'll stay in the cabin," I said to Robb as we climbed over the railings and ropes to our cabin.

"Why?"

"I think I overdid it today. I think I blew it. Maybe I better stay in the cabin for the rest of the trip. I'll be sick, and you can bring me meals."

"That's ridiculous!" he said. "I think you're underestimating what happened."

"I think I am, too, but in a different way than you mean."

Breakfast was standard. Two slices of bread with lard and a choice of tea or coffee that suspiciously tasted alike. Robb did not allow me to hide.

"You might as well face them now," he said. "Don't let them think they won. We've got almost two weeks left on this boat." Cringing, I allowed him to lead me on a shopping tour of the vendors' stands.

Instead of mockery or hissed insults, I was greeted throughout the boat by deep bows, imitative of what they had seen on kung fu movies. I was called "Mama," a term of respect. Everyone wanted to touch me; they wanted us to sit with them and talk about the night. Although my conduct had been egregious, the incidents awarded me celebrity status. We were adopted into every tribe on the boat. As the days passed, my legend grew. The bows and greetings multiplied to such great length and number it literally took two hours to reach the bows of the barges. It was so important to maintain friendships that we could not slight anyone—not even the first-class women, who now grudgingly admitted me into their fold on my terms.

The tailors made me a gift of a patchwork dress I could only call "cruisewear." It was long and blousy—Robb said it made me look pregnant—but it was perfect for the heat. Justine, an assistant barge captain, tied my stubby hair into protruding rods-a popular river style called the Antenna. It was a painful ordeal, and I pulled it out that same night. The boat moguls praised my Zairoise adaptation, but I had had enough of being a celebrity. I wanted to reclaim femininity in favor of karate queen.

I formed a great alliance with a woman named Justine. She wielded great power after nine years of traveling the river on the boat. She summoned me to her cabin the morning after the karate exhibition. Not a day passed when I didn't visit and share with her a Primus beer. Our status mutually blossomed from our alliance. Justine's eyes, face, and body moved with such extraordinary intelligence that I easily forgot where we were, who we were. The rift in cultures and experience disappeared. Just as important, I got food from her. I pounded the green plantains for her, and she gave us smoked eel in a spicy sauce. When first-class dining served bread and coffee for dinner or something else equally inedible, I went to Justine. The rule of the boats was that everyone dined in their assigned kitchen with no switching allowed. Justine supplied us with fresh fish, or the daily kill—antelope, monkey, rice, or fou-fou. When I thought we would languish from scurvy if we did not soon eat a vegetable or some fruit, Justine got me a pineapple. Fruit was so rare it was gobbled up the instant it was brought on board. She sent a request for fruit with the canoes that traded with the boat. Three days later the pineapple magically appeared in her hands. I was sure she exerted some pressure to get it (and to refrain from eating it). I gave her my best shirt as visible repayment.

Robb soaked the pineapple in rum. He threw a sunset cocktail party on a barge roof for the members of the white tribe—the *mundeles*. The red sky and the silent jungle slid past our juicy feast. The only thing better would have been if I had eaten the whole pineapple myself.

Desiree, one of the Dutch medical students, succumbed to malaria, dehydration and malnutrition—all the factors of their research. Ironically, neither she nor her colleague Ien diagnosed it. As we had learned, malaria is deceptive. Robb took over Desiree's care. He rehydrated her, packed her with wet towels to bring down the fever, and tucked bread-wrapped pills into her mouth. At Mbandaka on the equator, he carried her from the boat to where they were met by mission doctors.

Stephanie, another of the *mundele* tribe, contrived a sick act in order to get Ien and Desiree's vacant cabin. More than twenty people shared the four bunks in Stephanie's second-class cabin. She eventually got Ien and Desiree's cabin, along with a Zairean woman who complained vociferously about having to share it with a white person. For us, it was convenient to have someone on the other side of the adjoining bathroom who agreed to leave the doors open for cross-ventilation.

Nights were hot and steamy. The steel cabins baked by day and radiated still, hot air by night. The worst nights were when the boats were tied up to trees on shore, which blocked the breeze altogether. The gossip-line said it was because sandbars prevented nighttime navigation. We abandoned our beds and slept on the deck with the other passengers. Everyone slept side-to-side or back-to-back—women, men, and children. Our room was nothing more than a place to go.

An occasional flash storm provided diversity in the weather, but never made it cooler. Late one afternoon, a huge swooshing gust blew all the boats onto shore. Giant trees got tangled in the cluttered decks and impaled open doors. It looked hopeless. We'd be stuck for weeks. We became a tree house and not a boat, as the brown water of the river swirled past indifferently. Ropes were strung from trees like spiders' webs to help kedge the boats, while the mighty engine of the *Ebeya* churned mud from the bottom. It worked! The bars reopened for the celebration.

The pungent aroma of potent Congolese marijuana hung over the barges like a cloud. One barge bow in particular seemed to be the smoking loge. It was the area most popular with the security forces. Although they had hung up their uniforms upon departing Kinshasa and wore civilian clothing like everyone else, I recognized them. I remembered their faces from when they wore uniforms.

Josef hadn't that advantage. They laid a trap for him and sprang it tight.

Josef, with cropped curly hair, a sweet smile, and dressed in a *kitanga*—a skirt worn by men in east Kenya—bunked in Stephanie's old second class cabin. He carried a backpack constructed from bamboo and cloth. "The first day I was in Nairobi, off the plane from Germany and looking for a room, a man dropped a piece of paper. I picked it up and followed him trying to get his attention. He turned into an alley. Suddenly I was surrounded by six men who beat me up and took from me everything I owned...my passport, money, and clothes. I was surprised, because this man was white and looked like a tourist. Never again will I pick up a piece of paper. But, as for me, I am fine. I have much less to worry about."

So he said until the night he was dragged, screaming, past our door by the police. "Robb, Pam! I've been arrested for smoking ganja. I wanted someone to know in case you never see me again." His voice receded along with the sound of marching heels. We sat up straight. Josef was our tribe. One way or another, he was our responsibility. We woke up Stephanie, the only one among us fluent in French. Robb and Stephanie represented Josef as his attorneys. The police wanted $500 cash American for his release, or he would be imprisoned when the boat reached Kisangani, the last port.

Josef had nothing. He could not pay the fine. Nor could we. Kisangani was ten, maybe twenty, days away; until then, he would be under boat arrest, which was no big deal since the boat rarely stopped anywhere. Ultimately, Josef's arrest led to extortion requests on his behalf. From six in the morning until late at night, the police hunted Stephanie, "When will your friend pay his money?"

They threatened to kill him. We shrugged indifferently. "Kill him then," we said. "He isn't our tribe, he's German." Meanwhile, we snuck Josef choice tidbits from our dining room to his bowl, and when we had nothing he snuck food back to us. Yes, we were the same tribe. His best defense, and ours as well, was to disavow mutual responsibility and defuse the situation by acting indifferent.

Otherwise, the days and nights blended together with an undisturbed monotony. Sunsets, sunrises, increasingly bad meals, the swirling muddy water, a gray sky, dense forested banks, an occasional village, and trading by canoe were all as constant as the engine's guttural hum.

The market expanded with the hours: mirrors, nail polish, skin lightening lotions, soap, cloth, fishing line and hooks, racks of smoked monkey and eel, banana-wrapped bundles of quonti or manioc, and a proliferating array of medicines and syringes. The medicines were bundled into plastic bags, sealed by a flame, and hand labeled to represent a pharmaceutical supply never available in Kinshasa. We suspected they were all sugar encased in colorful ampules.

The decks were impossible obstacle courses. Each barge had a set of showers and toilets to serve maybe a thousand people. Water perpetually sloshed the steel floors. The pens filled with feces and animals until they flowed into the walk space. Flopping, whiskered fish, from three to twelve feet in length, were butchered and shared among the various kitchens. Next to the fish laid a huge bongo, an antelope-like animal, and a tusked warthog. Their throats were slit, and their blood and life drained across the deck. Their legs thrashed the air and desperate eyes begged for deliverance. Crocodiles with sticks between their teeth, their snouts knotted in nooses, were tied to every post on every barge. Monkey, eel, and fish filled the roofs where we had once exercised and prayed. They had to be turned frequently in the sun, or maggots would wriggle through their mouths and eyes. Laundry flapped from every railing and line.

Termites were deep-fried and sold in paper cones. Robb loved them. "They're like popcorn," he said between crunches. High in protein, they were a healthy addition to our meager diet. Giant beetles flew into the lamps at night and were served for breakfast the next morning. The first class women giggled when we picked wings and legs from our teeth the rest of the day.

We hungered to taste the legendary, giant white palm grub roasted on a skewer. It was the coveted food. Eels, beetles, monkey, and the white slug were considered delicacies. When we finally got invited for slug, it was chewy, and tasted O.K. going down, but within minutes it wanted to come back up again. We had to leave our hosts abruptly. It was the only food we ate that caused a strong visceral rejection.

I tried to count the canoes, the *bwotos*, tied alongside the barges. They came and went with such movement I could only estimate between 150 and 200 at any one time. The boat, the *masua*, never stopped at a town. Instead, the river villagers who traded into the interior would paddle upstream maybe a day or two ahead laden with food products. When the boat came in sight, the canoes paddled out and tied onto the barge with jungle vines. They would trade with the shipboard *commercantes,* drink a beer if a profit was made, then drop off within proximity of their village. It was a tricky maneuver and good timing was essential.

A small canoe held three people; the large ones carried up to ten. Many women filled the boats. Everyone stood in the unsteady boats and rowed with heart-shaped paddles. Quite a few canoes tipped. Sometimes it was funny, and the wet passengers splashed playfully. Sometimes it was sad seeing a valuable cargo lost to the current. Other times it was so nearly disastrous that everyone on the boat gasped in horror. Many of the women wore children strapped to their backs. If one of them went under, the mother might live but certainly not her child. Once a canoe and its passengers was swept under a barge. An alarm of screams and whistles ordered the engines to stop. A fearful silence floated over the water. Divers searched. Finally, a big cheer announced that the canoe and all six passengers had miraculously bobbed up behind the transom.

Nights were more active than days. Certainly the best foods, such as oranges, came on board at night. Some mornings we found orange rinds, but no oranges, on the decks. When a particularly good shipment of food arrived, cloth bundles were thrown from the decks onto the cargo. The cloth designated the buyer. Sometimes, several cloths would go down at the same time, and arguments broke out. Usually the bottom, or first cloth down won.

There were changes from day to day, and events that loomed large, but, for the most part, monotony sunk in. Many of the vendors had been doing this—riding the boat up and down the Zaire River—for ten or twenty years, some their whole lives. Watching the same cavalcade, they knew no other life.

Several times a week, video movies were shown in the first class dining room. They were free and open to all passengers who could fit into the small room, so places were reserved early. They were always kung fu movies. I saw one. It opened with a massive rape scene. The white woman at first protested against the twenty men, then begged with a nymphomaniac's panting delight. I was all too aware of the New York skyscraper background, the whiteness of her skin, the violent male-portrayed sex, and of my own recent tae kwon do exhibition. I got up, left, and never again watched another movie. Robb said the movie got better after that. The rapists were all killed or kicked to smithereens, and I should not have walked out. I would not have watched it at home, and I could not see any reason for watching it there. Especially with five hundred eyes burning into my back.

Ngaire and Lynn came on in Bumba. We heard a rustle at our door, and a soft voice said, "Your tribe is here, you must come." The two New Zealand women were distraught, visibly upset. They were surprised we had not already heard of them, and it took three days to glean this story from them:

"We were on an overland truck from London, but in Ghana we decided to go on our own. That's when we met Rick, a Brit, and traveled with him. He had cerebral malaria, but we did not know it then. We only know that some days he felt good, and other days he was very sick. We tried to get him to a hospital, but he refused. We tried to give him medications, but he refused that too. If we mentioned these things, he would get angry. We did not know him and thought we had no right to impose ourselves on him. What were we to do? Hold him down and force medications into him? Against his will?

"At Lisala we took a barge to Bumba. It took four days. On the second day Rick went mad. He screamed until he suddenly died. The Africans made a big circle around us and said we were responsible, that he was from our tribe. They would not otherwise speak to us, and we had to sleep with his body at night. We did not know what to do. When we arrived in Bumba, a missionary family took over. They called the American embassy who called his mother in Britain, a widow without the money to fly his body home. Anyway, his body was too far gone. We buried him in Bumba with a proper ceremony. We took pictures and sent the film to his mother. She may not want to look at it now, but sometime, maybe. . . .When we went through his belongings, we found all the medicines, everything he needed to live. The Africans said horrible things about us. Then, while we rested with the missionaries, overland trucks arrived. The story circulated among them too. They did not understand what happened, they were too protected from reality. . . .They came up to us and asked if we were the women with the man that died. Some even accused us of murdering him. They were cruel. We do not want to see them or talk with them." Ngaire and Lynn were passed into our care from the missionaries who wanted to shield them from the overlanders, who had also boarded at Lisala.

Robb, the social worker/psychologist, burrowed his way into Ngaire's confidence. He held her and encouraged her to let go. Lynn was unreachable. She teetered on madness.

The arrival of at least fifty new passengers from overland tours disrupted life as we knew it. It was an unwelcome invasion. For twelve days Zairean music had blared from the bars, and people had danced and hugged babies. Life on the riverboat had been orderly, safe. But on the thirteenth day, the white tourists commandeered every cassette player in the community. When constant Rolling Stones' music invaded the peaceful kingdom, the community sneeringly called the fifty new passengers "white tourists."

During the final three days, relationships on the boat became tenuous. Open hustlings, stealing, racial comments, and rudeness replaced harmony. We were protected by our African friends, but it was an uncomfortable atmosphere.

After 1,734 kilometers and fifteen days on the Zaire River, Kisangani was the end of the boat ride. Mixed feelings twisted our spirits. It was good to touch ground again, to get out from under the watchful eye of the community, to escape the horror of Mick Jagger in the Congo jungle and the rudeness of the last few days.

The last morning, Josef was escorted to Stephanie's cabin by the now-uniformed police. He had to pay his fine or go to prison. After an hour of haggling, his fine was whittled to one *kitanga*—a cloth from Kenya. He was freed.

Stephanie, however, brawled with the cabin chief. When she upgraded to first class, her old ticket was taken, and a new one never reissued. Yet the chief demanded she surrender her ticket to disembark. She and the chief had not been friendly. His final revenge was to reduce her to self-effacing tears in recognition of his power.

Justine and a force of twenty merchants swiftly accompanied Robb and me through the corridor of immigration and security police. Safely on the other side, we touched hands, hugged, and kissed. They would go back to the river, and we would go into the jungle. A part of our souls went with them to perpetually ride the currents of the great Zaire River.

- 22 -

East to Burundi

Kisangani, Zaire, was almost comatose. It was the fifth largest city in Zaire, but it looked like a town. It looked as if not much had happened since Stanley stopped there on his search for Livingstone. Dust clouds billowed down wide, deserted streets. People were friendly, but indifferent to the cavalcade of boat migrants. Kisangani provided sustenance for the onward trek. The quietness, spaciousness, and indifference were all luxuries after the closeness of the riverboat.

Miraculously, a pile of mail awaited us, which fed our spirits while food, hot and delicious, fed our lean bellies. The showers in the campground at the Hotel Olympia spewed clean, clear water. I was alarmed to see clumps of my hair wash down the drain.

We knew the next few weeks of our journey would be the toughest. With passable, dry season roads and good luck, it would take two weeks to cross 580 miles of Zairean jungle to Goma. It hadn't been dry, though, and few trucks chugged east out of town. We were prepared to wait when the sweet hand of irony tapped us on the shoulder. After having snickered at overland travelers, we would join them. Economic Tours, a group out of London, offered us a ride. They had missed the riverboat at Lisala and so had traveled overland to Kisangani. They knew nothing about Ngaire's and Lynn's scandal, and their offer was too good to pass up. Robb and I, Stephanie, Josef, Ngaire and Lynn swallowed our pride and signed on.

We had to first find money, though, which is always a problem on weekends. I arranged to change with a business woman who was as skittish as I over black market dealings. She locked the door to her office and pulled the blinds. Together, we counted the money back from $100. Something was wrong with the amount, I sensed. A new fever sprouted in my head, and I could not even add the change. We decided to trust the calculator.

I went back to Robb, who sat at a restaurant with a group of people. I whispered, "The amount somehow seems wrong." He counted it, several other people counted it, and it added up right. Call it a testimony to our weakness, loss of concentration, or fevers, but it took an hour for six of us to figure out I had been paid exactly double!

All our companions had been ripped off in transactions, so they argued that the profit was a karmic payback. If so, then Robb and I were not due, because we'd lost nothing. But $100 was too great a loss, I thought, for the woman to suffer.

Mama was elusive. I didn't find her for another three hours. "I think we made a mistake," I said, shoving all the money across the table to her.

"What are you doing?" she whispered sharply.

"We change money in the morning and the amount is not correct. Count it yourself."

Mama counted it, several times, and looked up at me with astonishment. "It is too much," she said.

I nodded. "Let us make it right."

Mama grabbed her heart and collapsed in a chair. I was debating the risks and ethics of CPR when she popped up and slathered me with kisses.

A while later, I returned to our table where money stories were still being spun. None of them would have returned it, they said. Just then the waiter bustled up with a feast of food and drink we had not ordered. We protested until the waiter confessed that Mama had. I found her watching from behind a reed fence. She followed me in order to show her appreciation. "Come eat with us," I said, taking her hand.

She said that she was not a money changer. She had done it this day only because she needed medication and treatments. Her husband had cancer and was dying. If she would have lost that money, they both would have lost all hope to save him.

Ten days and 312 miles later, in a small market near the town of Epula, a man came up to me. "Mama sends you a message," he said. I did not know him, nor did I know which Mama he spoke of. "She said to tell you that Papa died from the cancer last week. She said she is grateful to you." Unaccountably, I was stricken with grief, then by wonderment. We were accustomed to the rapidity of the African gossip line, such as advance announcements of our arrival; but this was the first time that a messenger had been sent to us.

Three trucks made up the Economic Tours caravan. The lead truck carried supplies, and the other two carried passengers. They were converted garbage trucks with built-in lockers and benches. Scaffolding supported a tarp roof that could be draped over the open sides when the weather turned bad. A small observation area was built over the cabin. Economic Tours was a no-frill, six-month expedition from London to Nairobi. Unlike other overlanders, they camped in the bush on the outskirts of towns and rarely visited restaurants. We liked them for that.

We were all assigned to the "couples truck," which was made up mostly of Australian professionals. The party truck of "singles" brought up the rear. The people on the tour were nice and polite, and they tried to make us feel comfortable by assuring us that the only sacred rule pertained to the rotation of cooking duties. They were scarcely aware of routines after four months of closeness. We volunteered for all work details, yet we were constantly pricked for our mistakes: "Greg always sits there." "I always pitch my tent next to Sally's." "Only non-meat eaters can have vegetables." The novelty of group travel quickly wore off.

The mindlessness of it robbed all the adventure of discovery.

There was none. The drivers worried with the road, where and when we camped, and supplies. The community within the truck found their own culture more gripping than the country we passed through. And, as a group, they were never free to step out of that role and experience any other.

The trucks roared through towns as fast as the engines would push us. The people saw us as one alien creature. A single white organism. Probably lifeless. The two-handed waves so common in central Africa were open-handed demands, "Give me a book, give me a Bic, give me, give me." Rocks were thrown and taunts of *musungu,* whitey, were meant to insult. We stopped in a few towns, and we quickly learned why the drivers avoided them. In Oysha, many hundreds gathered to watch our traveling, roadside attraction. They tried to enter the trucks with food bowls in hand. The police had to avert a nasty situation. The Africa and Africans of our hearts were beyond our reach, beyond our experience. They became a glob, a single organism, existing outside the boundaries of our trucks.

Once a day, we broke by a river for exactly thirty minutes. We'd run as fast as we could, juggling soap and shampoo, dirty clothes and detergent, and water bottles. To accomplish all the tasks in the allotted time called for creativity and total disregard for modesty.

Lynn ran away the second day. Her mental health was precarious; her departure abrupt and crazy. No one escaped feeling anguished worry for her, least of all Ngaire, who was already worn down by her own struggle with death. Stephanie and Ngaire left us several days later to look for Lynn. They survived two days on the Zaire trucks and came back. Lynn was alive. She had been spotted, but was totally unapproachable. Ngaire said that Lynn looked wild, as if she had flipped out. Another day, we all saw Lynn flitting through a village. She ran when she saw us. Ngaire plotted ways to kidnap Lynn home to New Zealand once we were out of the jungle.

The road to Goma in eastern Zaire was a mere red gash in green walls. Tall stalks of bamboo intertwined high overhead like a dense thatched roof. Wild pineapples, bromeliads, and bananas struggled for light and space against the greedier big trees. It was beautiful and dangerous. Branches lashed through the open-sided trucks and slashed at our heads.

Killer bees attacked when the lead truck grazed their hive. One of the overlanders in our truck, Clyde, instantly swelled like a lumpy blimp. And with it came the onset of respiratory cardiac failure. "Get out of here! Move! Now! Now!!" We screamed and thumped the sides of the truck. The drivers heard our alarm and, without questions, moved through the potholes at reckless speed. Clyde went into shock. We pumped antihistamines into him, and at the first stream, carried his near lifeless body into the cold water. Slowly, his breathing and heart rate regained strength.

Although Clyde's life was probably saved by basic first aid, the two nurses in the group stood by helpless—just as the Dutch medical students had not recognized their own symptoms of malaria and dehydration. Robb and I fumed at them until I remembered something told to me by Linda, the American doctor in Liberia. "We are so accustomed to diagnostic equipment, consultations, gleaming clean facilities and medicines, that we are almost paralyzed here. We don't know how to transfer our knowledge."

Often thunderstorms (Thor's hammer) pounded the earth like a drum, and a thousand jagged fingers of lightning clawed the night sky. Wind-whipped tree canopies sang. Somewhere in the deep forest the roots of a giant tree would rip free and the long crash to the ground could be heard for several minutes. We troughed around our tent each night. The baked mud would merely chip under the blade of the juju cutlass. The next morning the ground would be squishy and slippery.

The second night out the ground quaked. It was so imperceptible that no one noticed but us. We had survived a devastating earthquake in El Salvador, and it was embedded in our memories. The slightest shiver set off panic alarms.

It happened again on the third night, and still no one remarked on it. We sweated with anxiety, clasped hands, and tried to still our runaway fears. On the fourth night the ground beneath us heaved. The trucks swayed as if they would topple. The overlanders screamed as they crawled from their tents. Wide-eyed, Robb and I assessed our position. We were in a large clearing, a mud bog. Even if the tallest tree fell, it would not touch us. No escarpment or hill loomed to slide its mud-and-rock face upon us. "It's time for us to face this," said Robb. "We are in a good spot to live it through." We laid down again. Together, we tried to relax by imagining we were on a vibrating bed in an American motel. Mentally, we dropped quarters into the locked box. The muddy ground shook. I guess it was fun after a while.

With each day out from Kisangani, travel got more treacherous. The clay road deteriorated under the nightly storms. Then, early one morning, we ground to a halt. Steve and Janet, the drivers of the lead truck and "our guides," lept from their cabs.

"It's a mud hole," bellowed Steve with a New Zealand accent. "We'll need all the shovels and help we can get! It's a big one, too, so you better hop to or we will be here tomorrow."

Slowly my eyes took in the scene. I counted twenty-three trucks, twelve stick houses, one mud church. Several dozen people squatted by the roadside on the fringe of a bamboo forest with metal pointed spears, bows and arrows, and one antique musket. Mired in the middle of all this was a truck towing two trailers. They were almost completely buried in one giant red mud hole. The truck drivers had been standing around scratching their heads since the previous afternoon. It did seem like the appropriate gesture.

Steve grabbed a chain saw from the back of his truck and, without a word, stalked to the edge of the forest. The rest of us grabbed shovels or machetes and followed. A small group of women cranked up a fire and cooked pancakes and tea. Although it was our first mud hole, we went to work as if it were something we did every day of our lives. Actually, it was quite simple to figure out: the truck and trailers would have to be dug free, trees felled and split to use as ramps, the truck towed and pushed free, and then the hole would have to be filled in to make a passable road. Simple, but very slow and laborious—especially after the chain saw broke.

At least four layers of trees, laid in a crosshatched pattern, were swallowed in the soft mud of the pit. The next four layers raised the slippery pit to chest height. Each truck was towed by the one in front and pushed from behind. We cringed with each threatening wobble, with each splintering crunch of logs breaking under such great weight. Between each vehicle, the road had to be rebuilt. Then, after six hours, we broke free to the other side.

We did not rest until eleven-thirty that night. Every few kilometers another yawning mud pit entrapped yet another truck. Some had toppled in the deep ruts and laid on their sides. A major rear spring broke in one of our trucks. Steve replaced it at one in the morning, but the next day it broke again. A block of wood was jammed into the undercarriage, but the truck tilted precariously to one side. The days seemed endless. Up at 4:00 A.M., to bed at 1:00 A.M., and in between we dug, cut, built, pushed, pulled, cooked, and cleaned. We crawled into our sleeping bags covered in red mud and bug bites.

Camp was often made in the road because of the density of the surrounding jungle. It was also Pygmy country. It was not unusual to see them squatting by our camp, in the periphery of the firelight. In the cold, predawn darkness, they would still be there. When we were fortunate enough to find a bathing stream, a tribe might quietly emerge from the forest to watch. They were as fascinated by us as we were by them.

The Pygmies are super short. The children appeared to be of normal height, but when their heads scraped three feet they seemed to simply stop growing. Of normal proportions, they are simply short. One young girl carried a baby on her back. I thought she was maybe five years old and helping her mother. What a shock when she put a prepubescent-looking nipple into the baby's mouth to feed! They are accomplished hunters. They use small bamboo bows and arrows, with dry leaves instead of feathers to control the flight, to hunt birds and small animals. They use large nets to snare the larger animals. Hunting camps dotted their territory. The huts were half shells constructed with a crosshatch of pliable sticks and covered with leaves. They were prone to leak, as we learned one day when we took shelter during a storm. I think the Pygmies stayed too stoned to ever finish them completely; even children puffed on fat, cigar-sized cannabis joints.

Epulu was a breeding station for the rare okapi. A thick-necked animal that looked like a big-eared zebra, the okapi was in the camel family. The breeding station was a much-needed rest and recreation stop.

A small town provided a source of Primus beers, but little in the way of much-desired fruit and vegetables. Only a few stalks of ripened bananas hung from the rafters of the meager market. Oh, how our bodies ached from nutrition depletion! Several weeks without sufficient fruit or vegetables had ravaged our bodies' stored resources. I examined my face in a hand mirror and barely recognized myself. What little hair was left on my head was white. Robb's beard was streaked with a zone of grey, and his hair was so thin it wasn't worth combing. Deep lines etched our gaunt faces. The youthful, elastic glow of health we had at the start of the trip was gone. I read that one year in the tropics would sap ten years from your life. We had lost perhaps thirty.

A lovely river ran alongside the Epulu campgrounds. Fast-moving, smooth rock rapids were great for water races. But the races came to a screeching halt when someone slid down the back of a mammoth crocodile. Mr. Croc staked out our swimming grounds as his hunting grounds. His big eyes bulged above the waterline as he waited to wrestle one of our bodies to the river bottom.

We quickly and abruptly broke camp late one afternoon after the arrival of an overland truck from the opposite direction. The road ahead was in such bad condition it had taken them four days to pass the 75 kilometers from Komanda to Beni.

Travel throughout the next afternoon was light. We emerged from the thick, fluorescent green of the jungle to open sloping hills and tall elephant grass. The sky again! Shortly past the town of Komanda, an oil leak demanded emergency attention. I walked ahead of the trucks for solitude and sunshine. Down the road danced a man totally oblivious to all but his private music. He strummed a thumb piano held between his hands as gently as if he were plucking the morning sun's rays. The tune and his movements were haunting, the rhythm mesmerizing. During those minutes, I thought I was hearing a movie sound track. Sometimes reality can be understood only by its imitation.

The road ahead turned into a redundant bad dream.[1] It was more of the same, except now the trucks chugged up deep mountain passes. We could walk faster and frequently did so, then waited several miles ahead for the trucks to catch up. It was misty and bitter cold. One of the most uncomfortable nights yet was spent on the equator.

The Zairean jungle changed abruptly in the region of the tea plantations. Alpine-like meadows, mud houses with steep pitched roofs, and tall trees strung with spidery, light green Spanish moss gave the impression of tropical Swiss villages. Herds of cattle with big u-shaped horns ambled to the prodding of blanket-wrapped Masai herders. We learned the Kiswahili greeting *jambo hibari* when we stopped for the joy of joys—a vegetable and fruit stand! That night we feasted on vegetable stew: cabbage, tomatoes, and onions followed by mangos, pineapple, paw paws, and tree tomatoes. It was like the antidote to the sleep of zombies.

Virunga National Park is a wildlife reserve on a vast open plain bordered by distant volcanic cones and, on the far side, by Lake Idi Amin. Steve finagled in-transit passes, which circumvented the park fee of $100 U.S. per person. The condition was that we could not spend the night in the park. Both by plan and by accident, we missed the sunset deadline. The unavoidable delays were in digging our trucks, and other trucks, out of the mud. The plan was to see as much wildlife as possible without paying. Topi, Ugandan Cob antelope, horned warthogs, baboons, and buffalo bounded across the plain. Fat hippos snorted from mud baths and flocks of brilliantly colored birds arched through the sky like rainbows. A lovely sulfur spring bubbled from crystalline rock. The water was almost too hot to touch and stung divinely on our blister-studded hands.

The gate guard would not let us exit since we had tarried past sunset. We'd have to wait until morning and pay the park fees, but "No camping allowed! No cooking fires!" Three local trucks were caught in the same snare, yet they were allowed to tend blazing fires and to sleep by their warmth. Janet, one of the tour leaders, brushed her golden red hair over her shoulders and seductively hunkered down with the guards to negotiate our release. She got us through.

It was midnight before we stopped to camp next to Rutshuru Falls. The full moon lit its frothy cascade and fern-covered banks. While others waded in the icy pool, Robb and I worked dinner and breakfast detail. We were too tired to fully erect our tent, so we let its middle droop over our middles. Night was transformed into dawn with barely time to flutter an eyelash in sleep.

The camp broke into groups. Some would pay ($100 U.S.) to see the lowland gorillas, while others would do something else. It was time to part company. Ten days with an overland expedition was

enough. They got us over the worst roads of Africa intact. Economic Tours and its passengers demonstrated a strength and endurance that was irreproachable; at the same time, we were not
pack animals. The infighting and secret rules, and the isolation
and taunts from the Zairean people got to us. Freedom was
sweeter than the sadness of separating from friends.

Goma was only twenty-eight kilometers from the point where
we began walking and hitching. It took eight hours and three vehicles to get us there: there were beer stops, stops to pick up charcoal and lime, more stops for passengers, and stops for flat tires
until there were no more spare tires. Six of us waited under a rain-
heavy sky for another ride. A little Toyota pickup truck groaned
down the road under a seven-foot mound of potatoes, tires, and at
least twelve people crowned that. Their legs bounced over the
sides. "Come with us," they called gaily. "Come up tourists." We
hesitated. An old man urged, "Go with them, little Mama, before
the rains come." From the truck the invitation was chorused,
"Come next to me, Mama. There is room for you and Papa." We
waved farewell to the other waiters as we creaked and tottered off
to Goma.

I would have fallen off if an old man with long, sinewy arms
and knobby hands had not hugged me tightly. Robb clung onto
my leg, a woman and her child on my right arm. I could not see
the face of the grandfather who anchored us all, but I loved him.
We were home again in the cradling bosom of Mama and Papa
Africa.

Laughter and squeals bounced off the truck as it entered
Goma, a frontier town at the migratory juncture of truck, car,
boat, and plane routes. A resortish atmosphere garnished Goma.
White block walls spilled over with bright pink, red, and orange
bougainvillea. Moss-strewn oaks shaded the streets, and, in the
center of town, wood promenades were shaded by roof overhangs.
Extinct volcanic cones jutted in the distance. Blue Lake Kivu
shimmered fancifully. I was told, though, that no one swims or
fishes in the alkaline water.

We wanted from Goma a shower, rest, food, and transport out.
They all came, in time. Stephanie came too. We thought we had
separated when, at Rutshuru Falls, sweet Josef left for Ruwenzoris in Uganda, and Ngaire and Stephanie left to see the gorillas.

Stephanie, however, had to be rushed to the Goma hospital when malarial fevers racked her body. Typical of malaria victims, she discharged herself from the hospital and did not follow up on the medication. For weeks to come her moods and strength vacillated with the fever.

The Lake Kivu ferry from Goma to Bukavu was, of course, crowded. The character of the people was different from any we'd met. Babies whined stridently for seven nerve-racking hours. These were the first babies we heard cry in all Africa, and they made up for every other silent one. The elders bickered relentlessly over seating and leg space. They also got hostile when we refused to give them our food. "It is our way of life to share," said one man. Yet, when we demanded food from them, the sharing concept broke down. All of the behaviors were of unmitigated self-indulgence. If community spirit ever existed, it was long ago ruthlessly torn out by the roots and left to wither from greedy neglect.

We did not expect such a change in behaviors and were unpleasantly shocked. North, west, and central Africa had been homogenous with respect to courtesy. Military personnel and police were brutes, but people were kind and considerate of each other. Lake Kivu, for me, was like crossing an invisible line dividing west from east.

Bukavu town was more picturesque than Goma and also more confusing. Little finger peninsulas, harbors, and bowl valleys made the structure of town somewhat difficult to navigate and neighborhoods were fragmented. It was remarkable in one aspect: real cheese and sausages! While waiting for Burundi visas, Robb and I hosted a cheese-and-sausage dinner party for the other *muzungus,* the Kiswahili word for whites.[2] It had taken us fifty-nine days to cross the heart of Africa. We had only one day left on our Zaire visas, so we had no choice but to leave early the next morning. I regretted leaving central Africa as much as I rejoiced in the nearness of the Indian Ocean, which was still a month away.

At the border of Rwanda, we got in-transit visas, real coffee, and a lesson in *trompo*—standing at attention while the flag was raised. Rwanda was hilly, almost mountainous, and beautiful where the land hadn't been stripped of every twig. This minuscule country supports almost seven million people and an enormous flux of refugees. To compensate for what the land cannot provide, tourists from the east are exploited through high prices. The major tourist attraction, a visit to the mountain gorillas of Dian Fossey fame, was $150 a day. A portion of the money probably maintained the parks, but more likely the hard currencies were absorbed by the government like a thirsty person on the Sahara absorbs water.

Like the nationals, we had little or no access to hard currency. It would have been folly to carry it that distance. A mere $50 American cash remained to pad us in an emergency. None of us who had traveled independently from west to east or long-term, had the cash, even if we had the means, to pay for the parks. I think bitterness set in with the discriminatory policy. From Rwanda on, we would meet tourists who described the African experience in terms of safaris, wildlife parks, and souvenirs.

Burundi. We spent a week in Bujumbura, the capital, while waiting for the Lake Tanganyika ferry to Tanzania. The ferry had been out of commission for three months, so competition for a ride was keen. We had to inquire daily at the harbor office to find out when it would run, which meant we could not stray far from the city.

We stayed at the Johnsons, a missionary family who ran schools and clinics, and hobnobbed with the national and international power elite. It was a wise alignment since they had been threatened with eviction from Burundi several times. For travelers and savvy short-term tourists on the cheap, the Johnsons were parents, friends, and shelter, who asked little in return except a helpful hand. Breakfast was served with a non-denominational prayer that was acceptable to even the quasi-animistic.

In Bujumbura, Burundi, Robb shaved his beard of fourteen years. Without it, he looked ten years younger. I sulked with jealousy. There was nothing I could do to shed my grandmotherly appearance. At the start of the trip I was called "Sister." Then, gradually, I became "Mama." Now, more frequently, "Grandmother."

Beyond the prying eyes of Africa, I resumed exercising and walking through the hills. Movement was such a part of our lives I felt vertigo standing still, and walking took us away from the other travelers. After months together on riverboats and overland trucks, and in one-room, shared accommodations (like at the Johnsons), I yearned for private time—to know my own thoughts and make my own decisions without having to seek a group consensus. With many people traveling the same road at the same time, claustrophobia was inevitable. As Robb pointed out to me, "We are on the tourist route now. This is east Africa, and it's June, the start of tourist season. It will be like this from now on, so get used to it."

Lake Tanganyika defined the limits of Bujumbura. It gleamed under the bright sun like liquid mercury. Other days, low dark clouds and murmuring thunder rolled across the water to nestle in the surrounding hills. A local celebration was marked by ululations and drumming. A poor row of shacks lined the dirt path that led to the main road. "Hello Johnsons," people called to the white tribe.

Robb and I joined our African neighbors for the five o'clock beer hour.[3] The kids were pesky and their parents oblivious, until we took the strategic offense of creating a diversion for the kids. We made instruments with bottle caps and a cooty catcher from a scrap of paper. Each corner of the cooty catcher was labeled with a number, a color, and prizes they knew and valued: Primus beer, Fanta, five hundred Burundi francs, and a Corolla car. The silly game captivated the adults as well. Within hours everyone at the brochette stands had cooty catchers. The children were shooed outside the circles of dancing adults, who were singing, clapping, and whistling to the rhythmic snap of tambourine bottle caps.

Several nights we went into Bujumbura city and partied at the clubs that started rocking only after our usual bedtime. They were clubs without names, where live bands pumped reggae and Zairean music into our veins like heroin. Dancers got so drunk they'd fall, lift their bloodied faces, and stumble on until sunrise. Abandonment was inseparable from the night. Regardless of initial pairing on the dance floor, men took men and women took women. The drunken mood was volatile. Robb and I exchanged glances over our partners' shoulders. During one slow dance, Robb waltzed with a man who grabbed at his testicles, while two fat mamas sandwiched me in undulating rolls of sweaty fat. With a smiling grimace, Robb said, "I should have shaved my beard earlier."

Late one night we got a ride home with a "Short," a Hutu, who wanted to know Americans. "They are not friends with the people, we know nothing of Americans. I don't want to go to America though. I think life is too hard, you must work too much and life here is easy."

It was four o'clock in the morning when we encountered a military blockade in the road. Unfortunately, they were bored. They were Tutsi, the "Talls," the tribe who slaughtered 200,000 Hutus in 1972 and sent 100,000 more into exile. So the Talls hassled our Short friend, the driver, then honed in on me and Robb. We went limp. We did not respond to their French, but acted with stupid docility. Our new friend was in jeopardy because he was with us. In total frustration, the police spat at our feet and ordered us to leave. "Whew!," our Hutu friend said later, "the military are barbarians, and that was close. Thank you. They were jealous of me, they wanted the money and gifts that you give me. That's Africa for you. Stronger than friendship is greed. But I think you know this. Your stupidity saved us."

Between the Johnson's breakfast table and embassy newspapers, we caught up with three months of news. The Zairean military had massacred 125 students asleep in their dormitory, an earthquake in Sudan had left 300,000 homeless (must have been the same one that rocked us), 20,000 Cameroon people had clashed with the military and six were dead, the French had been evacuated from Gabon and possibly from Cote d'Ivoire in the near future. In Liberia, Charles Taylor led his group of rebels within twenty miles of the capital and missionaries had been slaughtered. Gorbachev was in trouble with an insuppressible demand for autonomy coming from dissident republics. Cameroon was advancing in the World Cup of Soccer—a celebrated first for Africa.

We also caught up with news from home. The Johnsons allowed us to receive calls from home. An international phone call, like mail, was a rare event.

My mother's speech was so sharp that her acerbic humor cut through the miles. Unsanctimoniously, we were basted and carved like turkeys without reprieve.

Robb's mother was diagnosed with Parkinson's, a disease that debilitates the nervous system. So we transferred worry from one mother to another.

Travel philosophers sometimes romanticize "letting go" as a hedonistic voyage into a void. Letting go is certainly necessary to experience. But what are we if, in letting go, we forget those whom we've loved, and who have loved us in return?

PART V

Tanzania, Kenya, and Uganda

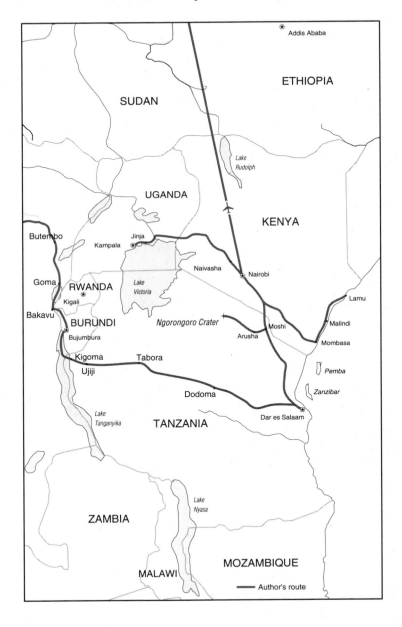

- 23 -

Where Stanley Met Livingstone

The Tanganyika ferry was mad! The entire crew, from the most petty level employee to the first chief officer, was piss drunk. No one could stand upright. They staggered off walls and grabbed imaginary props for balance. It stormed that night. Wind blew rain and spray across the open face of the metal deck, and the bathrooms flooded, which added treachery to the slippery surface. But it wasn't so rough that the reasonable person couldn't walk straight. Lake Tanganyika was thankfully narrow, or the navigator would have lost his way in drunken delirium. If it were daylight, I am sure we could have seen the boat weaving on its course.

Throughout the night, the ferry plied the dark waters south and east to the docks of Kigoma, Tanzania. The boat would lay over in Kigoma almost two days before it continued south another five days to Zambia.[1] Stephanie and a group of other travelers would take the boat to Zambia then cross overland to Malawi. Originally, they had planned to accompany us across Tanzania to Zanzibar, an island possession in the Indian Ocean. But overnight, Stephanie had grown suspicious of her boyfriend's fidelity and decided on the straight route home to Malawi. Despite urging us to alter our course, too, Robb and I disembarked in Kigoma. We had neither visas nor money for such a detour.

We parted company from Stephanie with only polite hugs, which was sad. We had shared much since Kinshasa: the Zaire riverboat, hitchhiking with Economic Tours, Stephanie's malaria, two ferries, and a cold. The stress of the travel had taken its toll. Weary of the necessary allegiance to one another, we waved to Stephanie like distant relatives glad to see each other go.

On our way into town we passed the train station. Robb and I ducked in to check on the schedule to Dar es Salaam, the capital of Tanzania, 720 miles to the east on the coast of the Indian Ocean. We were told the train ran sporadically. It would not be possible to get one for probably another five days. We were so accustomed to waiting that all of Africa was beginning to feel like one large waiting room. Kigoma was just another seat in it.

Every sign was printed in Kiswahili, so it was easy to learn the language. Yet, when the first person said, "You must learn Swahili. I will begin your lesson," something in me snapped. "I refuse to learn another language," I protested. Kiswahili would be the twentieth, maybe the hundredth, language we encountered since leaving home. Long gone was my enthusiasm for learning new languages. I was burned out. We barely spoke English any longer. It had degenerated into simple, present tense forms between ourselves. "See big man in rich car," adequately replaced oncefamiliar words like envy, affluent, and pomp.

Kiswahili, however, was the strand of homogeneity that wove east African people together: the African tribes, Indians, Arabs, "coloreds," and whites. It would be one of the most useful of all the languages. It was the first language since Arabic in which abstract concepts and future tenses could be expressed, and verbal communication took precedence over the physical, non-verbal type. With reluctant grumpiness, we began our first lesson.

Kigoma was a small town, so it did not take long to explore it and the hills bordering Lake Tanganyika. On the urban side, a strong Muslim presence dominated. Framed portraits of the Ayatollah hung over entryways. We found only two places in Kigoma that survived the Muslim influence: the Kigoma Hotel that doubled as a whorehouse, and the Railway Hotel that catered to upscale safaris.

They were a welcomed alternative to the Lake View Hotel where we stayed. It was predominantly African, which should have made it pleasant, except the new Africans were rude. Mothers regularly opened our door to thrust their bawling child into our faces. We suspected them of telling the children, "I will feed you to these *muzungu* monsters who eat babies." The game did not stop until we turned on the mothers with great roars, gnashing of teeth, and a monster-like stance. Then they would run. Our action preyed on their deepest fears—in their hearts, the mothers believed their own monster stories. We deeply resented the hostility and fear of whites these mothers were instilling in their children. It was not the way of the Africa we knew so far. Maybe it was the way of east Africa.

The main tourist attraction in northwest Tanzania was the Gombe Stream National park, the site of Jane Goodall's chimpanzee research. Admission to the park was $150, which excluded us with as much certainty as a private club excludes a pauper.

Gossips in town told us that a group of Americans on a three-week safari had pulled into town. Other than embassy employees, we had yet to meet another American on our trip, so we curiously strolled down to the Railway Hotel where they stayed. Their Banana Republic khaki shorts still hung with creases. When they learned we hadn't yet been on a "safari," they wandered away to recount the animals they had seen. (This word, safari, gives me problems. It literally means "trip." To the tourists, it specifically means a trip to the zoo.) Our worlds were too different to be of interest to each other.

Their guide, David, invited us for a drink (with a whispered plea to save him from the banalities of his clients). We swapped stories of Africa late into the warm starry night over warmer, less stellar bottles of Safari beer. The dust-weary miles faded, and our hearts lightened with laughter. Laughter was something we'd heard less frequently than the call of the loon. Our muscles twitched with unfamiliarity. Somewhere laughter had stopped.

Not that there hadn't been smiles and discrete giggles; but big-belly, full-throated chuckles were a cultural expression. Hearing it, feeling it, almost made us homesick. It was like missing potassium from our diet and not knowing it until we got an infusion.

While waiting for the train, we quickly ran out of things to do in tiny Kigoma. Long hikes into the hills assuaged cultural, economic, and linguistic isolation. Under the dry, hot sun, Robb and I healed the resentful wounds we had inflicted upon one another over the past months. No matter how much two people may love one another, when thrown together for fourteen months without a break, wounds are inflicted.

We followed meandering footpaths as if we were reading a book on the organization of small villages. Some paths were heavily trodden, like unmarked highways. Others were grown over with brambles. They were used at certain times of the year to drive the domestic herds or to go to harvest. They led through compounds and dried yellow grass to distant hilltops where the sky was pristine blue. Crisp, white clouds contorted into puffy elephants, rhinos, continents, and people that we knew. Fishing catamarans, sail-driven downwind and motor-driven upwind, shoved into the twilight of sunset. Purple heather covered the hills of Zaire across the lake and glowed red like a flame under the last light of day. And the tall sun-bleached grass of Tanzania looked so golden you only needed to gather it in your pocket to be rich for life.

I recalled the first path we walked in Africa. I was reluctant to cross someone's field or go through the middle of their compound—their house. That was before I understood that property was communal, and paths, wherever they might lead, were public byways. In 23,000 miles, our right to walk had never been challenged.

But here, suddenly, a woman confronted us on a curve of a jungle path. She was snarling like a bulldog.

"What is your tribe?" she growled. "What is your reason to be on our land?"

We calmly stood still and lowered our eyes to the ground in respect. "Mother, we are walking only," we said. "May we walk?"

She too stood silently. A bold, brightly colored print cloth wrapped her hips, another bloused from her shoulders. She carried nothing on her head nor a baby on her back. She emanated power. Likewise, we were scrutinized.

"Yes," she said finally. "Go in peace. Walk well."

A magpie group of naked children hounded our heels with cries of "Good morning, good teacher!" A form of greeting so polite and innocuous that, after so many curses, we could not ignore them or shoo them away. "Good morning, good students," we responded. Their number swelled with parents, until under a baobab tree in the center of a thatched village, everyone sang, "Teacher, teacher, Good morning."

I tried to imagine the *muzungu* who had such an effect on this isolated village. I tried to imagine what he or she would say next. Our walk would be burdened by followers, maybe taunters, if we did not play the scenario correctly. "Good morning students," I said loudly with the authority of a teacher. "Please take your seats." Without hesitation sixty people—men, women, elders, and children—sat on the ground beneath that baobab tree. Their eyes peered back unafraid but patiently waiting. Uh, oh. What came next? A lecture? In simple English I sallied forth among uncomprehending eyes. "We are from America," I began. Then I warmed up and talked about the regions of Africa and about millet. Robb gave me the signal to wind it up. I didn't want to, but I must admit I'd carried the story too far. I ended the lesson as I thought the white teacher might have ended hers: "Now, we will all stand and sing." It worked. All sixty stood up and started singing one song. I would have liked to have known more about that song, but Robb grabbed my hand and pulled me out of town.

"You carried that much too far," he remonstrated.

Yeah, but it was fun.

Ujiji was a nearby town, but far enough away that we needed to take the *matatu*—the local truck. Ujiji isn't a name that attracts recognition like Mecca, Mombasa, or London, yet it fills a niche in history. It is the site where Stanley met Livingstone in 1871 and where Burton met Speke in 1858. These four men and their dogmatic clashes probably did more to change central and east Africa than any other four men in contemporary history. For different motives and with very differing results, they opened this region to colonialism, Christianity, and resource exploitation. A small building, garden, and two bronze plaques commemorate their visits. Two stylized, caricature-like statues depict Stanley and Living-stone doffing their helmets. Something about it reminded me of the town in Nigeria where the slave traders and missionaries had first arrived. The water of Lake Tanganyika had receded a quarter mile, just like the memory—but not the legacy—of their explora-tions had receded. The legacy of life before their explorations was also preserved. It was painted on the mud walls of the few stores and restaurants in town—proud paintings of local life, of the mar-kets and fishermen, of life without the white man.

Finally, the whistle of the train blared its departure for Dar es Salaam. First class accommodations were great—great in the Brit-ish colonial style. It was a slice of time preserved, except the faces were all black instead of white. Meals, consisting of curried meat, rice with cloves, and cabbage salad, were announced by a me-lodic, hand-held xylophone. Clear glass goblets, porcelain plates, and only semi-used linen napkins welcomed the diner into an-other world. By night, cabin stewards turned down cracked leather bunks, polished cinders from the mahogany furniture, and wrapped beds in swaddling blankets. Very civilized.

Otherwise, everything was as we knew it to be. And that was good, reassuring. The narrow passageways filled with commuters and their bundles. Sunrise was a ceremony of teeth-brushing that would satisfy the heart of any dentist but make a fastidious per-son cringe. Every window and doorway was crowded with twig-brushing, spitting people. Frothing spittle flew out one window and blew into the next. The floor became slimy. There was no electricity and no running water. We spat on our hands to clean them.

The train rumbled past withered plots of corn, brown grass as high as an elephant's ear, plains, and distant mountains that, upon approach, weren't mountains at all, but clouds. It rolled past tiny stations, rectangular houses with mud walls and steeply slanted tin roofs. One dusty road, little more than a footpath, ran parallel to the tracks through the grass and shrub. The sky was brilliant azure by day, and by night, a midnight blue irradiated the cabins.

The train made frequent but short stops. Like the Zaire and Ni-ger riverboats, the train was a market. One stop was for carved animals—giraffes, wildebeests or flamingos all striped or dotted with shoe polish. Another stop was for cornstalk weavings—mats and baskets. At another, sabers in wood sheaths. And at another, used shoes. The merchants hung from windows to shout their bids for quantities too big to compute. Boys with white painted legs ran the length of the train to deliver the goods through any open window and collect the money, which was passed hand to hand. The most important stops, however, were those for food—tomatoes, raw potatoes, fruit, grapes, honey, curried brochettes, and samosas.

We had tickets for as far as Tambora, which was not quite midway to Dar. A policy of the Tanzanian railroad was to reserve first class cabins for university students returning home at the end of the school year. Tambora was the site of a vocational college, so our pleas for a straight fare to Dar yielded nothing more than advice from the TTT, the ticket taker, not to give up our seats—no matter what. Twenty-two hours out of Kigoma, with 520 miles dividing us from Dar, we reached Tambora. Our cabin was sold to a university woman, a secretarial student on her way home, traveling alone but in the company of friends in flanking cabins. When the demure young woman claimed our cabin as her own, we struck a deal to share it. That was fine with her. We consummated the deal with food and an agreement that we would watch each other's belongings while the other roamed.

A new TTT boarded at Tambora, and he had a different idea. It was illegal and immoral for people of different sexes to share cabins. The student and I could stay together, but Robb would have to stand in the corridor. That was unacceptable to our agreement, and all three of us argued eloquently. The student said she would only keep her things in our cabin and would sleep with her friends.

"No, no! It is not permitted!" the TTT ranted.

Finally, after rambunctious argument, the TTT moved Robb and me to his own cabin. Indignantly, and probably just to irritate the TTT, the women invited us back to our cabin.

"We don't like being told what to do," she said in halting English. "Leave your things here and come stay with us. We make a nice lunch." For the next twenty-four hours, until the train chugged into the Dar station, we stayed together. The TTT scowled his displeasure with all of us.

At first glimpse, Dar Es Salaam, the capital of Tanzania,

looked seedy, worn down. The skyscape was dominated by pre-modern buildings inscribed with dates and names like "Aga Khan 1883." Others were lattice-laced like wedding cakes. Spires of clock towers poked above the low skyline. The hands of the clocks were frozen. I imagined them stopping at the exact hour of independence from British domination. Who needed reminders that things ran late?

Many businesses were closed, attesting to economic hard times. Many streets were unpaved or deeply rutted by overuse and capital neglect. The hotels were all full. We found a room in Hotel Internationale next to a Pentecostal church that rocked every evening with country/western guitar-picking, hallelujahs, and hand-clapping.

The hotel was run by three Indian brothers who also owned the one remaining drive-in theater. They invited us out several evenings, and on the way we toured the posh suburbs of embassies and mansions.

Our hosts bemoaned the advent of VCRs. "They've wrecked the movie business. We used to get three thousand people a night, but now we get only a hundred or so." Whereas imported films were government-regulated, videotapes were smuggled past their scrutiny.

The Indians of Dar were in general a gregarious lot, whose hospitality seemed to include generosity to strangers. We met many while waiting for the boat, a sailboat called a *dhow*, to Zanzibar. One Indian, who owned a stamp kiosk in the big Kilimanjaro Hotel, took us home every night because he didn't like us out on the streets at night. Others invited us to tea or to the Sunday sunset vigil on the banks of the Indian Ocean. Thousands of Indians in silky saris contemplated the sunset glow until it ceased to reverberate in the eastern sky. The *dhows*, introduced by the Arabs, filled the harbor with full, billowy sails that changed color with the light.

The waterfront of Old Town was always active: food kiosks, impromptu bands, the arrival and departure of buses, people pressing for home, and children frolicking. Containerized freighters unloaded at the many docks under bright lights or the even brighter sun. If other sections of Old Town suffered from unimportance, the waterfront did not.

Scarcities of everything had plagued the Tanzanians, *Tangazos*, since independence in 1961. President Ali Hasan Mwinyi, the second president, was as strong-willed as the first president, Nyerere, had been. Nyerere had led the nation into a brand of socialism with the formation of village cooperatives called *ujamma*. The *ujamma* forced relocations of people and even towns. The *ujamma* were never successful, and resentment ran as deeply as economic failure.

"The marketing boards buy up everything that is produced at a price that is below the market. Then the farmer has to buy it back at a higher price in order to consume it himself. Often the products are not picked up, and the farmer cannot afford to pay the price so it sits and rots," said one man.

At the time of independence, sisal and groundnuts were the main export items, and in the early 1990s they still remain the main products.

"Look at all this sisal here," said a dock worker poking a mound with his toe. "It goes nowhere. There are many new fibers that are as strong. Who will pay to export this when they can produce something as good?"

We traversed all of Dar in search of seafood, but there was none to be found except the small fish netted in the interior lakes.

"Are there no ocean fish here?" we asked.

The reply was often a shrug. "Who knows? Who knows why we don't have the food we produce."

One young man whose father had been an official with the East African Community—a trade alliance between Kenya, Ethiopia, Uganda, Burundi, and Zimbabwe—said, "We need a common currency to make the trade work. As it is, we are supposed to sell our products to each other first, but at a preferential price below the world market. Foreign exchange is such a big problem for our countries. Why would Kenya, for example, sell to Tanzania and convert their shillings for ours when they can sell to Europe and get hard currency? The PTA, Preferential Trade Agreement, works only on paper. Maybe it will get better with the new credit checks that can be cashed at equal value in another member country. I don't know. It is paper."

He was articulate and savvy. We asked him if he had attended the university.

"I cannot go to college," he said. "It is too expensive. Only those with scholarships from companies or the government can attend." Opportunity in Tanzania, as in all the African countries, was based on tribal affiliation. Until the ruling tribe stepped down from power, or a benefactor appeared, he would never gain access to the wheels of influence.

Underlying the complaints repeated throughout the country was a tone of hopefulness, and not resignation. "We hope it will work, we hope it will get better. We will work hard for a few more years and see what happens." Much blame was passed to Idi Amin, who invaded Tanzania in 1978 intending to annex it to Uganda. The war was bitter, and it cost thousands of lives and "all our resources."

Newspapers labored under government censorship, but still managed to print far more news of the nation and the world than any we'd read in Africa. While other dictators brutally tried to stifle the movement for pluralism, President Mwinyi declared a period of open debate on the subject; the will of the people would be followed. The moratorium was met with skepticism.

"We will talk about it. Mostly the government will talk about it, and it will do as it has always done. Nothing will change. A multiparty system will never work in Tanzania. We are too many people with too much hate."

– 24 –
The Spices of Life from Zanzibar to Safari

Zanzibar is an enchanted island that lives up to all the exotica its name and reputation implies. It is a gastronomic paradise. My dreams of pizza and tacos faded to insignificance in this gourmet's heaven. I cannot speak the name Zanzibar without recalling vivid images of food and the sweet scent of cloves, without remembering its incredible lightness and abundance....But, like a hedonist relating an orgy and skipping the build to the climax, I am getting ahead of the story.

The *dhow* puttered out of the Dar bay with at least fifty people on its thirty-foot wood deck. For a while it ran parallel to the shoreline and squat waterfront buildings. Hundreds of pillowy sails skimmed the mirror-like water. The mainland looked so surreal I could not imagine we had ever actually stepped foot on the continent.

A gentle, warm breeze licked the morning chill. The sun toasted the moist sails, and the rising heat filled them. Away from shore, the engine was cut and we sailed free. The rope lines and wood hull creaked musically. The bow dipped into the waves of the Indian Ocean and tossed spray on our sizzling skin. Once dried, the salt made us look like a pride of white spotted leopards. The sight of fifty people huddled on that little boat looked no more real to me than the receding view of land. I chuckled thinking of the boarding procedure. The port officials had adamantly segregated us into two lines—one for men and one for women. Ritualized propriety was abandoned once on board. We were an indistinguishable heap. A canvas canopy, meant to shade the hold, merely baked the people beneath it like a convection oven. As the sea swelled and the sun burned more intensely, several passengers clawed to the rails. Regardless of sex, someone, anyone would hold them fast while their faces hung overboard.

The day was glorious. Even the sun was beautiful. There wasn't a cloud in the blue sky, and the water was a deep turquoise. With physical familiarity came jocular companionship. Two *muzungu* women rode the freeboard with us. We met while trying to get the dhow tickets. (We had camped out for two days at the Dar ticket office.) Blonde Kristin was a Peace Corps volunteer in Tanzania so she spoke fluent Kiswahili. The other woman was a Chinese-American whose name was Evonne. In a vague, roundabout way, Evonne was traveling toward "home" after a stint at Peking University, and she had stopped in Tanzania to visit Kristin, her college roommate.

The men around us gaped in wonderment at our animated conversation. Kristin translated their comments, which were directed toward Evonne.

"They say they are surprised she speaks our tribal language. They want to know what tribe she is from, and where are the others."

We all failed to convince them that Evonne was a member of our tribe. The men giggled as if it were a joke.

Before the old Arab fort or the towering facade of the Beit-el-Ajaib could be seen, Zanzibar could be smelled. Over the crashing waves wafted a perfume of cloves and jasmine. It was like a heady aphrodisiac. Such scents and spices were once more valued than gold. They had lured many foreigners to these shores: Sumerians, Phoenicians, Assyrians, Indians, Egyptians, Chinese, Portuguese, Indians, Arabs, and Germans. Zanzibar was so important that Oman claimed it as its capital. It did not unite with Tanzania until their independence from the British in 1963.

It still maintained a spirit of independence and historic pride separate from the mainland (six hours away by *dhow*). Immediately upon arrival, everyone was ushered through Zanzibar's own customs and immigration. They required a separate currency declaration and mandatory exchange of $40. Robb and I took advantage of the confusion and snuck away.

The Malindi Guest House could have been the Taj Mahal: large breezy rooms, woven rugs on the floor and walls, clean mosquito nets billowing around each broad bed, and walls that changed color like the sails of the dhows at sunset. It even had large, clean bathrooms! We had not realized how far we had strayed from "niceties" until the western guests stared when we buttered our breakfast toast with our fingers and picked up our eggs with our hands. Surrounded by cleanliness and neatness, we appeared scraggly. Our frayed backpacks were sewn with dental floss. Our clothing hung on skeletal frames, and thousands of miles of travel grit was imbedded under our fingernails. Our minds were accustomed to darkness: the darkness of the jungle and dirt, the darkness that absorbs a kerosene lamp or a ten-watt light bulb in a cheap room, the darkness of night when refugees from the hot sun come out to play, the darkness of mammy wagons crowded with so many people that light cannot penetrate the dusky interior.

Conversely, Zanzibar was lightness and sunshine. It was resplendent with perfumed odors, colors, tastes, flowers, and cultures. It beckoned us to come out of our silent dark world.

We went reef snorkeling from a dhow several times. Clear water rippled over us where, before, only brownish water from a bucket had trickled. On the often-empty beaches the sun was no longer an oppressor; it became a gentle lover. Zanzibar gave graciously, but its best gift was that of food.

By night, Zanzibar twinkled like the indigo heaven. Thousands of cooking fires enticed everyone into the streets to savor the fruits of the day. The waterfront park was a veritable carnival of food. For just a few cents a serving, you could choose from a smorgasbord of octopus, squid, kingfish, or shrimp marinated in coconut

milk and seared over a charcoal fire. Wads of flavored rice or potatoes came wrapped in paper or leaves. Brochettes of liver or
chicken were rolled in fresh *pili-pili,* a spicy hot sauce. Cane juice
was squeezed from a press. Ice cream was churned into creamy
scoops, topped with nuts, and dripping with fruit—mango, paw-
paw, banana. Peanut brittle was dessert. Our taste buds erupted
with delight after a diet of bland, nutrition-deficient fou-fou.

Mr. Mitu operated the most expensive spice tour on the island.
His trademark was a dilapidated yellow taxi with "Mr. Mitu"
scrawled on the door. He never solicited clients. Tourists had to
beg him while the imitators hawked. Evonne and Kristin found
him and signed us up for a tour before asking us. We went anyway
and spent a pleasant day eating beyond fullness. An Australian
family peddling by bike from South Africa to Egypt also joined us
with their two tow-headed daughters.

Zanzibar was hostage to a crime wave. The ills of mainland cities had invaded paradise. Theft was rampant and stories proliferated of *dala-dalas* (the island name for a mammy wagon) being
robbed by knife- and machete-wielding miscreants. Many *dala-
dalas* cut back service to remote areas of the island, and night
service was eliminated altogether.

One islander said, "Each year at Ramadan, theft increases because people must buy four new outfits and food for the feasts.
All three hundred police on the island are paid by the company
who owns all the food. These police do nothing to stop the crime
and this year, after Ramadan, the thefts do not stop but get worse.
We do not know what to do. We have no protection."

Mr. Mitu worked for his reputation. Unfortunately, less ethical
impostors exploited it. We heard of several groups of tourists who
were taken to the pirate caves, robbed, and left stranded in the
countryside.

It was easy to get disoriented among the narrow, twisted streets
of old town Zanzibar. Doorways were studded with silver and or-
nate carvings of lotuses. The "brring-brring" of bicycle bells temporarily parted the waves of Muslim women draped in *fatu,* black
dresses, men in spotlessly white long shirts, black Africans in col-
orfully patterned garments, and Indians in saris. Shops were iden-
tically filled with dry goods, spices, silver, and gold. The only
scarce item on the island was beer. Two restaurants served it after

sunset. Ironically, a twenty-four-hour liquor store on a small alley did a fast-paced business in the world's finest rums, whiskeys, and vodkas.

From Zanzibar, our plan was to take a dhow north to the Pemba Islands. From there we would take another *dhow* to Mombasa on the Kenya mainland. This was sometimes possible according to the Malindi Sports Club, who kept track of the boats. We extended our sojourn in Zanzibar several days while waiting for the "wrong winds" to swing "right." They never did. Pemba was out of reach for another two, maybe three weeks. Zanzibar had seduced us for ten days, but to remain much longer and take the iffy *dhow* route through Pemba was a pragmatically unrealistic course.

We needed money, and Nairobi, Kenya, was the first possible place to replenish our supply. Our money stash had dwindled to less than $200 since Nigeria, where we had last drawn travelers checks from our American Express account. Also nagging our minds was what to do about work: Robb's leave of absence expired in twenty days. We were beginning to dream of home, but not so much that either of us wanted to call it quits. There was so much more to see! We finally decided to procrastinate our decision. We would head on to Kenya, restock our money supply, and there decide our fate.

We took a dhow back to Dar Es Salaam and, from there, the eighteen-hour train north to Moshi at the base of Mt. Kilimanjaro. Our seat faced a short Muslim man who simmered in smoke. Great puffs and wreathes of smoke secreted from his ears. The man did not seem to notice. I tried not to notice. If water had been nearby I would have doused him. Finally I said, "Excuse me, you are on fire."

He flipped a cigarette out of his mouth with a flick of his tongue, then flipped it back into hiding. Then he explained. "The British made a law making it illegal for *Mussulmen* to smoke or drink. It was their joke against our religion. We still have this law, though, and one year in prison is the penalty." His eyes closed. Smoke emanated from his ears. "We know each other. We know who does what and when. If someone does not like you, they can go to the police and say this man who is a *Mussulman* smokes a cigarette. He would be arrested. Many people are jealous for one reason or another, and they will accuse this thing." He then smoldered in silence.

There wasn't much in Moshi to keep us there for long. As a city, a newness surrounded it. It was devoid of personality and lackadaisically accustomed to the tourist horde who roosted there only long enough to put together a climbing expedition. The mysterious and mighty Kilimanjaro was tamed. All but the infirm could go for $150 a day, plus guides, plus food, plus the fee of the refuge, plus rental of equipment—sleeping bags, boots, rope, wood—plus transportation to and from. The climb totaled approximately $700 per person in hard currency. We stayed in Moshi long enough to witness the clearing of clouds from the famous peak. It lasted only five minutes.

Further to the west of Moshi was the town of Arusha, which was more to our liking. It too was a tourist town because the wildlife reserves of Lake Manyara, the Ngorongoro Crater, and the Serengeti encompassed much of the land to the west. Somehow Arusha escaped blatant commercialization and manifested the unique character of a small dusty town going about its own business. Long-legged Masai tribesmen loped through the unpretentious streets. The Greenland Hotel was a popular hangout for them to go drink coffee. They stared at us, and we stared at them. Dark blue blankets wrapped their red cloth skirts, beaded earrings and stacks of hoops looped long necks, hand-polished staffs laid by their sides. Stylishly elongated upper and lower earlobes were stretched with a sundry of weights. One of the most bizarre was a ceramic light socket and light bulb. The man looked like a floor lamp.

Kristin lived in Arusha, and it was not long before we bumped into her and Evonne arranging a safari to Manyara and Ngorongoro Crater. They convinced us to join them because Kristin, as a resident, was eligible to pay regular fees in Tanzanian shillings. We would book the trip in her name and share the expense. Somewhere along the way we were joined by a tall goofy German man, Dietrich. He was forever lost. He could lose himself standing still. Yet including him meant the fixed price would be even cheaper split five ways.

The morning we were leaving, part of the Australian bicycle family arrived in Arusha. We ran into Camile on the street. While her husband climbed Kilimanjaro, she had brought her two daughters to Arusha. We added them to our group. "No problem!" we all chorused, "We've got plenty of food and we'll share the tents. No problem!"

The proprietor of the tour company wagged his head. "Never before have I sent so many people in one car." We grinned like fools who thought they understood the punch line of a joke but had missed it all together. We were soon to dub our Safari "Adversity Tours" and adopted as our motto, "This too will pass."

Dietrich the German was six feet three. His stooped shoulders bounced off the roof, and his chin bumped on his knees. Every time we stopped, Dietrich got lost, and we'd spend an extra hour searching towns or Lake Manyara or hillsides calling his name until it became the only thing silly about the safari.

Our driver dumped us at a campground on the misty ridge of the Ngorongoro Crater. What ensued was the classic camping scene. We had two small tents, both of which lacked crucial poles and pegs. The two sleeping bags were flimsy cotton that soaked up the humidity, then froze stiff in the cold cloudy night. We had a small, single-burner kerosene stove and water from our canteens, but no firewood or anything to cook in. Dietrich had not bothered to bring any food at all. The driver left to get both firewood and another tent from the "Big Lodge." He didn't return for four hours nor did he bring back any of the desired objects. The driver left again early the next morning, and we were stranded for another two hours while he looked for a coffee pot, which he never found. He probably ate and drank well in the Great Dining Hall, warmed by a log fire at the Great Lodge.

When the sun set behind a mountain, chill and desolation set in. Wet and shivering, we wrapped ourselves in the one piece of cloth and dismally cleaned the raw vegetables for a spaghetti stew thickened with a can of sardines from the bottom of my backpack.

We might still be on that mountaintop, if a fancy safari hadn't shown up. They looked like they stepped out of a television advertisement for some glitzy travel outfitter. We crouched in the darkness, our faces smeared with dirt. Sixteen hunger-dulled eyes watched twenty waterproof tents go up—each big enough for eight people, with screened porches, cots, and downy sleeping bags. Then long tables draped with white linen, crystal, and china were set up. The odor of food steamed from iron kettles.

"We've got to do it for the children," we said. "They need to eat even if we don't."

Yeah.

"You go."

"No, you go."

"We'll all go."

We startled them. We were like warrior apparitions stepping from out of the darkness into the circle of their lanterns and camp fires. They had not noticed us huddled under the piece of cloth.

"Please, may we have some firewood and borrow a cooking pot?" we said, thrusting the two tow-haired girls in front of us like a pathetic plea for "Feed The World" or "Adopt an orphan for only $20 a month."

By the time our driver returned, we didn't need him any longer. We were self-sufficient, crowded, wet, and cold, but with warm food in our bellies.

The next day the clouds did not lift until one-thirty in the afternoon, and then a haze hung in the crater. Crackly brown grass, patches of green scrub, thistle bushes, and a copse of trees were the major flora. We saw The Big Five: rhinos, elephants, lions, leopards, and Cape buffalo. We also saw giraffe, wildebeest, hartebeest, zebra, jackles, warthogs, elan, Thompson and Grant gazelle, spider monkeys, lesser and greater flamingos, eagles, plovers, pelicans, ibis, ostrich, cranes, bustards, and souvenir Masai warriors.

A group of Masai hung out at the bottom of the crater. They charged 500 Tanzanian shillings (TS) for a photo of one, or TS 1000 for a photo of three. They were cloaked in red clay with bangles and beads on every appendage. Others were all in black with white, painted faces. Kristin said these were the recently circumcised, and those with long braids down their backs were still undergoing initiation to become warriors. They must leave their own villages and travel for one year.

We were too bedraggled from the night before for Masai warriors-in-training to seriously bother with us.

"Big, rich *muzungu* Safari come now," we said.

Yes, they smiled, and leaped in a perfect display of delight at their future earnings. They trickled the fine, corn-colored hair of the two girls through their fingers, giggled, and said we could take their photos free.

A kind of artificiality hung over Ngorongoro and Serengeti. It reminded me of Africa's museums, in which history was portrayed as beginning with the white man and gave only his perception of what was real or useful. This same attitude was reflected in the game parks. Animals attracted hard currency from the environmentally conscious or daring, danger-seeking tourist. Human life did not. So the Masai who had managed the land for so long were banished in favor of the white man's perception of wildlife management. Hotly debated in Tanzania and Kenya, and probably south in other vast preserves, was whether the *muzungus'* dollars preserved the land and animals or was bringing them to a slow unnatural extinction.

We were all struck by the docility of the animals. The ones shown in documentaries must be in a migratory rampage or spooked by a camera crew for the sake of action shots. These had the meekness of those in American zoos. Radios linked the safari jeeps. A radioed announcement of "A bull elephant!" or "Lions feeding on a gazelle!" brought jeeps hurtling from every direction. Cameras and video recorders whirred. The animals looked blase, as if to say, "What's new?"

– 25 –
Kenya

Nairobi rose from the plain like a concrete phoenix. "Dar compared to Nairobi is a small village," someone said. Indeed, with its tall buildings, lights, loud busy streets, and traffic stampedes, Nairobi reminded me of London, Philadelphia, or any large, modern city. There were miles of African art shops, gem stores, bookstores, a Woolworth store, street corner acrobats, drinking halls, and millions of tourists. The tourists looked the same in multi-pocketed khaki uniforms, pith helmets, and with several cameras slung over their shoulders. Their voices could be heard over the din of traffic a block away: "Well, on my safari, blah, blah." It was all a game of one-upmanship.

A not-so-quiet refuge was the Iqbal Hotel, a low-budget travelers' flophouse. Long lines queued down the staircase each morning for rooms. Whether you got one was decided by a Muslim named Ali. He operated the house by a strict code: no alcohol, no visitors, no noise, etc. More than one woman was sent into the streets with "Whore!" shouted at her back. The Iqbal was quiet; the street noise was loud. A bus stop, and the raucous Modern Green Day and Night Club added to the din.

Nairobi is in the middle southeast interior of Kenya. It is the hub of all Kenya traffic—all roads lead to it, not around it. As a result, everyone passes through Nairobi.

In the Iqbal we met up with Michen, a Danish woman whom we had met in Mali nine months earlier. Back then, she and her boyfriend were planning to cross Zaire; now she was alone.

"My friend got pneumonia and flew home. Then I got malaria and was hospitalized for several weeks. I flew here from West Africa. Neither one of us made it to Zaire."

Michen was depressed. "I've been in Nairobi for two months, but I am so sick of travel I can't move. I will soon, though. I'll go to the island of Lamu. This place is getting too crowded with stupid tourists. If I hear one more sing the praises of *ugali* (fou-fou) I'll throw up or kill him. Maybe both."

On the street we ran into Janet from Economic Tours. She and her husband Steve had been the leaders of the trucks that took us across the mud holes of eastern Zaire. They had unloaded their overland group in Nairobi a month earlier. (As usual, Robb and I were the laggards.) With a sigh Janet said, "Soon we start back the other way with a new group."

Evonne and the Australian cycling family passed through Nairobi several times. We never saw them, but kept up a lively exchange of notes on bulletin boards.

And Josef, sweet Josef from the Zaire riverboat, celebrated his last night in Africa with us. We went on a sleazy tour of bars and built walls across our tables with empty brown bottles. The Modern Green Club, across from the Iqbal, had never closed its doors (nor changed its jukebox) since opening in 1968. Josef was quite smitten by one of "the young ladies" who worked there, so we stayed polishing the tabletop with our elbows until it was time to put Josef on the bus to the airport. He had spent all his money by then, and we had to give him enough for the airport tax and a bus home.

We also received mail in Nairobi. Home! Josef's departure made our own yearnings more piquant after fourteen months of nomadism, eleven of them in Africa. During that time, our mothers struggled with illness, a boy was born into our families, we'd received mail four times, connected four phone calls home, and taken only four hot showers. We were tired and wanted to see our friends and family again. Yet, the thought of returning home was scary.

Josef expressed it well. "I am terrified of returning to Germany. When I pass a stranger here, I stop and exchange greetings. What will happen if I do this in Germany? How will I feel when no one answers me?"

Would we find friendliness at home? Would we find our jobs again?

When we began our journey, we had decided to let our fate roll with the toss of the dice. Robb was supposed to be back at work in two days, but we still teetered with indecision: would we take the next flight home to Florida, or would we stay? We called his hospital from a pay phone in Nairobi and were greeted by a prerecorded message. Something new. Our phone didn't have push buttons, so it cost us $25 to listen to a long recording until we got to the operator. The operator connected Robb with personnel, but the entire staff had turned over! They had never heard of him. Another $30 was added to our bill while personnel searched for his record. "How may I help you?" the voice from Florida asked icily.

"I am calling from Kenya to tell you I won't be back to work on Monday." In hindsight, we knew all along what he would ultimately decide. Maybe Josef's confession of terror at returning to an impersonal homeland instigated fears that were further provoked and confirmed by the telephone recording.

Robb hung up the phone and wrapped his arms around me. "Well, where would you like to go next?" he asked. "We still have valid visas for Uganda?" It was craziness, but incredibly delightful craziness.

With rather misty eyes, I gazed into his. "Does this mean the trip has begun?"

"Pami, whether you've noticed it or not, the trip began a long time ago." Neither one of us could stifle our laughter a second longer.

Our pockets were once again full of money (thanks to American Express) and temporarily banished was any necessity to return home. We lingered in Nairobi a few days more because things, politically speaking, were beginning to get interesting.

All but the government-owned newspaper sold out by nine o'clock each morning. Copies were passed hand to hand for days. In public, they were read without comment or expression, but in private, momentous debates raged. President Arap Moi was becoming so repressive that *uhuru*, independence, took on new meaning. First he accused the American government of making their people stay home in order to economically destroy Kenya. He couldn't fool us—a quarter of the U.S. population seemed to be on safari. People just snickered.

But it was the start of an "uprising" that escalated with the arrest of two outspoken lawyers. Matiba and Rubia were in the forefront of a movement for pluralism, a multiparty state. Moi revoked their passports and reputedly ordered one of the wives beaten. A public rally in support of multiparties was declared illegal. People who attended might be shot.

The American embassy denounced the actions and denied Moi's accusations that Americans would be evacuated. Moi condemned U.S. intervention in internal security, then followed up with threats of "love us or leave us." He likewise renewed the threats of retaliatory action against pro-multiparty rallies and arrested the lawyers who defended Matiba and Rubia. The U.S. gave them asylum.

Only the day before we'd watched a news broadcast in which an Israeli official said, "Americans are naive. They know nothing about the world." Everyone in the room laughed so hard that there was no doubt as to their concurrence. But with the American Embassy standing toe-to-toe with Moi, public opinion shifted like the wind.

"America is a great country," said several Kenyans, showing us the article. "You are free to say anything about your Bush; even we can laugh. But if we say anything about our country, we will go to prison, we will be tortured, we will be killed. Watch and be careful."

Police patrols roamed the streets along with rumors that gangs would stone any citizen out of their area at night. Buses reduced their routes. Nervousness coursed through everyone's veins like caffeine. "It will happen. Be at sssspssp Saturday," people whispered in the streets. Anger was ignited with the increased repressions.

"Our President is not a good person. His is the only voice in this country, his ministers do not speak. All voices are silent. It is not good. I will go to the rally and then to Tanzania, where there are many people who speak."

"We are frustrated and very angry. There is no opportunity, no voice. It might take two years, maybe more, but we will win."

It was a good time to flee Nairobi. Our visas to Uganda were about to expire, so we hopped the overnight train to Malaba on the western border where Kenya meets Uganda. The train was delayed by rioting near the National Stadium. Buses burned, police were stoned and *wanachies*, the people, were teargassed. But once under way, all tension slipped away with the clacking and swaying of the train. Giraffe and zebra grazed on the plains that swept up into mountains. Fir trees laced the red setting sun; the full moon lit our compartment more brightly than the dim yellow bulb. We had thought the Tanzania train posh, but by Kenya standards, it was a cattle car.

"I could get used to travel like this," I said to Robb.

We went to Uganda with a mixture of curiosity and a set of weary expectations. Although the terror of Idi Amin was over, we could not shed the specter of his reign. Travelers had reported Uganda to be very cheap despite a food scarcity. The people were eager for tourists to return. Three days before our arrival in Uganda, prices doubled, then tripled; a 50 percent currency devaluation would nudge prices even higher. It was not cheap, but the people were very nice.

Our experience in Uganda started with the immigration official who ordered us past the jail and into a small interrogation room. We were nervous.

"In Kampala you must renew your visa," the official said.

We looked at him quizzically because our passports were stamped for two weeks.

"Is there a problem?" we asked. The walls of the room were closing in all too rapidly. Nothing but bad had ever come out of our meetings with officials. We braced ourselves for the inevitable, morbid punch line.

"I think you will find Uganda very interesting and will want to stay for a much longer time. Welcome to our country." He stood and smiled. We gasped for air and wobbled out with relief. A car going to Kampala tooted its horn, and we jumped in it before anyone else could welcome us.

Kampala looked like a bombed city. Dead rats and garbage littered the streets. Empty buildings were grim monuments to the Indian population who had been slaughtered or evicted by Amin. Now Uganda was trying to lure the Indians back. Their entrepreneurship was needed to rebuild the country. In the center of town, a traffic sign attested to the slow pace of progress: "Slow, Zebra Crossing."

Some of the best live music in Africa pounded compulsive dance rhythms until dawn at the day and night clubs. Rebel skirmishes in the north effectively cut off that region to travel, but the lovely Ruwenzoris mountains to the west were easily accessible. And the source of the 4,160-mile long Nile River at Jinja inspired us to later follow its length in Egypt.

Yoweri Kaguta Museveni, president of Uganda, and president of the Organization of African Unity, gave a stirring statesmanlike speech before the OAU delegates in Addis Ababa. His speech went something like this:

"It is time that we Africans stop blaming all our problems on the white man and slavery. We've had more than one hundred years to heal. It is time for the leaders to listen to their people, for African nations to open dialogue not only within their borders but among nations. Stop crying about the past and decide our future. Foreign aid, which we've become so dependent on, will go to the Eastern European nations, and unless we work together to find solutions to our own problems, no one will do it for us." I stood and applauded the radio voice. They were enlightened words from the leader of a humbled nation.

We stayed in Uganda as long as we dared—a week—before we high-tailed it back to Kenya. We liked Uganda; it was a country quietly struggling to its feet. It was expensive though. And the news from Kenya was ominous. More people had been killed. More attorneys sought asylum in the American embassy. Moi threatened to evict all Americans. The American embassy issued a travel warning for Kenya. The borders might close. The police were arresting the clergy, calling worship services "secret meetings." The archbishop railed from his pulpit, "Those who live by the sword will die by the sword, those who shoot to kill will be killed also." A priest from Mwangi added, "Unless the government allows dialogue, the church and the public will continue to oppose the leadership of one political party." The Youthwingers, a government-sponsored group of adolescent thugs similar to Hitler's Youth League, were granted "powers of arrest" and encouraged to turn in their neighbors.

The Ugandans shook their heads as if they read the obituary of a friend. "You would think they would have learned a lesson from our history. They learn nothing. They will kill themselves by their own hand. You must not go to Kenya. Stay here where it is safe." We returned to Kenya before Moi evicted all Americans—most of what we still owned in the world was stored in Nairobi. Also, we were very curious.

Again, another immigration officer detained us upon leaving Uganda. "You must stay here with us," he said. "I will find you employment as teachers if you will stay. We have very good schools, and our teachers are paid very well." He quoted a salary roughly equivalent to $12 a month plus room. "I will get you a job with my school. Yes? Stay in Uganda where we have learned our lesson."

The buses and trains between the border towns of Malaba and Nairobi were delayed by mutual violence. We were stuck again; this time in Malaba, a one-street town lined with rickety food kiosks and tractor-trailer trucks. There was also one train station, one bus stop under one baobab, and one hotel whose only name I could figure was "Bottle of Fun." We slept when the sun was high and crept out at night to scoop *ugali*, beans, fried bananas, and freshwater fish. A grandfather softly strummed a guitar and crooned from the shadows of a food stall. Rain pattered on the tin roof like a water drum. In the nearby fields voices raised in song and a cow brayed.

Nairobi was in semi-chaos. Nothing much operated except the gossip line, which whispered of more arrests and more demonstrations. In front of the American embassy double lines of "asylum seekers" wound down the block. A pony-tailed consular official commented with excitement, "Isn't it great? Whoowee! Were you here last weekend? It'll be even better this weekend." We decided we'd read about it in the newspapers. After we picked up our things from storage at the Iqbal, we left for the Kenya island of Lamu.

Lamu lies a short distance from the Kenyan coastline. It is so far north that the country of Somalia is right above it. To reach Lamu from Nairobi requires twenty-four hours of travel on various conveyances. The train went as far east as Mombasa on the coast, one bus went as far north as Malindi. Another bus went to Lamu. (Actually, the bus went to where the road ended at the Indian Ocean, and a dhow completed the journey to Lamu Island.)

The entire journey was fascinating. The overnight train to Mombasa forged through the Masai-Mara reserve with giraffe, zebra, gazelle, duiker, and wildebeest grazing alongside the tracks in the dun-colored grass. Included in the price of a train ticket was the most overlooked budget safari on the continent.

From Mombasa to Malindi the road wove along the coastline through verdant, neatly cultivated fields. Sailboats bobbed in the many protected bays. The atmosphere was more laid-back than inland and in the highlands. A long wait for the ferry at Kalimi added to the sense of laziness.

Laughter flowed easily too. A very popular clothing style among women was to wear a big bustle of cloth called a *hondo*. Some were so enormous that the wearer could barely squeeze through the door of the *matatu*. The driver would chide them, "I will have to charge you two fares. Maybe you hide another person there." Old men in their *kanga* skirts would wrinkle their weathered faces and giggle.

We stayed in Malindi several days. While on the train, Robb was struck with a high fever. A swollen toe painfully spread infection through his body. Like anyone unaccustomed to illness, Robb stubbornly denied the problem. Only when he couldn't walk did he finally agree to find a guest house in Malindi and rest.

A man spied Robb's limp and offered us a ride in his dune buggy. He said his name was Fondo and that he and his wife owned a small guest house. Luckily, it was perfect. As the door swung open to our new room, Robb used his last ounce of strength to fall face-forward on the bed. For two days he laid there shivering, delirious with fever, mumbling senselessly, and occasionally getting up as if to leave. He was an object of great concern to everyone. Perhaps they were afraid he'd die there.

When not caring for Robb, I walked the beach and explored Malindi. At first glance it was rather glitzy, with posh, beachside hotels, souvenir shops, and European-style restaurants. Germans and Italians huddled in this area. Rarely did they venture beyond the pool to the beach. Behind the strip throbbed the real village of Malindi, where people greeted each other, corn and brochettes roasted over fires, and homes turned into beer parlors after sunset.

Lamu is often compared to Zanzibar by people who have been to one but not both. They are both islands reached by sailing dhow, and a Muslim population dominates both.

People who have never been to Zanzibar claim the food is better on Lamu. Fresh fish in coconut milk was certainly tasty, but Lamu served all its fare in restaurants, not in the street, and high prices reflected upscale patrons. Only in dimly lit cafes in narrow alleys could you find simple fare for simple prices.

Lamu's charm exceeded that of Zanzibar. A smaller island, more quaint, the town twisted along hallway-like streets. There was not one road nor a single vehicle. It was also a donkey sanctuary. In Lamu, the donkey enjoyed the golden life. They roamed freely and grazed on garbage put out for them. Their working hours were few, if any.

Hustlers flocked to greet each boatload of arrivals. "Wanna room? I take you to fine place. This is paradise island. Wanna dhow to the beach? Snorkeling, the monument, fishing? The ruins? Wanna a sunset cruise?" One luckless hustler confided, "This is a very competitive business." The ruins were recent Portuguese, no one seemed to know anything about the monument, the nearby waters were fished out, and the seasonal trade winds stirred up the reefs. As in many tourist towns, once the hustlers learn your face and that you are not buying, you are left alone.

A terrific beach could be reached by a forty-five-minute walk along the quay, or along paths winding through sand dunes, or by dhow. The biggest dilemma of each day was whether to walk or sail to one of the most beautiful beaches in Africa. The beach seemed so endless I could never imagine it crowded. One man sold coconuts he carried on his donkey's back. The duo would first appear as a mere speck, hours away in the distance.

The mornings reflected the unhurried breeze, the poky pace of a sleepy donkey. If you hesitated, or sat too long in contemplation of movement, then you were likely to do nothing at all for the rest of the day. Josef had called Lamu timeless. Many days, we got tangled in the ephemeral bonds of eternity.

Newspapers and news were so hard to get that problems on the mainland receded into an obscure dream of a faraway land. Quite a few people had fled to the island paradise. They gathered each morning to peer over shoulders and around heads at the headlines, "Multiparty System Guilty of Coup Plot. Anyone collaborating with foreign governments will be tried for treason and hung." "International Law Conference Called Off." The fault was laid on America and Britain. "If you are American," commented one man, "I wouldn't go back to Nairobi." The best source of news arrived on the dhows with the refugees from the mainland. People knotted about them as if they were newspapers and listened to tales of buildings in flames and riots.

One day tragedy struck. A *dhow* arrived with different news. It was announced with long, loud wails of grief and terror. The bus from Malindi had been attacked by Somalian bandits who opened gunfire on the passengers. Three people were killed and four critically wounded. Confusion, trauma, and wailing shook Lamu. Litters bearing the injured were strapped to donkeys, who were urged to trot to the hospital.

Paralysis gripped Lamu. People almost tiptoed for two days, all except the white holiday tourists who packed the dhows and charter planes with puckered faces of fear. Rumored among the dead was a German tourist. It made no sense to me to jump from the pan of security into the fires of Nairobi.

Then a funeral procession filed along the quay. Women in mourning *bui-buis* accompanied the body. Shops locked up. The town stood still. At the same time, a *jahazi*, a large, deep-keeled dhow, broke the ocean breakers to enter the Malindi harbor. From the flower-festooned boat came blaring horns, throaty woofs, shrill ululations, drums, clapping, and singing. It was a wedding party from another island. The sounds of life and death, joy and mourning, became one.

Michen, the Dane we had met in Mopti and Nairobi, was living on the island in a small room rented from a T-shirt artist. For once she looked happy and healthy. Away from the fatty palm oil diet of the continent, Michen lost weight. Her cropped, curly hair bounced, and her cheeks positively glowed. Not once did she complain, a habit of hers that had always kept us at a distance. She had a new habit though—*miraa*.

Miraa looks like scrawny twigs. When the bark is peeled and the core masticated, it produces a high that "keeps sleep away." The slimy, slightly bitter pulp is spit out. It is also addictive. Robb and I bought a small bundle tied and wrapped in banana leaves for freshness. We immediately and prematurely fell asleep.

"The effect is cumulative," explained Michen. "If you are just starting you need to chew a kilo to feel the effect." A kilo? It had taken us two hours to consume our little handful. I could not imagine us chewing our way through a kilo in a month.

"Tonight come to my house," she said, "I will have a very big bundle of *miraa* for us. Then we'll go to the dance at the police station." It turned out that Michen knew not only the secrets of *miraa* but the whereabouts of every party on the island.

We went with her several times but could never keep up. The *miraa* continued to tranquilize us. The police parties were surprisingly fun. Music—Zairean and American rap—propelled the dancers into a frenzy. The room sweated alcohol. Unlimited, hot beer frothed through bodies like fermentation tanks of a bootleg still. And bootleg it was, almost. Only Petley's Inn in town sold beer, and then only between 6:00 P.M. and 10:00 P.M.

Several weeks earlier we bought plane tickets to Egypt after learning that the overland routes north to Egypt, through Ethiopia and Sudan, were closed because of fighting. I compared the date on the tickets, August 10, with my calendar. We had four days to make the plane. Regretfully, we left Lamu, the paradise island where time stands still and the donkeys roam free.

The bus back was heavily guarded by the military; passengers fought for seats. Two more ambushes had occurred since the massacre, and it was those who were standing who died. The eight-hour ride from the Lamu ferry to Malindi was tense; it was like waiting for the executioner's bullet and not knowing when it will come.

Trains from Mombasa to Nairobi were overbooked, and a first

class cabin wouldn't be available for at least a month. In all but the first class cabins, gender segregation was strictly enforced on the Kenyan railroad. (Women and men traveled in separate-but-equal cars, supposedly to protect women from the unwanted advances of men's uncontrollably lusty hormones.) Robb and I were not willing to travel separately, so we took a bus back to Nairobi and, this time, passed through Tsavo National Park, more green and fruited than Masai-Mara but still with rhinos and elephants and tribes of baboons loitering on the road. One adolescent male baboon charged the bus with such fury that everyone lept up, laughing, to get a better view.

Nairobi was much the same as before—politics, rumors, and opinions. One man told us, "We are training people in Libya. You see the street boys? Those who eat out of the garbage bins? We send them from here for guerrilla training, then smuggle them back through Uganda. They're mean. They aren't like you and me. They have no mother and father, nothing to stop them."

At the Iqbal, tales of street scams were sniffled through tears. Three or four travelers daily handed over $500 to $1000 at a time to total strangers. Why? The stories were similar. "A man approached me on the street and said he was a refugee/student from South Africa/Libya. We'd talk a while, then he would leave. Minutes later two men came up to me and identified themselves as the police and said I was under arrest for keeping company with terrorists/spies/political criminals. They said they would take me to jail and torture me into a confession unless I paid the fine." Some of the victims cried publicly, others hid with shame. It was incomprehensible craziness.

The night before we flew to Egypt, we laid awake listening to the cacophony of traffic horns, music, trucks without mufflers snorting down the alleyways, and screams from jealous prostitutes fighting over a john.

We imagined Egypt would be refreshingly different. We looked forward to seeing her great pyramids and comparing them to the ones of Central America we knew so well. In our minds, we thought we were doing the right thing to fly from Nairobi as quickly as possible.

– 26 –
Egypt

Egypt taught us that you can't run away, especially from one big city to another. The grass is always greener on the other side of the fence, especially the grass of Kenya, whose sweet aftertaste lingers like an aperitif. If Egypt were our first taste of Africa we might have loved it. Instead, it came at the end of our trip, like an unscheduled layover on the route home.

Our companion passengers on Air Egypt should have been a portent of things to come. Shortly after take-off the entire crew filled the aisle and bowed in prayer. It was not noon, nor was it sunrise. The timing was unnerving. A chatty group of Canadian tourists decked in khaki, with plastic name tags and bundles of tacky souvenirs, hollered the length of the plane, "Shopping in Cairo will be great!"

An enthusiastic young Irish woman on a four-day tour of Egypt, Kenya, and Israel lectured to the rapt Canadians. "Oh,

Egypt is lovely! So well organized too—not like Kenya. You can buy everything there. But it's shitty hot!"

"Did you hear that, dear?" said Marge to Harold. "Cairo is beautiful and cheap!"

"So where are you going, buddy?" A voice boomed over our shoulders and an even bigger paw fraternally slapped Robb's back. His name tag said Charles. "What did ya think of the safaris? Something, eh? Nice, real nice, but those black people are lying thieves, eh? If you leave your tent for a minute it will be gone when you come back. They aren't even human." He shook his head sadly. "Heh, cheer up. We're headed back to civilization. Eh? You never did tell me, did you and your li'l woman here see The Big Five?"

We gazed at him in our best blank, uncomprehending look. The same one we'd given all the police who demanded money. Robb said something nonsensical like "Ouagadougou sango nini ugali, ca va?" And shrugged his shoulders. "Oh, you don't speak English, sorry." Charles lumbered away in search of a more agreeable conversant.

Robb squeezed my hand. Tears clouded my contact lenses. We kissed ever so slightly and silently turned our faces to the window to watch the silhouette of the plane glide over the quiet sands of the Sahara. Somewhere down there a dung beetle was leaving its tracks, and a young girl was digging the sand for water to fill her goat-belly sacks—a history swept by the wind.

Egypt, beyond a doubt, was a net consumer of the world's total oxygen output. The only greenery sprouted along the Nile and in the Sinai Peninsula. Holes in the ozone not burned by cars and buses were burned by the acerbic bickering of the people.

I guess everything is relative; all realities are true. It might have been fun—all the argumentative negotiation, that is—if we hadn't come from polite, quiet, black Africa, where correct change was always delivered after a wait and not magically absorbed by last second-price increases as in Egypt. We were used to the ways of black Africa; it was what we knew. Egypt clashed against our cultural reference.

Nairobi was as quiet as a library in comparison to Cairo. My positive opinion of Egypt wilted with every second we spent in Cairo. Simple things were monumental hassles. The taxi driver from the airport dropped us at the center of town because he got lost. A price had been agreed upon. We paid him that and a tip. The tip was not enough, so he wouldn't give us our luggage. We scuffled. Robb snatched the luggage, and I snatched the tip. "Okay, Okay I take it," the driver recanted.

Every pension in Cairo was located at the top of eighteen flights of stairs, and we had to climb them all to learn that every pension was full, although everyone complained about the lack of tourists. Finally, we got a room and paid for the night. Then the manager said if anyone else showed up she would put them in our room. What? Where? "Two can sleep on the floor," she said. "Give me two pound more." Why? "I take your passport to the police to be stamped." (We did it ourselves for free in Luxor.) Bedbugs nibbled at Robb, whose face swelled and drooped like Igor the Monster's.

Our biorhythms were not in synchronization with those of Cairo. As long as we did not have to deal with money or people everything was pleasant. Money made everything go haywire. We ordered a bowl of lentil soup and got vegetable consomme.

"Excuse me, please, I ordered lentil soup."

"I give you lentil soup. What? Are you stupid or something? That is lentil, you don't know what are lentils. Give me five pound more."

"But the price on your card says three pounds for lentil soup."

"It is wrong."

I felt like a novice tourist. Simple conversation occurred on two different levels and mingled different subjects.

On the premise that people in rural areas are less rude than their brethren in the cities, we caught the southbound train to Thebes. The train tracks run parallel to the Nile. Dense populations congregate along the narrow green banks of the river. It took hours to get out of Cairo. A few towns, like Haj Hammadi, got fat and wide with people and buildings, but mostly the land was given over to agriculture. Every inch of arable soil was cultivated. I guess the regular flooding of the Nile, now stopped by the Aswan Dam, made the Egyptians more dependent on the river than ever.

The train broke down. I heard breakdowns were so common they were scheduled as part of the run. We spent the night on a side rail listening to the drunken babble of the man across the aisle.

Thebes. Finally, a town, and not a megalopolis. It was slow enough to sort through all the mixed messages, and small enough that incidents occurred one at a time and not twenty simultaneously. Thebes is the jumping spot for Luxor, Karnak, and the Valley of the Kings. For that reason it is also a big tourist port. Luxury cruise liners tie up among the hand-built sailing *feluccas*. Pretty people clank champagne glasses and waltz under chandeliers. For the most part that is all we saw of the tourists. Big, airconditioned buses whisked them to the sites, and guides escorted them to the nearby tourist bazaar.

Thebes was funny at times. Like the pension where we got a room, it had hot showers. In Nairobi, where it was cold at night, a hot shower would have been lovely. In Thebes the daytime temperature was between 112 and 120 degrees Farenheit. Who needed a hot shower?

And vendors dickered with themselves. Prices for the horse drawn buggies were posted as one pound per person anywhere within the city. In a typical scene, the whiskered-chin driver would trot up and start bargaining, "Carriage? Carriage? Cheap price! Two pound to your hotel. Okay? Okay? Make it four pound for both of you. Six?" And the curio and spice dealers would say, "Just five pounds...O.K. three. Make it two pounds and you take it." The really odd thing was that the vendors bartered without any reference to anything in particular and with no one but themselves. No response was required. It was almost as if we were cardboard cutouts with wallets.

We went to Egypt to indulge our love of archaeology. Guidebooks adequately cover all pertinent information, so I made only critical summaries in my journal. Luxor and Karnak are both impressive, but they are almost too overwhelming for a layperson to absorb. They lent themselves to cursory perusal. Every inch of surface was devoted to hieroglyphics—from below the ground to the topmost lintel. Statues were massive. They imparted the impression that these kings were giant gods who must have shook the earth when they walked. Such self-apotheosis makes me irreverent. I felt sorry for the sculptors whose task it was to replicate in stone the ego of their human model. The stylized forms used by the artisans were surely a safe way of suppressing their own emotions.

The Luxor Museum housed an outstanding display of second-rate artifacts that might have been educational if they were labeled. Nevertheless, the museum was a lovely place to cool off and bask in tranquility.

There are many ways to tour the Valley of the Kings. We opted for the Rent-a-Donkey-and-Guide itinerary. Imagine a middle-aged Egyptian tour guide, missing a few teeth, in a dirty white robe, without any special talents, and you've got Achmed, our guide. He was a nice guy, though. He offered little information, but he didn't intervene either. He wasn't obvious about cheating us, and never once did he beat the well-behaved donkeys, so we never felt bad about him. All in all, he was more like a tag-along who knew the paths.

The terrain is dry, chalky limestone, with a smattering of alabaster rock. From above the ruins of a Roman town and looking east, the Nile valley is a green agricultural shawl draped over the shoulders of the Nile. A white haze of pollution hangs over the scrawl of civilization. Further into the mountains, alone under the pale blue sky, with only the steady clip-clop of the donkeys' hooves, time went backward to centuries gone by.

The Valley of the Kings looked like all the other dry, rocky valleys we'd skirted since sunrise. No wonder it laid hidden for so many centuries. Erase the Rest House Cafeteria and five hundred tour buses in the paved parking lot and nothing much was left on the surface. It took some minutes for our minds to reorient to present time. Achmed nudged us down the steep walled bowl to join our contemporaries.

Entrances to the tombs are carved into the mountainsides. The rubble that once hid them like natural camouflage has been pushed to the side. Inside, long, deep tunnels plunge through the grandeur of the pharaohs. Magnificent architectural and artistic achievements of the past centuries open like a book—the early pages depict simple, stick-like figures; the later pages are three-dimensional, full-figured gods and goddesses. I guess it's human nature to depict ourselves as evolutionarily improved.

More and more tourists thronged the chambers, so the only view was the backs of heads. Kids shrieked to hear their voices ricochet off the walls. If any pharaohs still slept beneath the canyon walls, they probably did what we did: we left.

The donkeys clopped over hills to the valley of Queen Hatshepsut's temple. The pillars were slim; the design was almost sensual. Without serpentine lines and a thousand voices droning aloud from guidebooks, it was hospitable to a languid contemplation of eternity.

Next we went to the Ramesseum, a garden of colossal statues of Ramses II. The difference between the architecture of the king's temples and that of the queen's was like a neon poster alongside a poem. His enormous ego was chiseled into multiton pillars and statues. Time had wreaked appropriate vengeance. As my mother was fond of saying, "What goes up must come down." Most of the statues had come down.

Achmed suggested we stop at Ramses Rest House to water the donkeys and ourselves. The owner of the rest house claimed to have accompanied Howard Carter into King Tut's tomb. A yellowed photo of him as a young man standing next to Carter was brought out and held alongside his now-withered visage as proof. Carter, who died from the curse of the mummies, was recognizable, but there was little similarity between the robust young man in the picture and the gray-whiskered man before us. But he presented a vivid, "I was there" story of the tomb discovery.

A fat and greasy-looking man clinked scarabs and coins in his hand throughout the recitation. "These came from tombs," he hissed in a fat whisper, although no one else was around. "You know Mr. Carter took many things from the tombs that no one knows about. Many fine things they say." Hint, hint. "Do you want to see more? Come to my house, I will show you more. It is just over there. My name is Mohammed, everybody knows me, you can trust me." What is a trip to Egypt without an encounter with the Great Antiquities Hoax?

We followed Mohammed to the nearby village and into his house, where he made a big show of ordering his wife to bring tea and sending everyone else away. The samovar and cups were placed in the center of the room. Mohammed locked the door, then removed a stone in the floor beneath the rug and unearthed relics in sealed plastic bags. The statues, heads, and miniature sarcophagi were slightly better executed than the shiny ones sold in souvenir stands.

"Five hundred dollars for this one," he whispered, "In the United States you pay $2,000, maybe more....It's good price. Take your time."

When we showed no inclination to buy anything for $500, Mohammed left the room. Achmed leaned over the objects conspiratorially. Casting anxious glances at the door, he whispered, "No, it is not a good price. I am ashamed. I bring you here because Mohammed is my trusted friend, but he does not give you a good price. Three hundred dollars, that's all, tell him three hundred and he take it. Shhhh, here he comes."

"They say $300," Achmed volunteered to Mohammed while we sat dumbly. As with the carriage drivers and falafel vendors, our participation was not required for the scene to unfold like a play.

"What!? You insult me with this little money!" Mohammed said, flashing dagger eyes at Achmed. "You come to my house and rob me!"

Mohammed started packing his trinkets, twisting each one in front of our eyes like a belly dancer promising something more. The two men wrangled over prices, and accused each other of mutual treachery. The whispered conspiracy was replaced by the yells of two best friends. Achmed was sullen on most of the ride back to the donkey stables. Only near the end, in hopes of a good tip, did he perk up.

Late in the evening we took the Nile ferry back to Thebes. On the boat, a boy told us that Iraq had invaded Kuwait several days earlier. It was astounding, ominous news, but he knew nothing more. We scoured town in search of a confirmation, but news in English was as hard to come by as pizza.

The road south to Aswan cut through rocky, brown desert. It was so hot it singed the hair in our nostrils. Not a beast moved nor did a window shutter flutter in any of the small, colorless villages. If it was 120 degrees in Thebes, it was 140 in Aswan. We went there not so much to see the dam or Abu Simbel, where the temples were moved when the dam was built, but to hire a *felucca* sailboat for a downriver trip back to Thebes. For days we watched the smooth surface of the Nile. Not a single boat moved in the lifeless air. The few that took sunset charters drifted broadside. The sails flapped uselessly. The crew would pole, paddle and swear for another two hours, only to moor again at the corniche. We had to scrap the planned boat journey.

No one in Aswan moved during the day. Not even the lure of a profitable sale induced the shops to open before evening. Everyone slept. Oppressive languor and heat-induced irritation rose with the relentless sun. With the coolness of night came fun. The *souk*, the market, was lively, even festive and jovial. Families strolled and licked ice cream, and laughter rolled down the streets.

I would have liked southern Egypt if not for the male attitude toward non-Muslim women. Men thought nothing of grabbing my breasts, hissing, and clutching their penises with gyrating motions. On the crowded buses, they rubbed their organs into my shoulder. I felt abjectly humiliated by the culture. I feinted with shrill objections and began to dislike myself. I bought a Nubian walking staff with a sharp gazelle horn mounted on the handle. When my vocal objections were ignored, or a swift kick in the butt was impossible to execute, I would accidently gore the offending member with my staff.

I don't think I invited their rudeness. We had lived among modest people for the past year. I had been tutored by savvy women from—Morocco to Kenya—on the nuances of behavior. And in Kenya, when we decided to go to Egypt, I commissioned a Muslim seamstress to make me an appropriate dress. Nevertheless, the negative experiences cremated forgiveness. I turned my humiliation and anger on all Egyptians. It was a lousy way to experience a culture.

Early one morning in Aswan, Robb and I took a ferry across the river to visit a group of nobles' tombs. The tombs honeycombed a gold-colored mountain crowned by a tiara-like, eighteenth-century mosque. The town at the base of the mountain was lovely, bucolically peaceful. The view from the mountaintop overlooked several valleys. The blue Nile and Aswan glistened. By the first light of day, it was spectacular.

If there is a profit to be made in something, then the Egyptians will find a way to exploit it. Although the site of the tombs was not fenced, a kiosk was clearly labeled as an office where admission tickets were sold. It took a while to hunt up the ticket seller. I don't think he expected tourists so early. Indeed, we saw no others. When we finally found him, he accused us of trying to sneak in and demanded *baksheesh* in repayment for our attempted deceit. Enough of him. No sooner had we started up the first path when another fat, huffing Mohammed (my new generic name for Egyptian men) bullied us with unfriendly threats that he must be our guide. The more he bellowed, the more we squawked, "No! We do not want a guide. We will not pay you! If you come this way it is on your own." Fortunately, Mohammed was too overweight to ascend past the first switch-back in the trail.

Many of the tombs were locked with iron grills, and the entrances to quite a few were half-covered with rubble. Those with crawl spaces large enough to wriggle through crumbled with debris, and human and bat excrement. The opened tombs were totally stripped, even of the wall murals, or defaced with graffiti dating back to 1382. It made us realize that "the ugly tourist" was not a modern phenomenon.

Robb, however, made a real discovery in a very remote sector. He'd wriggled into a chamber through one of those nasty tunnels. The rooms were quite splendidly intact, the murals still vivid with colors. Then, under the sweep of the flashlight beam, he noticed a small tunnel off to one side of a room. The dirt and debris looked recent, so he crawled into it for a further look. His hand grasped something big and round. It was bitumen, a black, hardened substance used by early Egyptians to preserve bodies. The piece he held encased half a cranium. Broken food bowls, beads, funerary cloth, and splintered pieces of painted wood from a shattered sarcophagus laid strewn around. This was not the work of an archeologist, but of a looter, who destroyed everything of little value to him. It had been done quickly and very recently.

Judging from the dates of surrounding tombs, this one must have been four thousand years old! With suspended breath, we listened to the silence of the grave—the sound of eternity disrupted. The seclusion was awesome. Only the fragments of another life linked us to our own.

That might have been the end of the story if we didn't hate tomb robbers. But, having worked as documentary videographers at several spectacular archeological sites in the Americas, we did not have to be Egyptologists or physical anthropologists to read the evidence of destruction. Robb photographed the looted burial and its location while I stood guard outside on the deteriorated causeway.

Aimlessly, I swept the ground with my foot and fumed over Mohammed, the antiquities dealer at Luxor. Maybe what he sold was truly authentic loot and not just hasty hoaxes. That's when I spied funerary cloth in the dirt. I had taken a scrap of it from the dark tomb to examine its weave by light. It crumbled quickly in the sunlight. I knelt and compared the crumbling scrap in my hand with the pieces on the ground. The rust colored weave was identical. Considering how rapidly my piece of cloth had deteriorated in light, the tomb must have been looted that night!

Just about then, a workman sauntered listlessly past with a broom. Because he swept nothing, he made me nervous, and I whistled for Robb to hurry it up. Robb and I crouched along the path comparing soil samples and cloth when behind us came a very large, very black hulk of a man.

"Doctor?" he asked respectfully.

We stood up. His eyes flared like torches imbedded in a rock hard face.

"You are not the doctor," he said. "Come here."

We didn't move. Our feet were pinned to the ground with the intuitive knowledge that this man knew what we knew.

"I order you," his voice boomed like a denizen from hell.

"We've seen the tombs," we said weakly.

He was visibly frightened and started toward us aggressively. He suddenly stopped. "Your tickets! Give me your tickets," he shouted.

I could feel my knees beginning to quake. "We have tickets!" we hollered and waved the two paper stubs in the air.

"I said, come here!"

"No!" Intuition warned us not to go near him.

"Give me your tickets!"

"No." This man was the embodiment of evil. Never before in my life had I looked into the face of the devil.

He cried with the fury of fire emanating from his throat. He lurched toward us, and we ran nonstop to the ferry.

We no longer felt safe in Aswan. The ticket seller, guards, the black hulk, and maybe even this doctor person were all tomb looters. We were certain they did not like the idea that we knew it.

In Cairo, a person could easily hide. We left for there that same afternoon.

Apparently, Egyptian troops were mobilizing, because the train station in Cairo was thick with uniformed men. They filled every seat of every train. Iraq had captured Kuwait! The U.S. was amassing troops in the region. Egypt's President Hosni Mubarak hosted a pan-Arab conference. Tension crackled like a live electrical wire.

We were planning to go to the Sinai next, but a phone call home nixed that. "What are you doing in Egypt?" screamed our mothers. "Are you crazy or what? I suppose you're planning to go on to Saudi for front row seats? You're not going to be happy until you get yourselves killed?! Come home right now. Do you hear me? Do you? Say something...."

I suppose we were tired, or we might have gone to the war, or on to the Sinai and Israel. But, our mothers' pleas reminded us that we'd been gone from home long enough. We missed them. We had accomplished and experienced more than we could have imagined at the outset. Luck had been kind to us. There was no sense in pushing it. Besides, Crete beckoned. It lured us with promises of healing balms—sunshine, food to fatten our bones before our mothers hugged them, rest, and a chance to gently orient our minds to the west.

Greece and home shimmered in the near distance like the coast of Africa had from the shores of Spain. We grew impatient to leave Egypt, to recapture the security of belonging to one place, time, and tribe. Maybe that desire compelled us to breach our ethical code. Maybe the Egyptian Museum did it. Maybe Africa caught up with us. In over 28,000 miles, we had resisted all pressure to talk with money—*baksheesh*, a bribe, a tip, a *cadeau*.

But, at four o'clock one morning, we fingered a ten dollar bill outside the portals to the pyramids of Giza and asked for Pyramid Frank. "For *baksheesh*, Pyramid Frank will take you to the top of the pyramids for sunrise," someone had whispered. No one was permitted to climb the pyramids at any hour. Our intended peccadillo leered at us with the smirk of victory. Corruption had found the price of our souls.

During our last few days on the African continent, we tried to recover the peaceful rhythm with which we had walked in much of

Africa. We pressed it into our souls like flowers between pages of a book. But the flowers, the rhythm, crumbled in Cairo's harsh pollution.

We stumbled in total darkness over rocks dislodged by the sandaled feet of Pyramid Frank. We heard him whisper to the other guards, "It is me and my friends." He pointed to the soft, crumbling stairs of Cheop's pyramid and asked if we wanted to climb it. No, we want only to watch the sunrise. Frank led the way through ruins undergoing reconstruction less rapidly than the smog eroded the block. "We climb here," he said at the foot of the smallish pyramid of Mycernius. Cement reinforced the giant-sized steps that led to the peak.

In the azure sky, stars—many millennia away—blinked red, blue, yellow, and white with their undecipherable history. We waited as patiently as waiting for a mango to turn ripe, as silently as the moon over Timbuktu.

Roosters crowed. The cry from the *muezzin*, like we first heard in Morocco, announced the sun before we saw it peak above the tip of the great pyramid of Cheops. It radiated at the tip of the apex like a bright diamond. For a few, glorious moments we understood something profound, but the thought left on the sun's chariot before it could tell us its name.

That day we bought tickets for the ferry to Crete. It would leave five days later from the port city of Alexandria. With nothing more to hold us in Cairo, we left immediately for the northern seacoast of Egypt.

Alexandria is a city that has been conquered, loved, fought over, and immortalized in song and literature for many centuries. It was our final face of Africa. It is like a city veiled with mystique. We tried to brush the veil aside during the sultry days waiting for the ship to Crete. But the face underneath was as disarranged as a Picasso portrait. So many layers of life existed simultaneously in one spot, like a baklava of history. We could no more know Alexandria than we could know ourselves.

We strolled the corniche along the harbor, our own faces turned toward the wind and rain; followed crowded neighborhood alleyways through bazaars, weddings, and funerals; and watched black-draped women buy crotchless panties and gold at the million boutiques. We felt disembodied. Alexandria was surreal. Our thoughts strayed to the future, while our hearts yearned to return to black Africa.

It did not seem like a year had passed. It did not feel like we had experienced enough. We had accepted Africa on its own terms. It had been fun—it was hard work, and physically and mentally challenging, but fun. Africa had been very kind to us. It had embraced us to its heart with motherly protection. We walked well because people took care of us like an extended family, and not through any superhuman feat of our own making.

Within twenty-four hours we would begin re-entry into Western culture, linear thought, and homogeneity, where nothing is unexpected, and everything is predictable. Trains, cars, and buses delivered people according to schedule. Showers were reliably hot. Accomplishment was measured by money and not by knowledge. Back to a civilization where strangers in the streets might not greet us.

I touched the lion-tufted gris-gris around my neck. The juju doctor in Cote d'Ivoire had made it for strength and courage.

"How long is juju good for?" I asked Robbie.

"I don't know, why do you ask?"

"I was just wondering how much time we had left on this gris-gris. It brought us all the way through Africa safely and with few problems. Will it protect us at home?"

"I doubt it," he said, "everyone knows that white men don't have juju."

Epilogue

We've been home for almost a year now. We are still changing. I know, because life and people around us are as stationary as watermarks. It is as if we are still traveling, but this journey is inward. Our fears of boredom, isolation, or assimilation never materialized. We learned to live without such fears, just as we learned to live without a clutter of possessions. Our cottage is quite small, but it is bigger than a backpack.

We came home slowly, via Greece and Czechoslovakia, which meant we overstayed our leaves of absence. We came home to no jobs, the fervor of the Gulf War, and the economy in a sling. Robb feared unemployment. That fear didn't materialize either. He was offered a new job before we were unpacked. It was much quicker than he wanted. One day he was a nomad, and the next, he was the director of a social work program for families who had abused each other for so long the state threatened to split them up. In a daze he put on a necktie and fumbled through bureaucratic systems like a lost man.

I am a trader now. I trade odd jobs, dog walking, yard work, etc., for fruit and other gifts. I also wrote this book.

Our concept of time and distance was completely askew. We drove from Cape Cod, Massachusetts to Merritt Island, Florida. Thirteen hundred miles in just twenty-eight hours. Such a distance in Africa would have taken weeks! We felt like we were in a time machine that warped distance into wrinkles.

At first I thought I would walk everywhere instead of driving a car. Brevard County, Florida, sprawls over seventy-two miles and was developed on the equation of one car for each adult. My mother lives on the other side of the river. It takes me two hours to walk each way or fifteen minutes by car. My best friend lives a day away by foot or twenty-five minutes by car. We succumbed and bought a used second car.

I had forgotten about packaging. The grocery store was within a walkable distance, but minimal purchases produced maximum bulk. Outside the store, I stripped unnecessary layers of packaging from the items so I could carry them home. The stares of my fellow shoppers soon put an end to this practice. It was just too eccentric. Now I drive to the store and bring home more cardboard and plastic than food. As we learned in Africa, a can or bag are valuable, reusable items. I save them all until we can't close the one closet door.

The grocery store, or any store, overwhelmed us with the selection available—shelves and racks were stocked with different brands of the same item. It was just too much. Several times we ran away without getting the item we went for. As a result, we go to the smallest stores and buy only what we need for the moment. I cannot yet grasp the concepts of planning ahead and hoarding things.

I read that the average American showers for thirteen minutes. I also read that water shortages are a critical problem. It makes no sense to me. I flashback on hauling water from a well, and I am quite happy with a three-minute, cold-water shower. What do people do in the shower for thirteen minutes?

The telephone still intrigues me. I feel self-consciously disembodied whenever I use it. I hear myself speak, then the other person speak. Sometimes I do not understand what the other person is saying because I cannot see gestures. One aspect I like about the phone is that it is a single conversation, not multiple and loud in the typical American tradition. We get totally confused by several people talking simultaneously.

The United States is green. After fifteen months of brown stubble, desert, and windblown topsoil, even New York City looks like a lush garden. Florida is a veritable fruit jungle.

The sky is drab though. There is something about the sky in Africa that is dramatic and distinctive. Unknowingly, I had memorized it. Now when I see a photo of an African sky, just the clouds or sun, and I can identify it without context. I miss that sky. I miss the upside down new moon.

We really looked forward to reunification with our friends and family. The greatest of all joys was seeing our mothers. They are terrific women whose personal strengths sustained our own. We grinned idiotically, then settled into contented silence. Friends politely asked a few questions. We are experts at reading body language, so it is easy to know when the listener does not listen. One friend admitted, "I am sorry. What you describe to me is so different from anything I know that I cannot imagine it or comprehend it." A cruise to the Bahamas or a canoe trip down a local river were identifiably real experiences.

Our friends still think we are crazy, and at times we almost agree. They have been very kind and patient with us however. We could not have made it without their help any more than we could have made it through Africa without the help of the Africans.

Africa began to feel like an amputation. Like an arm or a leg that no one could see but we could still feel and miss. Until I wrote this book, it has been a secret knowledge shared between Robb and me.

The most rewarding aspect of travel is new friends. They are, in a way, closer friends than the ones at home. Maybe because the experience of travel is intense and personal, and because the range of human experience and emotions are so compressed, that friends on the road know each other more intimately than many of us know our brothers and sisters. We helped each other then, and we are still helping each other. Weekly we get a card from someone we met on our trip. Most went home for a little while and found the adjustment difficult. Some of them fled. They went back to Africa or traveled on to Australia, Asia, America. I am not sure that there is any "right place" for any of us. Africa changed us too much for any one egocentric society—and all societies are egocentric to some extent.

Dave, the systems analyst, and Linda, the physician, whom we met in Liberia, are back in Minnesota. Our first week home in Florida they came to visit. They told us of their last few hair-raising weeks in Liberia as the rebels marched into the capital. Missionaries and refugees were slaughtered at the mission guest houses where we had stayed.

"We've been home almost seven months, and the culture shock alone is much worse than we expected," they said. "We work closely with refugees and present benefit programs on their behalf, but inside us is a knowledge we can't express. You had to be there," Linda confessed. "I don't know that we'll ever fit in again. Supermarkets overwhelm me, and as for things, well, none of us want or need anything."

Stephanie from Zaire went back to Canada and immediately signed another contract for Malawi. "Canada has been fun—lots of culture shock, friends, and family, but I cannot remain here. People's values are not mine." She went to Australia for a while with Drew and Blue, two Australians who connected with us at the end of the river voyage. None of them feel comfortable in their societies any longer. "Home is a drag. All our friends talk about is buying things. I look around, and there is nothing I want."

Josef, who was arrested on the Zaire boat, went back to his family farm in Germany, lasted two weeks, and returned to Kenya for another six months. He is back in Germany again and completing a university degree in social work. "I dream of building a big canoe, loading it with termites, banana, smoked monkey, live crocodiles, and tortoise, and then going along the Danube trying to trade with the riverboats. Maybe home is the wrong place for me."

Debbie and Jane, the stiletto-heeled duo from Guinea-Bissau, made it to Zaire where Jane caught encephalitis (sleeping sickness) malaria, typhoid, and pneumonia. Jane was hospitalized in England for a month. Shortly after she was discharged they flew to California and continued their travels through the east. "Nothing we've experienced is quite as difficult as Africa."

After two months at home, Jane wrote, "I have to try to keep calm and realize that the majority of people live a pretty boring existence, and that's why most people are dissatisfied and grumpy and rude. It's a world of rushing around from someplace to nowhere. It makes me laugh when someone says, 'So how was the trip?' and I really can't explain that it's just there, engraved in my memories and my heart. All I know is, it's made me a better person."

Ien and Desiree are finishing medical school in Holland. Desiree wrote to thank us for saving her from malaria on the Zaire boat. "The first months I really got nervous from all the hurry. I take my time when I talk to people—this is important to me now."

Evonne, our safari companion from the Chinese-American tribe, continued through Turkey, where "the testosterone level was a little high," and then returned to New Jersey. "It's crazy, they keep throwing money at me," she complained of her job. When Kristin was released from the Peace Corps the two moved to San Francisco where they are doing nonprofit work and planning another trip.

We separated from Golo and Walter at Niamey after the Sahara. Golo came to visit us from Germany. "I was afraid you would have changed," he said, "that you would be different from when I knew you in Africa. You haven't..." Golo hadn't changed either. He was fuller of frame, as were we, and had signed a contract to work in Ghana as part of his university degree. He and Walter both got malaria, but Walter was hospitalized in Ghana. Walter is now driving trucks around Austria, but wants to go to South America.

The Africans—some have written, some have not. Postage fees are high and a low budget priority when ranked against food. I remember the difficulty of mail, and I wonder if they get my letters. Many of their countries are in turmoil. Many did not read or write English or French. I send them postcards.

Africa is changing too. Subtly but irrevocably. Niger has a new president, Liberia fell to an upstart faction of rebels, violence has torn Zaire apart, and Mobutu is being forced to implement his promises! Moi in Kenya has also acceded to the demands for a multiparty system. Algeria is in open conflict between the secular government and the Islamic fundamentalists. In country after country democracies are emerging. It will be tough going for them; they have no experience in self-determination. But until they shirk the yoke of their own military dictatorships, they will never be able to move their goods to market or solve their problems.

When in Africa, I spent hours plotting our escape. I thought it hard and expensive; that I'd never return again. When in Africa, I tried not to understand daily happenings but accumulate the effect. I could not measure it then. We learned to live happily with very little, we learned patience, and to take time to enjoy life. Under the African sky, all things are both possible and impossible. "Expect the unexpected."

The juju gris-gris is still powerful. I wonder sometimes if I might not wear out before its magic does.

Our floor is once again strewn with maps. Home is a resting place between journeys. We hear the rustles of palm fronds, the shuffled rhythm of feet, the snort of the mammy wagon, and murmurs under an azure sky. They whisper our names.

Notes

CHAPTER 1
AFRICA AT LAST!

1. Daily car/passenger ferry service is maintained by three companies. The least expensive point to cross the Mediterranean is from Algeciras, Spain, to Ceuta or Tangier in Morocco. Tickets are available at the terminal building on the dock.

2. Reaching Africa from the U.S. can be a budget buster. The cheapest way is to fly to Europe, then purchase a ticket from a bucket shop (a discounter). Budget travelers consistently use Aeroflot via Moscow. We purchased discounted tickets in Boston: $220 each, one-way to Portugal.

3. Morocco, Malawi, and Togo are the only nations that do not require Americans to obtain visas. Together we spent $1,850 for

visas and used three hundred passport photos to enter twenty-one countries. The most expensive visa was Zaire—$164 each.

US Embassies do not charge to add supplementary pages to American passports. All our photos, including negatives, cost $20 in Rabat, Morocco.

4. Thirty dollars a day for two people is unrealistically low in Central Franc African (CFA) countries. CFA is linked to the French franc and is used in most ex-French colonies: Niger, Mali, Burkina Faso, Senegal, Guinea-Conakry, Cote d'Ivoire, Togo, and Benin. The countries in west Africa trade CFA as a "hard currency" like US dollars, Germans marks, or English pounds. Since it is extremely difficult to buy US dollars, or any hard currency, in most of Africa, it is worthwhile to purchase CFA for cash conversion. In CFA countries, a more realistic budget is $20 to $30 per person, per day for eating at food stalls, using public transportation, and staying in budget accommodations. In non-CFA countries, you can get along on $10 a day. We had no problems using American Express travelers checks or converting American dollars. We reserved hard currency for emergencies only.

5. Our packing list is included here in full. We had everything we needed and were not overburdened.

Total weight, including water and food, was twenty-eight pounds each.

—Convertible backpacks with strong, well-balanced internal frames for hiking were ideal but heavy. (Two advantages of the packs were they could be locked and the fabric was sturdy.)

—Medium-weight, goosedown sleeping bags

—Three-fourth-length sleeping pads

—Sleeping sheets (hostel-approved, cotton, cocoon-like pouches)

—TEVA sport sandals (terrific for all terrains)

—Gortex hiking boots (We sent these back after North Africa and later regretted it around Kilimanjaro.)

—Two cameras (one automatic and one fully manual), batteries, one telephoto lens

—Thirty rolls of slide film at different speeds

—Two flashlights (Mini-Mag Lites are worth the extra dollar or two over cheaper brands.)

—Rain ponchos (served double duty as ground cloths, tents, etc.)

—Sunglasses (Splurge for good quality that wraparound eyes—these were the most coveted items we owned.)

—Folding hats

—A seal-tight plastic jug

—A one-gallon collapsible water container (We sent this home after the Sahara.)

—An AM/FM tape player and recorder with a splitter jack for ear phones and miniature speakers

—Blank tapes for audio letters home

—A small alarm clock

—Swiss army knife (We took the simple, bottom-of-the-line model, but one with a long blade, maybe four inches, would have been more practical.)

—Sierra cups and spoons (doubled as tiny cooking pots)

—First aid kit (Most valuable items were: Pepto Bismol, which really worked for minor digestive problems; Second Skin, adheres better than Band-Aids, cushions better, and can be used as a suture; strong anti-bacterial cream; different antibiotics and malaria treatments: quinine, fansidar, chlorquine, vibramycin, and tetracycline. We bought Paludrine in Europe.)

—Sewing kit (Dental floss is perfect for heavy-duty repairs.)

—Twenty-foot nylon rope

—Towels (small, chamois-like cloths)

—A nylon day pack

—Passport cases

—International Driver's Licenses (contact AAA), US driver's licenses, International Health Certificates, VISA and American Express cards, passports, and photocopies of everything

—Maps (Michelin Maps are unquestionably the best. We found them only in Ivory Coast and Kenya.)

—Notebooks and pens

—Toiletry items (easily and cheaply replaced)

—Eye care (My ophthalmologist recommended a commercial eye wash. I took hard contact lenses, one spare pair, my prescription, and two pairs of eyeglasses set in children's frames, which were extremely durable and inexpensive. I wore glasses in the desert and on trucks. The hard lenses were very practical in that they didn't require electricity or sterile water. Solutions were unattainable in all but big cities.)

—Plastic bags of various sizes (to protect objects from rain and sand)

—Books (We would walk ten miles for a book swap. Guidebooks are impossible to obtain in Africa. The best guidebook of Africa is *The Guide to West Africa* (Lonely Planet) by Alex Newton. The only guide to the entire continent is *Africa on a Shoestring* (Lonely Planet) by Geoff Crowther.)

—Clothing (I usually wore a long skirt or African dresses. We took rather drab, cheap, nondescript clothes. No one could guess our nationality or our wealth by our clothes.)

*Long pants—one lightweight pair and one heavy pair

*A long-sleeved shirt

*Two short-sleeved shirts

*Two tee-shirts for layering

*A pair of shorts

*A turtleneck sweater

*Silk long underwear (It folds up small, dries quickly and provides substantial warmth.)

*Socks, including "wicking" socks

*A lightweight, hooded, rain-resistant windbreaker

*Underwear

*Bathing suits

Another tip is to roll clothing and secure it with a rubber bands. Our packs were more compact and easier to repack after customs searches.

CHAPTER 2
MOROCCO .

1. For visas to Algeria, go to the consulate (not the embassy) located three blocks from the American Embassy in Rabat. It usually takes twenty-four hours to get the visas. (We got ours in two hours.) The visas require three forms, three photos, and cost approximately $6 each.

2. Independent entrepreneurs throughout Africa generate busi-

ness by preying on tourists fears. Exaggerated, imaginary threats are a disservice to the country and tourism. Ignore them.

CHAPTER 3
EASTERN MOROCCO

1. The Algerians check vehicle papers and passports at the Oujda/Tlemcen point of entry. The name on the title of the car and the drivers name must be the same. Passengers must somehow document their right to be in the car. We heard that official-looking typed and stamped rosters worked. Independent travelers are turned away.

CHAPTER 4
ALGERIA

1. To obtain visas, both Nigerian and Malian consulates require Algerian financial declarations (papers saying you have converted the required amount), International Health Records, passports, and three photos. The visas cost $45 each.

CHAPTER 5
DIGGING ACROSS THE SAHARA

1. The Algerian government reputedly instituted the registration procedure at the insistence of the French who are alarmed by the number of Europeans who are disappearing in the Sahara. Reportedly, 120 Europeans died in 1989 while trying to cross the desert.

2. A heavy, four-wheel drive is the ideal vehicle for the Sahara. Our vans were two-wheel drive with standard transmissions, so air was let out of the tires to increase traction. That's very hard on tires, and we used every spare. Mechanical repairs are available in the little town of In Guzzeman, at the Algerian border. Several decent books have been published on adapting vehicles for crossing the Sahara.

3. Border hours for Algeria and Niger are 8:00 A.M. to noon and 3:00 P.M. to 5:00 P.M.—give or take a few hours either way. Vehicles line up early on both sides, but friends and relatives get served first.

Financial declarations are stringently inspected for irregularities. Fines are often based on what the inspector thinks your pocket will bear. Keep receipts of all money exchanged and make sure you can prove that you changed the official minimum. Algerian dinar will be confiscated. If you are smuggling money, for whatever reason, be clever. Niger does not have a declaration.

4. A *carnet de passage* is a type of insurance that guarantees payment of duty if a vehicle is sold within the country. It can be purchased in advance or at the borders. Collision and indemnity insurance is also required. Most African countries do not recognize international insurance policies and require travelers to purchase their own, which are very expensive. International driver's licenses and clear titles of ownership are also required. Helmut forged all their documents, except the titles, by obtaining standard blank forms, typing in the ideal information, adding documentary stamps purchased from the Austrian rail system, scrawling an illegible signature, then embossing it with the equivalent of a notary stamp. It worked for him.

5. DO NOT take photos or write anything in or around border crossings anywhere in Africa. It's easy to innocently violate these two rules while delayed for hours or days at a time at a border crossing. Find something else to do because the military police are seriously xenophobic. If you are carrying a camera and are accused of spying, the simplest way to defuse the situation is to expose the film and hand it over. Similarly, be cautious of what you write in your travel journal. Journals are often seized in conjunction with infractions and reviewed for "seditious" or politically sensitive statements.

CHAPTER 6
NIGER

1. Arlit is the only town we heard of where the police hold on to foreigner's passports. Supposedly, all foreigners must register in

each town; however, the police will make you register everywhere they have a roadside station.

2. AIDS, or SIDS, "the slimming disease," is on the increase in Africa. Reportedly, Burundi, Rwanda, and Uganda have the highest concentration of HIV-infected people. In many countries, like Niger, diagnostic equipment is found only in urban centers and is not very sophisticated. Medical personnel routinely diagnose AIDS as tuberculosis and estimate the infection as "high." Both migrant prostitutes and travelers share the burden of its spread. An alarming number of Europeans adopt "temporary spouses" while in Africa. Women travelers also engage in sex for pay.

3. Registration with Surete, the head cop shop, in Niamey is required for entry and exit to the city. Photo permits are no longer required, but hell awaits anyone caught snapping a sunset photo of camels on the scenic Kennedy Bridge spanning the Niger River. In fact, just about any edifice is politically sensitive.

CHAPTER 7
BACK INTO THE DESERT

1. Supposedly, tourists are no longer required to register with each municipal police department and pay the 500 CFA registration tax. However, the police in Gao will hunt you down and make you pay. One photo, several long forms, and paying the tax will get you a rubber stamp in your passport. (One obnoxious foreigner was charged 10,000 CFA!)

CHAPTER 9
THE DOGON MYTHS OF MALI

1. SMERT (Societe Malian Explotacion d' Resources Turistique) is the quasi-official governmental arm of the tourist board. It was allegedly "fired" because tax revenues raised by SMERT were not reaching the capital. However, they are still operating without jurisdiction. SMERT does not operate in Bandiagara, nor are tourists required to take a guide into Dogon Land. Registra-

tion at the police station on the far side of the river is mandatory, but free.

CHAPTER 10
THE GAMBIA

1. The Gambia consulate in Dakar, Senegal, issues seven-day visas ($20 each and requires two photos). The visa is easily extended in Banjul at the Ministry of the Interior—however, you'll be escorted from office to office, as if they had never done such a thing. If planning to reenter Senegal from The Gambia, get a multiple exit visa for Senegal, otherwise you'll have to reapply. Also in Banjul are consulates for Guinea-Bissau and Sierra Leone.

2. At taxi stands, posted fares are titled "Tourist Rate" and are at least 800 percent higher than fares for locals. Buses and shared taxis are the cheapest. The unofficial tourist tax is charged all over Africa. The best way to circumvent it is to ask local people what they pay for a tomato, a ride, or whatever, and begin bargaining with that amount, or merely pay it. Resorts during tourist seasons are always more expensive, and there isn't much that a traveler can do except avoid them.

3. Gamtel, the Gambian national phone company, had direct-dial to the US.

CHAPTER 13
GUINEA-CONAKRY

1. A common sign of motherhood, or the female gender, is a cupped breast. Sometimes my own breast was touched this way to inquire if I were a mother. It is an unorthodox gesture for breastphobic Westerners, but it is not an offensive gesture in Africa. Robb and I do not have children, but we carried photos of our nieces for just such occasions. Only once were we referred to a juju man for help with our infertility. In Africa, childlessness is considered a curse, a spell, that can only be undone by a juju doctor. We told people that our children stayed with their grandmother, which in communal societies is acceptable.

2. Visas to Sierra Leone cost $19.62 each, required two photos, and took twenty-four hours to get.

CHAPTER 14
SIERRA LEONE

1. It is possible to avoid customs and immigration bribes. One trick the guards at some border crossings use is to first give you your money declaration, then count your money, hoping to find that you "miscalculated" so they can fine you for a lie. We declared every penny but our well-hidden emergency stash. It is illegal to import or export non-convertible, domestic currencies (eg., naira, dilassi, and leones). Spend it down before you reach borders, because few borders have banks and fewer still will reconvert.

Another treasure trove for extortion is the traveler's bundle, backpack, or suitcase. The guards are not interested in utilitarian, worn clothes or half-used bottles of shampoo. Merchants with new goods, or people carrying jewelry, fine lotions, etc., were more interesting.

The third scam for extorting bribes is to find fault with documents, e.g., an expired visa, an improper or absent entry/exit stamp, a South African visa, or an expired cholera shot. We painstakingly kept our paperwork in good shape.

At border crossings, be patient and helpful, but persistent. Keep quiet. When it is your turn, bumble through the process and languages. To avoid arguments, pretend you do not understand the request for bribes. Take your time—buses, trucks, boats, and taxis will not leave you, and the other passengers will arbitrate for you.

2. Correct change is always returned, eventually. The crux of the problem is no one trusts anyone else, so money boxes, cash registers, etc., are frequently emptied by the owner/manager. Change is also often treated as a floating credit, an honorary bond. Foreigners often cause nasty scenes when the correct change is not promptly returned. Wait and it will come. We even had change delivered to us a day or two later.

3. The Peace Corps Rest House charges one hundred leones per

person, per night. The Peace Corps headquarters in Washington, D.C., is halting this business throughout Africa, so I have purposely played down the occasional hospitality the rest houses offered. They provide an invaluable resource for the few travelers who penetrate remote areas. However, they are caught in a catch-22—the local embassy refers almost everything to them, and Washington mandates they can't do anything.

4. Poyo—palm wine freshly tapped from the crown of palm trees—is bubbly and refreshing. After several hours it ferments like a yeasty beer, beyond that, it is lethal—especially if diluted with well water.

5. Female circumcision is under attack by reformists. It is often performed under unsanitary conditions using a glass shard, ceremonial knife, razor blade, or, only recently, a surgical blade. At the very least it deprives the woman of sexual stimulation. The procedure often causes infection or hemorrhaging and can lead to physical complications with menstrual flow, urination, and childbirth. Infant mortality and mental handicaps are attributed to the practice. For a complete and candid discussion of the topic see *The Circumcision of Women: A Strategy for Eradication* by Olayinka Koso-Thomas. Nigeria was one of the first nations to "legally" ban the practice.

CHAPTER 15
LIBERIA

1. Immigration charges $5 each for fifteen days. An exit visa must also be obtained from the same place for another $5. Camera permits were required but useless.

2. Expediters are employed by embassies and multinational corporations to move their people through customs and immigration without problems.

CHAPTER 16
COTE D'IVOIRE

1. Get visas to Ghana in Abidjan. The visas are for three days and cost $27 each.

CHAPTER 18
THE GOLD COAST

1. In Accra, France issues visas for C.A.R. Nigeria didn't charge us, by some quirky mistake. After submitting our paperwork, we asked to "borrow" our passports in order to go to the bank. Miraculously, they were immediately returned with the visa stamps.

2. Headache, stiff neck, recurring fever, and loss of appetite are symptoms. Diarrhea occurs in the advanced stages of the disease. Cerebral Malaria is normally a killer disease unless treated in the early stages. One treatment for cerebral malaria is quinine and doxycycline.

3. We didn't meet other travelers until much later in Cameroon. They told us of relentless harassment by the Nigerian Secret Security Service in central and northern Nigeria. From Nigeria eastward, be cautious of people with fake identity cards claiming to be police. Since few police wear uniforms, it is easy to fall prey to the scam. Many travelers were robbed in this way.

4. Passage by boat through the Sea of Guinea is a lovely way to cross between the two countries. Unfortunately, it is not safe. The U.S. Consul in Cameroon told us that two Peace Corps volunteers had a similar experience and that he would issue a travel warning. We never saw it. I suspect that it was censored for political reasons. The U.S. embassies routinely suppress negative reports. This is a very dangerous disservice to travelers who depend on embassy travel advisories.

CHAPTER 19
CAMEROON AND THE CENTRAL AFRICAN REPUBLIC

1. In Yaounde you can get visas for Zaire—$164 each for a two-month single entry visa.

CHAPTER 20
ZAIRE

1. A letter of recommendation is sometimes requested as a condition of a visa. A citizens' embassy normally issues the letter. American embassies do not charge for issuing letters. The Zaire consulate told us that we needed the letters then changed their minds.

2. The Peace Corps in Zaire is very paranoid. They have twice been evicted from Zaire. Their meetings are attended by a government representative and the transcripts filed with the government. "We don't welcome tourists here," they say of Zaire. To be fair, they eventually assisted us with invaluable non-political resources, eg., Paludrine, and courier service to US.

CHAPTER 22
EAST TO BURUNDI

1. During the rainy season roads are virtually impassable. The rains came late that year and persisted through May.

2. In Bukavu, visas for Burundi cost four thousand zaire each, require two photos, and take twenty-four hours to get.

3. No alcohol can be sold in Bujumbura before 5:00 P.M. The Johnsons say that per capita nutrition consumption has increased since the law took effect. People are spending less on beer and more on food. "Friends" can buy at any time, and the amount consumed in the evenings makes up for what cannot be bought during the day.

CHAPTER 23
WHERE STANLEY MET LIVINGSTONE

1. If taking the ferry onward, it is possible to stay in Kigoma without a visa during the thirty-six-hour layover. To do so, go through customs/immigration and get a currency declaration form and change money officially. If travelers do not do this, they

are still allowed in Kigoma but they must be back on the boat by
6:00 P.M.

CHAPTER 24
THE SPIECS OF LIFE FROM ZANZIBAR TO SAFARI

1. The best safari deal in Arusha is to Ngorongoro Crater with
Adventure and Safari Tours located behind the museum. Resident
fees are $250 for transport, $15 per person park fee per day, $15 ve-
hicle fee, and $10 camping fee. You must provide your own food.